The Sustainable Development Goals

There have been significant efforts to implement the Sustainable Development Goals (SDGs) at multiple levels of governance across all regions of the world. However, the manner in which the global governance norms underlying the SDGs are actually being diffused is under-researched and not well understood. This book considers the promotion of the SDGs through the lens of norm diffusion theory, with a focus on three SDG policy areas; health, education and decent work.

A distinctive feature of the book is that it offers multiple original case studies of SDG norm diffusion involving Asian and European actors. A unique feature is that the case studies in the book identify relevant SDG norm senders and norm receivers, and examine the relationship between them. The book also challenges the assumption that the SDGs themselves are static and unchanging, and reveals how SDG norms are dynamic and can be reformulated as a result of contestation between norm senders and norm receivers. As well as introducing a diverse and original set of case studies, the book therefore allows readers to deepen their understandings of the policy diffusion mechanisms by which SDGs are diffused, and grasp the patterns of success and failure in the implementation of these policies.

Paul Bacon, PhD is a tenured Professor of International Relations at the Faculty of International Research and Education, and a Jean Monnet Chair in European Union Studies at Waseda University, Japan. His research interests include the SDGs, human security, EU–Japan relations, NATO–Japan relations, Brexit, liberal international order and human rights norm diffusion.

Mina Chiba, PhD is an Assistant Professor of Organization for Regional and Inter-regional Studies (ORIS), Waseda University. Her major field of study is international development and human rights. Her research interests include global governance in education and health, non-cognitive skills' development and regionalisation of higher education.

Frederik Ponjaert is Researcher and Lecturer at the Université Libre de Bruxelles (ULB) and Associate Lecturer in Comparative Regionalism at SciencesPo (IEP-Paris). His research is on comparative regionalism, with an emphasis on European and Asian realities.

Routledge Studies in Sustainable Development

This series uniquely brings together original and cutting-edge research on sustainable development. The books in this series tackle difficult and important issues in sustainable development including: values and ethics; sustainability in higher education; climate compatible development; resilience; capitalism and de-growth; sustainable urban development; gender and participation; and well-being.

Drawing on a wide range of disciplines, the series promotes interdisciplinary research for an international readership. The series was recommended in the *Guardian*'s suggested reads on development and the environment.

The Politics of the Sustainable Development Goals
Legitimacy, Responsibility, and Accountability
Magdalena Bexell and Kristina Jönsson

Ecological Limits of Development
Living with the Sustainable Development Goals
Kaitlin Kish and Stephen Quilley

Learning Strategies for Sustainable Organisations
Bryan Hopkins

Social Progress and the Authoritarian Challenge to Democracy
Donald G. Reid

Decentralization, Local Governance, and Localizing the Sustainable Development Goals in Asia and the Pacific
Edited by Bruno Carrasco, Hanif A. Rahemtulla, and Rainer Rohdewohld

The Sustainable Development Goals
Diffusion and Contestation in Asia and Europe
Edited by Paul Bacon, Mina Chiba and Frederik Ponjaert

For more information about this series, please visit: www.routledge.com/Routledge-Studies-in-Sustainable-Development/book-series/RSSD

The Sustainable Development Goals

Diffusion and Contestation in Asia and Europe

Edited by Paul Bacon, Mina Chiba and Frederik Ponjaert

Routledge
Taylor & Francis Group
LONDON AND NEW YORK

First published 2023
by Routledge
4 Park Square, Milton Park, Abingdon, Oxon OX14 4RN

and by Routledge
605 Third Avenue, New York, NY 10158

Routledge is an imprint of the Taylor & Francis Group, an informa business

British Library Cataloguing-in-Publication Data
A catalogue record for this book is available from the British Library

Library of Congress Cataloguing-in-Publication Data
Names: Bacon, Paul (Lecturer in international relations), editor. |
Chiba, Mina, editor. | Ponjaert, Frederik, editor.
Title: The sustainable development goals : diffusion and contestation in
Asia and Europe / edited by Paul Bacon, Mina Chiba and Frederik Ponjaert.
Description: Abingdon, Oxon ; New York, NY : Routledge, 2023. |
Series: Routledge studies in sustainable development |
Includes bibliographical references and index. |
Identifiers: LCCN 2022027808 (print) | LCCN 2022027809 (ebook) |
ISBN 9781032072180 (hardback) | ISBN 9781032072197 (paperback) |
ISBN 9781003205951 (ebook)
Subjects: LCSH: Sustainable development–Asia. | Sustainable development–Europe. |
Policy sciences–Asia. | Policy sciences–Europe.
Classification: LCC HC415.E5 S777 2023 (print) |
LCC HC415.E5 (ebook) | DDC 338.95–dc23/eng/20221011
LC record available at https://lccn.loc.gov/2022027808
LC ebook record available at https://lccn.loc.gov/2022027809

ISBN: 9781032072180 (hbk)
ISBN: 9781032072197 (pbk)
ISBN: 9781003205951 (ebk)

DOI: 10.4324/9781003205951

Typeset in Galliard
by Newgen Publishing UK

Contents

Illustrations

Tables

Figures

Box

About the editors

Paul Bacon, PhD is a tenured Professor of International Relations at the Graduate School of International Culture and Communication, and a Jean Monnet Chair in European Union Studies. His research interests include the SDGs, human security, EU–Japan relations, NATO–Japan relations, Brexit, liberal international order and human rights norm diffusion. His three co-edited Routledge monographs, *The European Union and Japan: A New Chapter in Civilian Power Cooperation?*, *Human Security and Natural Disasters* and *Human Security and Japan's Triple Disaster*, appeared in paperback in 2016. Bacon has carried out research on public opinion and the death penalty in Japan, co-funded by the European Commission, and the foreign ministries of Germany, Norway and the United Kingdom. He has an ongoing interest in the influence of Japanese elite opinion on security policymaking, and recently worked on a NATO project where he interviewed 30 senior Japanese security experts. Bacon co-administers a major five-year project funded by the Japan Society for the Promotion of Science on 'The European Union and Japan in a Fluid Global Liberal Order'. As part of this project he is working on several publication initiatives.

Mina Chiba, PhD is an Assistant Professor of Organization for Regional and Inter-regional Studies (ORIS), Waseda University. Her major field of study is international development and human rights. Her research interests include global governance in education and health, non-cognitive skills' development and regionalisation of higher education. She has field work experience in Benin, West Africa and Belize, Central America as a Japan Overseas Cooperation Volunteer (JOCV). Mina holds a Bachelor of Law from Waseda University, Master of International Politics from the University of Melbourne and PhD from Waseda University. Her recent publications include: 'Investigating effective teaching and learning for sustainable development and global citizenship: Implications from a systematic review of the literature', *International Journal of Educational Development* (2021; 81, [102337]; co-authored); and 'Promotion of school-based comprehensive sexuality education: building support from teachers and parents in Thailand', *Development in Practice* (2021; In press).

Frederik Ponjaert is Researcher and Lecturer at the Université Libre de Bruxelles (ULB) and Associate Lecturer in Comparative Regionalism at SciencesPo (IEP-Paris). His research is on comparative regionalism, with an emphasis on European and Asian realities. He equally works on EU external action and inter-regional partnerships, again with a specific focus on Euro-Asian dynamics. More recently, both of these research strands have focussed on the developing EU–Japan relationship in light of the recently signed Economic Partnership and Strategic Partnership Agreements. At the ULB, as both his teaching and research span both European and Asian realities, he is a member of both the Institut d'Études Européennes (IEE) and the East Asian Studies Center (EASt). He is also co-editor of two Routledge book series, the GEM series on 'Globalisation, Europe and Multilateralism' and the CES series on 'Contemporary Asian Societies'.

Contributors

Elena Avramovska is a Senior Researcher at the Friedrich Ebert Stiftung. Her research has been funded by the European Commission, the Swiss National Research Foundation and the Open Society Foundation. She holds an Erasmus Mundus PhD in Political Sciences from the Université Libre de Bruxelles and the University of Geneva, as well as an Erasmus Mundus Masters in Global Studies from the University of Leipzig and the University of Vienna. In the course of her PhD, she spent one year at the University of Oxford as a visiting researcher. Elena has worked for a variety of international and non-governmental organisations such as the United Nations and the European Parliament.

Stephanie Ghislain leads the 'Trade & Animal Welfare' Programme at Eurogroup for Animals, the pan-European animal advocacy organisation representing more than 80 members based in the EU and beyond. The Eurogroup for Animals' 'Trade & Animal Welfare' Programme acts as a constructive partner to EU decision makers offering the World Trade Organization (WTO) compatible solutions to problems identified in connection with trade and animal welfare. Before joining Eurogroup for Animals, Stephanie worked for six years in a consulting firm, primarily advising companies and governments on EU trade policy. She was a member of the European Commission's Expert Group on Trade Negotiations and represents Eurogroup for Animals on the EU Domestic Advisory Groups (DAGs) on the EU trade agreements with Ukraine, Canada, Japan, Vietnam and Singapore.

Makiko Hayashi, PhD is currently Assistant Professor at the Sacred Heart Institute for Sustainable Futures, University of the Sacred Heart in Tokyo, Japan. She received her PhD in International Studies from Waseda University (Japan), with a specific focus on policy analysis of comparative and international development of education. Her work covers issues on equity and inclusion in the area of inclusive education at the international policy level as well at the national level, conducting field research in Cambodia since 2006. Her current research interests relate to the dynamics of skills' formulation through inclusive education for primary school children without disabilities learning together with blind and deaf students in Cambodia, where she uses her sign language skills (ASL) to interact directly with deaf students.

Yasushi Katsuma, PhD is Professor of the International Studies Programme in the Graduate School of Asia-Pacific Studies (GSAPS) at Waseda University. He is Director of Global Health Affairs & Governance in the Institute for Global Health Policy Research (iGHP) at the National Center for Global Health & Medicine (NCGM). Prior to the current positions, he worked for UNICEF in Mexico, Pakistan, Afghanistan and Tokyo. He received his PhD (Development) from the University of Wisconsin-Madison; LLM and LLB from Osaka University; and BA from the International Christian University. His areas of expertise are global health affairs and governance, human security, human development and child rights. His recent publications include: *Leave No One Behind: Time for Specifics on the Sustainable Development Goals* (Brookings Institution Press, 2019; co-authored); 'Next steps towards universal health coverage call for global leadership,' *BMJ* (2019; 365: l2107; co-authored).

Jun Kawaguchi, PhD graduated from Waseda University in Japan. He is currently working as an Associate Professor at the University of Tsukuba. His major field of study is educational development and teacher education policy. His research interest for his doctoral dissertation lies in primary teacher education policy and inclusive education in Malawi. His professional experiences began when he was a high school teacher in Japan. After that he participated in volunteering at a teacher training college in Malawi. Next, he completed his master's programme and worked as a researcher in the Japan International Cooperation Agency (JICA). Prior to becoming an Assistant Professor at the University of Tsukuba, he was an Assistant Professor at Osaka University.

Shukuko Koyama, PhD is Associate Professor at Waseda University's School of Social Sciences. Between 2007 and 2015, she worked for the International Labour Organization (ILO) and engaged in post-conflict reconstruction and disaster response in sub-Saharan Africa and the Asia and Pacific regions. Before joining the ILO, Shukuko worked at the United Nations Institute for Disarmament Research in Geneva and the United Nations peacekeeping mission in the Democratic Republic of the Congo. Shukuko holds a PhD from the University of Bradford, the United Kingdom.

Kazuo Kuroda, PhD is Professor at Waseda University's Graduate School of Asia-Pacific Studies. His research fields include educational development and policies in Asian nations, global and regional governance of education, international higher education and history of international cooperation in education. He graduated from Waseda University (BA), Stanford University (MA) and Cornell University (PhD). Kazuo also serves as Visiting Research Fellow at JICA Research Institute, as well as an executive board member of the Japan Society for International Development (JASID) and Japan Comparative Education Society (JCES), and chair of the Research Standing Committee of the World Council of Comparative Education Societies (WCCES). His recent edited book publications include *Japan's International Cooperation in Education: History and Prospects* (University of Tokyo Press).

Leyla Radjai is a PhD candidate at the Graduate School of Asia-Pacific Studies, Waseda University and a Programme Adviser at the Secretariat of the International Peace Cooperation Headquarters, Cabinet Office, Government of Japan. Previously she worked as a Project Coordinator at the Center for Research on International Cooperation in Educational Development (CRICED) at the University of Tsukuba. In 2017–2018, she also served as a Youth Engagement Officer at the United Nations Volunteers in Sri Lanka. She holds a MA in International Relations with a concentration on international education policy and her research interests include internationalisation and regionalisation of higher education, internationalisation of curriculum, and multicultural and intercultural education.

Thais Favero Souza, PhD is a former doctoral student at the Graduate School of International Culture and Communication Studies, Waseda University. She has a Bachelor's Degree in Law from the Federal University of Juiz de Fora – UFJF (Brazil), and a Master's Degree in International Law from Waseda University's Graduate School of Law. Her research focuses on international human rights, women's right to work, gender equality, feminism and theories of norm diffusion. Her most recent publication is an article titled 'Improving the Conceptualization and the Implementation of Women's Right to Work: The Importance of Adding a Feminist Dimension to the Spiral Model of Human Rights Diffusion' (*Transcommunication*, Vol. 6-2, Fall 2019). She is active as a member of the Sophia University Committee for the Promotion of Diversity.

Nishkhan Usayapant is a young professional with research and policy advocacy interests that lie at the intersection of business and human rights. She holds a Bachelor's Degree in Law from Chulalongkorn University, Thailand, and has just completed a Master's Degree in Development Studies from the Graduate Institute, Geneva. She has over four years experience working with and closely following policy development with regard to trade and labour conditions in Thailand. While working at the Human Rights and Development Foundation, a leading Thai labour rights NGO, she played a leading role in legal and policy advocacy towards the elimination of forced labour and human trafficking in the seafood industry. Her contribution to this chapter draws on her direct professional experience. She is currently based in Geneva, Switzerland.

Acknowledgements

This publication offers the latest research produced as a result of what is now a deep, multifaceted and long-standing relationship between Waseda University and the Université Libre de Bruxelles. The authors would like to thank the Japan Society for the Promotion of Science (JSPS), as the book was produced with financial support from the JSPS Core-to-Core Program, A. Advanced Research Networks 'The European Union and Japan in a Fluid Global Liberal Order: Establishing an Inter-Regional Studies Centre' (grant number: JPJSCCA20180002).

Paul Bacon, Mina Chiba and Frederik Ponjaert,
Tokyo and Brussels, May 2022.

Abbreviations and acronyms

AHTA	Anti-Human Trafficking Act
AITC	Animal Issues Thematic Cluster
APCEIU	Asia-Pacific Centre of Education for International Understanding
APEC	Asia-Pacific Economic Cooperation
ASEAN	Association of Southeast Asian Nations
BCR	Biopharmaceuticals CEOs Roundtable
CBCP	Catholic Bishops Conference of the Philippines
CEDAW	Convention on the Elimination of All Forms of Discrimination Against Women
CENN	Caucasus Environmental NGO Network
CETA	Comprehensive Economic and Trade Agreement
CSE	Comprehensive sexuality education
CWDs	Children with disabilities
DAC	Development Assistance Committee (OECD)
DAG	Domestic Advisory Group
DCFTA	Deep and Comprehensive Free Trade Area (Ukraine)
DG	Directorate-General (EU)
DG	MARE Directorate-General for Maritime Affairs and Fisheries (EU)
DOH	Department of Health (Philippines)
DSWD	Department of Social Welfare and Development (Philippines)
EAPRO	UNICEF Regional Office for East Asia and the Pacific
EFA	Education for All
EIU	Education for international understanding
ESD	Education for sustainable development
EU	European Union
FDA	Food and Drug Administration
FTA	Free Trade Agreement
G7	Group of 7
G8	Group of 8
G20	Group of 20
GCED	Global Citizenship Education
GD	Georgian Dream (political party, Georgia)

GFATM	Global Fund to Fight AIDS, Tuberculosis and Malaria
GHG	Greenhouse gases
GHR	Global human resources
GIP	Georgian Institute of Politics
HFA	Health for all
HLPF	High Level Political Forum
HSS	Health systems strengthening
ICCPR	International Covenant on Civil and Political Rights
ICESCR	International Covenant on Economic, Social and Cultural Rights
ICPD	International Conference on Population and Development
IDGs	International Development Goals
IFPMA	International Federation of Pharmaceutical Manufacturers and Associations
IHP+	International Health Partnership
ILO	International Labour Organization
IPC	Infection prevention and control
ITUC	International Trade Union Confederation
IUU	Illegal, unreported and unregulated
JMA	Japan Medical Association
LLINs	Long-lasting insecticidal nets
MDGs	Millennium Development Goals
MEXT	Ministry of Education, Culture, Sports, Science and Technology (Japan)
MoE	Ministry of Education (Thailand)
MoEYS	Ministry of Education, Youth and Sport (Cambodia)
MoPH	Ministry of Public Health (Thailand)
NAPAC	National AIDS Prevention and Alleviation Committee (Thailand)
NATO	North Atlantic Treaty Organization
NGO	Non-governmental organisation
NPE	Normative Power Europe
ODA	Official development assistance
OECD	Organisation for Economic Co-operation and Development
OHCHR	Office of the High Commissioner for Human Rights (UN)
OSCE	Organization for Security and Co-operation in Europe
OWG	Open working group (on the SDGs)
PATH	Program for Appropriate Technology in Health
PCW	Philippine Commission on Women
PDA	Population and Development Association
PHC	Primary health care
POHR	Power of Human Rights (book)
PPOHR	Persistent Power of Human Rights (book)
RBM	Roll Back Malaria initiative
RCF	Regulatory and Cooperation Forum
RH	The Responsible Parenthood and Reproductive Health Act (2012) (Philippines)

SDGs	Sustainable Development Goals
SPS	Sanitary and phytosanitary
SRHR	Sexual and reproductive health and rights
STI	Sexually transmitted infections
TICAD	Tokyo International Conference on African Development
TRIPS	Trade-Related Aspects of Intellectual Property Rights
TSD	Trade and Sustainable Development
TTIP	Transatlantic Trade and Investment Partnership
UDHR	Universal Declaration of Human Rights
UHC	Universal health coverage
UN	United Nations
UNAIDS	The Joint United Nations Programme on HIV/AIDS
UNDESD	United Nations Decade of Education for Sustainable Development
UNDP	United Nations Development Programme
UNESCO	The United Nations Educational, Scientific and Cultural Organization
UNFPA	United Nations Population Fund
UNGASS	United Nations General Assembly Special Session
UN HLM	UN High-Level Meeting
UNIAP	United Nations Inter-Agency Project on Human Trafficking
UNICEF	United Nations Children's Fund
WHA	World Health Assembly
WHO	World Health Organization
WMA	World Medical Association

Section 1

Conceptual frameworks

1 The Sustainable Development Goals (SDGs) as international norms

Mina Chiba and Yasushi Katsuma

Introduction

The Sustainable Development Goals (SDGs) are a set of international norms adopted at the 2015 United Nations (UN) Sustainable Development Summit. The UN stated that the SDGs offer the blueprint to achieve a better and more sustainable future for all by 2030. Although the formulation process of the SDGs was open to diverse stakeholders such as UN member states, international and regional organisations, civil society organisations and private sector actors, the SDGs are the outcome of international public policy dialogues. Therefore, to achieve the SDGs, we need to consider how SDG-related policies can be domestically adopted and implemented in each UN member state, rather than treating the SDGs as prescriptions for development projects.

In this volume, we explore through case studies the challenges and opportunities of SDG policy implementation, taking a norm diffusion perspective. When defining norms as ideas of abstraction and specification concerning fundamental values, organising principles or standardised procedures, the SDGs are regarded as a group of international norms. If we assume that SDGs are norms and their content fixed, it may be inferred that their delivery and implementation are automatically diffused from norm senders to norm receivers. However, we challenge this assumption and demonstrate that the SDGs are dynamic and constantly reformulated by contestations during the diffusion process. This volume highlights the way various actors deal with the norms and implement SDG-related policies and activities. The implications drawn from each case study contribute to further discussion on the challenges and opportunities for the achievement of the SDGs.

This book was written based on a joint research project between Europe and Japan, within the Japan Society for the Promotion of Science (JSPS) Core-to-Core Program A (Advanced Research Networks), *The European Union and Japan in a Fluid Global Liberal Order: Establishing an Inter-Regional Studies Centre*. As a result of active research exchanges, including multiple joint seminars in Tokyo and Brussels over three years, a diverse team of authors from Europe and Asia worked together on this broader theme and contributed to this volume. Therefore, it covers a wide geographical area with a focus on both regions. It

DOI: 10.4324/9781003205951-2

has three case studies involving European actors, including the European Union (EU) and Georgia, five case studies in Asia, including Thailand, the Philippines, Cambodia and Japan, and one case study from Malawi in Africa. The asset of this volume is the analysis of multiple policy areas by SDGs' and human rights specialists. Diversity is reflected in the authors' characteristics, including both women and men from different regions, as well as senior scholars, early career researchers and practitioners. We believe such a diverse team provides readers with more comprehensive ideas and broader perspectives on achievement of the SDGs.

In the following sections in this chapter, we will clarify the purpose of the book with a brief statement of its conceptual framework and areas of policy. To help the reader build a basic understanding, it presents the SDGs as international norms and traces the emergence of international goals and targets in the context of developmental policy. Finally, we introduce the structure of this book and its chapters.

The book's theme

This book regards the SDGs as collective international norms and highlights how they have been adopted, implemented and/or contested in different parts of the world. We explore the process of policy diffusion and implementation across different geographical regions and multiple policy areas. Based on the specialties of the authors, this book focuses on three different norms embedded in the SDGs: Goal 3: ensure healthy lives and promote well-being at all ages; Goal 4: ensure inclusive and equitable quality education and promote lifelong learning opportunities for all; and Goal 8: full and productive employment and decent work for all. The analysis of diffusion processes was made through case studies in most chapters. As each of these three goals have multiple targets, we do not cover all the norms embedded in each goal. Rather, chapter contributors selected relevant SDG targets in the policy areas they studied.
The objectives of this book are threefold, as follows:

1. To explore whether, how and why the selected SDG norms have been diffused, contested, transformed and implemented across a series of original Asian and European case studies.
2. To explore the roles of different actors such as norm senders and norm receivers in the diffusion and possible localisation of SDG norms as they are implemented.
3. To explain which policy diffusion attempts successfully result in SDG norms being incorporated in national policies and implemented following international expectations.

Our conceptual framework is based on norm diffusion theories including the spiral model of human rights. Although the analyses made in each chapter are not constrained by this theoretical base, the contributors were asked to connect their case study analyses to the ideas and perspectives underpinning these theories. The second chapter by Thais Favero Souza and Paul Bacon further explains the conceptual framework for norm diffusion theories.

SDGs' overview

The SDGs were listed in the 2030 Agenda for Sustainable Development and adopted at the UN Sustainable Development Summit held in September 2015. The SDGs comprise 17 goals and 169 targets, intended to be achieved by 2030. Overall, they aim to eradicate poverty and realise a sustainable world (see Box 1.1). The preamble of the 2030 Agenda states, 'The Goals and targets will stimulate action [...] in areas of critical importance for humanity and the planet'. Thus, the SDGs will be followed by different action plans worldwide.

Box 1.1 Sustainable Development Goals (SDGs)

Goal 1. End poverty in all its forms everywhere
Goal 2. End hunger, achieve food security and improved nutrition and promote sustainable agriculture
Goal 3. Ensure healthy lives and promote well-being for all at all ages
Goal 4. Ensure inclusive and equitable quality education and promote lifelong learning opportunities for all
Goal 5. Achieve gender equality and empower all women and girls
Goal 6. Ensure availability and sustainable management of water and sanitation for all
Goal 7. Ensure access to affordable, reliable, sustainable, and modern energy for all
Goal 8. Promote sustained, inclusive, and sustainable economic growth, full and productive employment, and decent work for all
Goal 9. Build resilient infrastructure, promote inclusive and sustainable industrialization and foster innovation
Goal 10. Reduce inequality within and among countries
Goal 11. Make cities and human settlements inclusive, safe, resilient, and sustainable
Goal 12. Ensure sustainable consumption and production patterns
Goal 13. Take urgent action to combat climate change and its impacts
Goal 14. Conserve and sustainably use the oceans, seas, and marine resources for sustainable development
Goal 15. Protect, restore, and promote sustainable use of terrestrial ecosystems, sustainably manage forests, combat desertification, and halt and reverse land degradation and halt biodiversity loss

Goal 16. Promote peaceful and inclusive societies for sustainable development, provide access to justice for all and build effective, accountable, and inclusive institutions at all levels
Goal 17. Strengthen the means of implementation and revitalize the Global Partnerships for Sustainable Development

Source: United Nations (2015)

The SDGs are based on the Millennium Development Goals (MDGs), which comprised eight goals agreed upon by UN member states for implementation by 2015. Despite this fact, the SDGs are unique in many ways, particularly their claim to a universal and inclusive nature. For instance, the 2030 agenda declares, 'these are universal goals and targets which involve the entire world, developed and developing countries alike' (United Nations, 2015, paragraph 5) and pledges, 'no one will be left behind' (United Nations, 2015, paragraph 4). The SDGs have a more comprehensive and broader agenda that includes environmental, social and economic sustainability, while poverty alleviation is a core objective. This suggests the SDGs reflect the view that development is a transformative process while the MDGs hold that development meets basic needs with a strong focus on economies' productive capacity to improve people's living standards.

From the perspective of norm diffusion, the SDGs can be regarded as a set of 17 different norms, but they are interconnected rather than independent. For instance, quality education and decent work are end goals, but they set the foundation for good health and poverty reduction. Several cross-cutting norms such as human rights and gender equality, are embedded in the SDGs. In particular, human rights promotion is not a specific goal but incorporated as a general principle.

The SDGs measure each goal's target outcomes with indicators. Like the MDGs, the SDGs are structured in three layers: (1) goal: a statement of social and political priority; (2) target: a time-bound quantitative outcome to be achieved; and (3) indicator: a measurement tool to monitor progress. However, it is a common critique that transforming norms into measurable indicators is likely to reduce their complexity and distort the original meanings. Some notions incorporated in the SDGs, for example, sustainability and inclusion, are particularly incompatible with quantitative measurement. Moreover, some SDG targets focus on quality aspects. Therefore, not all SDG targets and indicators are quantitative. Due to this feature of the SDGs, some scholars pointed out that the most transformative goals and targets might be neglected in implementation through selectivity, simplification and national adaptation (Fukuda-Parr & McNeill, 2019). The SDGs are characterised by an intention to be more comprehensive, universal and inclusive. As a result, they include various complex norms to diffuse and this creates a challenge for implementation worldwide.

The emergence of the SDGs and targets

In this section, we overview the prehistory of the SDGs by tracing the emergence of international goals and targets in the development context. By doing so, we demonstrate how international goals and targets were diffused as global norms over the decades in international society. This also highlights the uniqueness of the SDGs as international goals. When exploring the antecedents of the SDGs, we find seeds in the mid-twentieth century. The idea of reducing global poverty was embodied in the Universal Declaration of Human Rights, drafted by international representatives and proclaimed by the UN General Assembly in 1948. After this dramatic event, the first UN Development Decade was launched by the General Assembly in 1961, which called for global support to accelerate the economic and social development of developing countries. In this programme, a 5% minimum annual growth target by the end of the decade was set for developing countries, and the need for the concerted actions of the member states was emphasised (United Nations, 1961).

Although multilateral efforts to address global poverty were stalled in the 1980s with the rise of neoliberalism, ideas of poverty reduction and global goal setting dramatically evolved in the early 1990s. Milestones included the first publication of the *Human Development Reports* by the UN Development Programme (UNDP) in 1990 and the World Summit for Children held in New York. These UNDP reports defined human development and suggested a coherent framework for policy change in the development context. The World Summit for Children was held the same year and called for mobilising public support and political commitment by formulating specific goals for children's survival, development and protection. In terms of setting concrete targets to improve children's prospects internationally, it is considered an important forerunner of the MDGs as well as a reaffirmation that global summits can produce concrete improvements in human welfare (Hulme, 2007).

In the mid-1990s, when the world experienced declining levels of official development assistance (ODA), the Organisation for Economic Co-operation and Development's (OECD) Development Assistance Committee (DAC) adopted a report entitled *Shaping the 21st Century: The Contribution of Development Co-operation* (now widely known as the DAC's New Development Strategy) in 1996. This document declared an improved quality of life for all as its primary goal and articulated seven International Development Goals (IDGs). However, these goals were produced entirely by the donor club and lacked developing countries in the formulation process. Consequently, this initiative did not gain much attention or resonance from developing countries and was cast as 'aid agency rhetoric' (Hulme, 2007, p. 6).

In the year 2000, the UN Millennium Declaration was adopted. The MDGs were agreed on by leaders of 189 countries at the UN headquarters in New York, with a commitment to achieve a series of eight measurable goals by 2015. Although the MDGs were recognised as a predecessor to the SDGs, there are several important differences in their nature and formulation. The MDGs are a

Table 1.1 The antecedents of the SDGs

Global Norms	*Year*	*Characteristics*
UN Development Decades	Pre-1990	Formulated by UN member states for developing countries
World Summit for Children	1990	Formulated by UN member states for developing countries
OECD/DAC New Development Strategy	1996	Formulated by donor countries for developing countries
MDGs	2000	Formulated by UN member states for developing countries
SDGs	2015	Formulated by UN member states for all UN member states

North–South aid agenda, which was reflected by content targeting developing countries. Additionally, the MDGs were predominantly formulated by leaders of bilateral and multilateral development agencies. Consequently, the MDGs are often criticised as a top-down approach for meeting basic needs, promoting a target-driven strategy and as being de-contextualised from local settings (Fukuda-Parr, 2016).

Based on an overview of the IDGs and targets, it is remarkable that they were first formulated by the UN member states for developing countries, and then transformed to North–South aid agendas articulated by developed countries for developing countries (Table 1.1). This underscores the uniqueness of the SDGs' intention to involve developing countries *and* developed countries in global development.

Formulation of the SDGs

The 2030 agenda's formation began in 2011 and evolved over a long and complex process based on two parallel streams. Although explaining the details of this process is not the purpose of this chapter, it is important to look at the formulation process of the SDGs.

The SDGs' formation occurred in two parallel processes, namely, consultations over the Post-2015 Development Agenda, known as the 'post-2015 debate' or the 'post-MDGs debate', and the follow up to the Rio+20 Conference on the Environment and Development (Rio+20). The post-2015 debate was led by the UN Secretary-General to formulate a 'Post-2015 Development Agenda' which succeeded the MDGs at their expiration. To that end, task forces, consultations and high-level panels were established by UN agencies and the Secretary-General. Meanwhile, Colombian and Guatemalan representatives proposed the formulation of the SDGs and they were accepted at the Rio+20 UN Conference on Sustainable Development in Brazil in June 2012. Based on this agreement, the open working group (OWG) was established and it involved UN member states, civil society organisations and private sector actors. Integrating reports from both streams, the 'post-2015 agenda' was finally formulated at the UN General Assembly in September 2014.

As seen above, the SDGs' approach is a policy-oriented project, like the MDGs. However, the formulation process for the SDGs was more open to multi-dimensional stakeholders. Particularly with the establishment of the OWG, various actors including governments, civil society, academics, business groups and UN agencies participated. Developing countries played a key role in the proposal made at Rio+20, and both Northern and Southern environment ministers drove the formation. Reflecting on the critique of the MDGs' formulation process, it is significant that the SDGs' formulation involved many constituencies.

Introduction to the book chapters

In this volume, we will examine the diffusion and implementation of the SDGs in multiple policy areas and different regions. The conceptual frameworks introduced in this chapter are more fully explained in the following chapter by Souza and Bacon. Their chapter introduces the constructivist theory of norm diffusion with a focus on the 'spiral model', which helps explain the processes that allow internationally sanctioned human rights norms to be diffused and implemented in various states. The model also clarifies who has the normative power to put such diffusion into practice. The chapter assists readers in building a theoretical understanding of norm diffusion and introduces the analytical perspective within which to read the following chapters.

The three subsequent sections of this volume focus respectively on the three different policy areas: health, education and decent work. Most chapters discuss SDG norm diffusion using case studies. The authors were guided by the following questions:

(1) What was the relevant actor's reaction toward the norms embedded in the SDGs?
(2) Who contested or accepted the norms and why?
(3) How have the norms been diffused and what was the role of relevant actors in this process?

The second section focuses on norm diffusion of SDG 3: health and well-being. Chapter 3 by Yasushi Katsuma highlights universal health coverage (UHC), which is an explicit SDG target (Target 3.8). The origins of the current movement towards UHC are analysed from the perspective of norm diffusion. The author aims to explain: (1) how a legal norm of the right to health translated into the goal of 'health for all'; (2) how terms such as primary health care (PHC) and UHC were used to pursue 'health for all'; (3) how the 'health for all' agenda became integrated into the SDGs; and (4) how a multi-sectoral approach is taken to promote the implementation of SDG Target 3.8: UHC.

Chapter 4 by Elena Avramovska highlights the protection of sexual and reproductive health and rights (SRHRs) and unpacks the interaction between various stakeholders aiming to redesign the SRHR agenda in the Philippines. This chapter's purpose is twofold: (1) tracing the evolution of the SRHRs and their inclusion into the SDGs; and (2) examining the compliance with SRHRs in the Philippines. While the Asian archipelago was a forerunner in the region regarding gender equality policies in political participation, gender budgeting and violence against women, compliance with the SRHRs has been sporadic, often contested and incomplete. This chapter specifically investigates the role of key stakeholders and institutions such as the Catholic Church, which do not belong to the traditional state vs non-state actor divide, and discusses their roles in weakening mechanisms of compliance concerning the SRHRs.

Chapter 5 by Mina Chiba focuses on the diffusion of school-based comprehensive sexuality education (CSE) through a case study of Thailand. Internationally, providing young people with CSE has been suggested as an effective measure to prevent HIV/AIDS and promote SRHRs. However, CSE is often domestically disputed due to its culturally sensitive nature and its implementation stagnates in many states. This chapter explores how CSE has been diffused, limiting its implementation in Thailand. The chapter investigates Thailand's policy development process and implementation with a focus on promotion and contestation against CSE among domestic actors, such as ministries, NGOs and school teachers. It also investigates the results of a national-scale project implemented by an international NGO to widen the implementation of CSE in schools.

The third section of the book sheds light on the diffusion of SDG 4: equitable quality education. Chapter 6 by Makiko Hayashi explores how and why 'inclusive education' is diffused and transformed (or not) across various stakeholders at the levels of intention, delivery and implementation in Cambodia. This chapter begins by illustrating the historical development of inclusive education discussed as an international norm of educational development. Next, it focuses on the Cambodian case to explore the relations between inclusive education and a body of key human rights instruments and policies. It analyses, with an application of the spiral model, how the concept of inclusive education is constantly reformulated partly through a 'cascade model' of training. It also investigates why inclusive education does not diffuse as originally intended.

Chapter 7 by Jun Kawaguchi and Kazuo Kuroda illustrates and discusses the diffusion of inclusive education as an educational policy norm in developing countries through exploring Malawi's primary school system. This chapter is based on a case study which uses extensive fieldwork: classroom observations, questionnaire surveys and interviews with teachers, principals and parents about the objectives for education and their evaluation of 'inclusive education' and 'special education' settings for children with and without disabilities. From the data analysis, the chapter discusses the complexity of norm diffusion of inclusive education from international to national and national to local levels. It suggests a more careful promotion of the new concept in educational practices, while fully acknowledging the achievements and potential of inclusive education.

Chapter 8 by Leyla Radjai focuses on SDG 4.7, which focuses on 'global citizenship and appreciation of cultural diversity and culture's contribution to sustainable development'. This new target, which was not included in the MDGs, emphasises the value and quality of education rather than access alone. This chapter highlights factors that affect the diffusion of Global Citizenship Education in higher education policies in Japan and investigates how the concept of global citizenship has been interpreted and implemented in this country.

The fourth section examines SDG 8: full and productive employment and decent work. Chapter 9 by Thais Favero Souza analyses the connection between gender equality and decent work, through a case study of Japan. Gender equality and the woman's right to work have become an integral part of the UN human rights agenda, incorporated respectively within goals 5 and 8 of the SDGs. However, a huge gap between state commitment and compliance remains. The author argues that this is clear in Japan, especially regarding the right to work. This chapter uses the spiral model framework, through a feminist lens, to analyse the processes of diffusing and implementing the female right to work in Japanese society. For that, it considers power relations between female actors and key institutional players in the translation of international principles, treaties and guidelines such as the SDGs into domestic laws and policies.

Chapter 10 by Paul Bacon and Nishkhan Usayapant evaluates the EU and International Labour Organization (ILO) roles in promoting SDGs in Thailand and in particular, SDG Target 8.7, which pledges to take 'immediate and effective measures to eradicate forced labour, end modern slavery and human trafficking'. In April 2015, the European Commission issued a 'yellow card' impacting the Thai fisheries industry, threatening economic sanctions and urging the Thai government to take action to eradicate illegal, unreported and unregulated fishing. The EU is one of Thailand's largest export markets and, as a result, the EU successfully pressured the Thai government to improve its fisheries governance and improve compliance with labour standards in the industry. The chapter attributes this success to the EU partnering with the ILO and benefiting from their expertise to diffuse decent work norms on the ground, while leveraging the threat of economic conditionality deployed in the form of the fisheries yellow card.

Chapter 11 by Shukuko Koyama highlights SDG Target 8.8 'Protect labour rights and promote safe and secure working environments for all workers, including migrant workers, in particular women migrants, and those in precarious employment'. This chapter explores dynamics in the process of adopting labour rights norms and analyses factors affecting the norm diffusion process by taking an example from Georgia. It examines political-economic interests among local political elites and how they determined the course of norm diffusion. It argues that norm diffusion research needs to advance a more nuanced understanding of actors and suggests meso-level elites' inclusion such as internationally educated Georgian staffers in international organisations and local elites in some opposition parties, civil society organisations and private sector companies, as a key unit of analysis in future norm diffusion research.

Chapter 12 by Stephanie Ghislain illustrates how implementing the SDGs made the issue of animal welfare mainstream and discusses the role of EU trade policy. Internationally, the UN 2030 Agenda for Sustainable Development, which contains the SDGs, envisages 'a world [...] in which humanity lives in harmony with nature and in which wildlife and other living creatures are protected'. This chapter introduces how SDGs interconnect with animal welfare, especially SDG 8, and studies how this norm, pushed for by the public, was gradually adopted by the EU. In addition, it demonstrates how the EU's trade policy can project this, more specifically through provisions on regulatory cooperation, trade and sustainable development, and the potential socialisation of EU trading partners.

Chapter 13 by Paul Bacon, Mina Chiba and Frederik Ponjaert gives an overview of some of the key findings in the book, and how each of the chapters in the book offers a contribution to our understanding of the challenges and opportunities in diffusing the SDGs. It is demonstrated that the spiral model remains an extremely helpful theoretical framework which was used productively by most of the contributors to the volume. In many of the case studies there remains a problem in moving from commitment to compliance—moving from a state of affairs where target states sign up to commitments, to a point where these commitments are implemented in a meaningful way. Lastly, most of the chapters in this volume are based on extensive and granular fieldwork, allied to cutting-edge conceptualisation; it is argued that this is necessary in order to fully understand the locally-mediated nature of SDG diffusion. There is tremendous scope to use this approach as the basis for a comprehensive research programme on the implementation of the SDGs.

References

Fukuda-Parr, S. (2016). From the Millennium Development Goals to the Sustainable Development Goals: Shifts in purpose, concept, and politics of global goal setting for development. *Gender & Development*, *24*, 1–10. https://doi.org/10.1080/13552074.2016.1145895

Fukuda-Parr, S., & McNeill, D. (2019). Knowledge and politics in setting and measuring the SDGs: Introduction to special issue. *Global Policy*, *10*, 5–15. https://doi.org/10.1111/1758-5899.12604

Hulme, D. (2007). *The making of the Millennium Development Goals: Human development meets results-based management in an imperfect world* (Brooks World Poverty Institute Working Paper 16). http://dx.doi.org/10.2139/ssrn.1246696

United Nations. (2015). Transforming our world: The 2030 Agenda for Sustainable Development. *Resolution adopted by the General Assembly on 25 September 2015* (A/RES/70/1).https://sdgs.un.org/sites/default/files/publications/21252030%20Agenda%20for%20Sustainable%20Development%20web.pdf

United Nations. (1961). United Nations Development Decade: A programme for international economic co-operation (I) (A/RES/1710 [XVI]).

2 Adapting and applying the 'spiral model' to the diffusion of the SDGs

Thais Favero Souza and Paul Bacon

Introduction

In this ground-clearing theoretical chapter we explain how constructivist theories of human rights norm diffusion could be adapted and used to explain the processes that allow internationally sanctioned Sustainable Development Goal (SDG) norms to be diffused to a variety of states, and to clarify who has the normative power to put such diffusion into practice. The work that represents the state of the art for norm diffusion theories is the 'spiral model', which focuses on the interactions of international and domestic institutions to understand the socialising effects of international society. However, even though the spiral model will be used as the basis of this analytical framework, it could benefit from incorporating improvements taken from other relevant approaches to norm diffusion. Specifically, this hybrid theory also features scope conditions, mechanisms of diffusion and modes of action from Ian Manners' Normative Power Europe and Börzel and Risse's Europeanisation/diffusion paradigm.

In this chapter, we will introduce the basic and most relevant points of the spiral model, including the improvements provided by the use of the aforementioned hybrid theory. The exposition will be divided as follows:

1. First, we will focus on the logics of action and socialisation processes present in the model, including here a clarification of the concepts of socialisation and persuasion based on Checkel's theory of different types of socialisation.
2. Next, we will introduce the model's scope conditions, under which such socialisation processes occur.
3. Then, we will focus on presenting the direct and indirect mechanisms of diffusion and modes of action which can cause states to internalise international norms.
4. In addition, we will explain the model's five phases of implementation (respectively, *repression*; *denial*; *tactical concessions*; *prescriptive status*; *rule-consistent behaviour*).

Also, the ways in which the theory has evolved through the years will be briefly touched upon, mostly as an introduction to our suggestion of other theoretical

DOI: 10.4324/9781003205951-3

additions that could be used to better apply the spiral model of norm diffusion to specific cases. As a result, we aim to make the spiral model an even more powerful tool to understand and thus, improve the results of norm diffusion and norm compliance in locations beyond Europe.

The spiral model of human rights change and the hybrid theory

The spiral model was created in the book 'The Power of Human Rights' (1999), and in its follow-up 'The Persistent Power of Human Rights', edited by Risse, Ropp and Sikkink (2013). Both publications have been continuously cited and successfully applied by scholars in many case studies, serving as a framework to analyse the diffusion and implementation of human rights in diverse countries from all over the world. According to Google Scholar, in November 2021, 'The Power of Human Rights' (1999) and 'The Persistent Power of Human Rights' (2013) have 4200 and 640 individual citations, respectively. However, before thinking about its material application and its adaptation for use in studying the diffusion of SDG norms, it is necessary to understand the theoretical basis of this model.

The theory of the 'boomerang effect', proposed by Margaret Keck and Kathryn Sikkink (Keck & Sikkink, 1998; Keck & Sikkink, 1999), is the stepping stone used to define the diffusion processes identified by the spiral model. The boomerang effect bases itself on the concept of transnational advocacy networks communicating, sharing information and services, circulating personnel and exchanging funds, all in a joint effort to influence policies (Keck & Sikkink, 1999, pp. 91–92). Through these networks (which include research and advocacy groups, intergovernmental organisations, local social movements, foundations, the media and others), there is influence from groups in one state in need of help towards citizens of another. This then culminates with those citizens pressuring their own government to make the offending regime change their ways. In other words, avoiding compliance at first could backfire on those states, since they could become the target of even greater international pressure and criticism in the future.

The spiral model uses this national/international interactive work between state and non-state actors and specifies the concept by identifying socialisation processes, phases of compliance, scope conditions under which socialisation mechanisms work and modes of social action to encourage compliance. All these theoretical points will be presented in this chapter, and then followed by the problematisation of some points of the model and by useful additions to it, all with the aim of easing and broadening its application.

However, as previously mentioned, our approach to the spiral model uses a hybrid theory that incorporates elements from three major theories in this field: Risse, Ropp and Sikkink's spiral model of norm diffusion (Risse, Ropp & Sikkink, 1999, 2013); Ian Manners' Normative Power Europe concept (Manners, 2002); and Börzel and Risse's Europeanisation/diffusion paradigm (Börzel & Risse, 2012). Thus, it is important to at least briefly mention the theoretical bases of the last two theories, especially since the spiral model will be thoroughly explained. For the Normative Power Europe approach (which, as its name shows, concentrates its explanatory efforts on the European Union (EU)), the normative basis that the EU is built on makes it inclined to also act in a normative way in world politics. Because of this and its strength, the EU is then thought to have the power to define what is considered 'normal' in world politics. However, the theory has been subject to criticism for focusing too much on questions concerning the EU's identity, rather than on its actions (Bacon & Nakamura, 2021). Börzel and Risse's Europeanisation/diffusion paradigm offers a powerful framework, but the authors limit the scope of application of this approach to look only at developments concerning acceding states, states in the European neighbourhood area or in relation to other regional organisations. As can be seen, there are pros and cons to the application of each of these approaches to norm diffusion. There is added value in creating a consolidated hybrid theory. In the following sections, we will introduce a tentative hybrid framework, centred on the spiral model and including additional important points present in the other two theories.

The interaction between logics of action and socialisation processes

The theoretical framework of the spiral model is permeated by logics of action and the respective socialisation processes they work at, all aiming towards the implementation of human rights. First, the logic of consequences sees political action and outcomes as the product of rational calculating behaviour designed to maximise a specific set of preferences. The question actors ask themselves here is 'how can I maximise my interests?'. The logic of appropriateness, on the other hand, understands action and outcomes as a product of rules, roles and identities that stipulate appropriate behaviour in given situations. This time, the question is 'who am I and how should I act based on that?' (Krasner, 1999, p. 5). These two logics are not mutually incompatible, in fact they are often mitigated by each other (Krasner, 1999, pp. 3–8), but their importance does tend to vary depending on the situation the state, its representatives and other actors find themselves in. They can also be seen at play in different mechanisms of diffusion and in their respective modes of action.

Concerning classification of socialisation processes, the spiral model has initially identified three distinct but interconnected types, named instrumental adaptation, argumentation and habitualisation. They are considered to be interconnected because they are indispensable for enduring change in the protection of human rights (and in our adaptation, to the SDGs) to happen. Respectively, we have:

1. Instrumental adaptation deals with the use of strategic bargaining by governments when they have to adapt to domestic and international pressure. In this socialisation process, states make use of concessions, try to bargain their way out of accusations of non-compliance with human rights norms, or resort to 'talking the talk' of norm compliance in the international scene,

without truly 'walking the walk' (Risse, Ropp & Sikkink, 1999, p. 12). Here, there is clear presence of a 'logic of consequences'.

2. The process of argumentation, which concerns argumentative discourses in the Habermasian sense, focuses on processes of communication, argumentation and persuasion, all based on moral discourse. It is used by states when they want to challenge the validity claims of the definition of human rights norms. It is not simply exchange of information, but using discourse to question information (Risse, Ropp & Sikkink, 1999, pp. 13–14). Here, we have what the authors call a 'logic of arguing'.
3. Habitualisation originates from the fact that the spiral model sees the difficulty the previous two processes would have to make states truly internalise norms by themselves. This internalisation happens gradually, when actors start to comply with norms regardless of instrumental considerations of personal benefit or loss, or of individual beliefs about norm validity. In this process of socialisation, compliance with norms is simply taken for granted as the right thing to do (Risse, Ropp & Sikkink, 1999, pp. 16–17). Finally, here we have a 'logic of appropriateness'.

This original formulation has been constantly updated in subsequent publications by the spiral model's authors and other scholars working with the theory. Specifically, Börzel and Risse reorganise these socialisation processes in their work on Europeanisation, as displayed below:

1. *Instrumental rationality or logic of consequences*: actors are conceived as (mostly self-interested) utility maximisers who select their course of action according to cost–benefit calculations.
2. *Normative rationality or logic of appropriateness*: actors are thought of as rule followers who 'do the right thing' because they want to be part of a particular community and have been socialised into following rules.
3. *Communicative rationality or logic of arguing*: actors deliberate and try to persuade each other about the validity claims inherent in any causal or normative statement. Arguing involves reason-giving and challenging these reasons as well as the legitimacy of norms (Börzel & Risse, 2012, p. 5).

When compared to the previous list, there is a clear inversion of the order of the logics of action. The logic of consequences remains top, but persuasion and moral argumentation have moved to the bottom, while socialisation remains second. This suggests that, for the authors, actors being socialised into following rules and actions just because there is a dominant idea telling them what is the right thing to do is a 'mere' logic of appropriateness. On the other hand, to reach the level of communicative rationality, actors need to be deeply persuaded of the importance of a norm, believing that it is substantively true or correct. However, this classification is not without some criticism, and to help understand the difference between socialisation and persuasion, and the importance of these processes for the successful diffusion and implementation of human rights, we must apply additional hybrid theory analysis. In this context, Checkel's theory of different types of socialisation helps understand the changes in the approach included in the spiral model.

Checkel's theory of different types of socialisation

As seen above, while in the original approach to the model there was an under specification of the concept of habitualisation and of norm internationalisation by states, this was somewhat remedied by the authors' following works on norm diffusion and by citing Jeffrey Checkel's theory of different types of socialisation (Checkel, 2005). Checkel divides socialisation processes into three different types: strategic calculation, role playing and normative suasion. They are based on the mechanisms of socialisation in use and focus on the interaction between different actors, looking at the socialisation initiated by international institutions and the results of this process at the domestic level (Checkel, 2005, p. 808). The types are defined as follows:

1. Strategic calculation: as a rationalist social theory, it deals with how incentives and rewards (material and social) are important to socialisation. Here, there is no true socialisation since there is only a logic of consequences. This type would be more like the starting point towards sustained compliance, needing other processes to reach that final goal (Checkel, 2005, pp. 808–810).
2. Role playing: for this type, which is also called Type I internalisation, actors are rational beings that cannot calculate pros and cons of every single interaction and thus, need to use certain hints and cues from the environment to decide how to act. Basing itself in organisation theory and cognitive social psychology, role playing (as its name says) does not use calculation or internalisation, but instead says that subjects act in a certain way because they think it is appropriate or because it is the easier thing to do. This is the beginning of the shift from a logic of consequences to one of appropriateness (Checkel, 2005, pp. 810–812).
3. Normative suasion: also called Type II internalisation, where we finally have conscious acts of persuasion, based on Habermasian social theory with the influence of social psychology. There is communication and attempts at suasion between subjects and finally, they actively and reflectively internalise what they must do. The sole logic here is that of appropriateness, with true persuasion at play (Checkel, 2005, pp. 812–813).

Checkel believes that socialisation should aim to reach Type II internalisation so that it can be more stable and enduring and thus, criticises the spiral model on that point, claiming that it focuses too much on the necessity of social mobilisation to jumpstart strategic and rational reactions from target actors (Checkel, 2005, p. 807). Risse and Sikkink do address this criticism, saying that the distinction between Type I and Type II socialisation might be helpful, but they still affirm that Type I would be considered sufficient for compliance (Risse & Sikkink,

2013, pp. 284–285). In other words, it is not important whether governments comply because they are completely and truthfully persuaded, or because they have no other choice (even if this decision was caused solely by instrumental reasons). This approach to the logics is similar to the aforementioned division between normative rationality and communicative rationality of Börzel and Risse, and can easily translate into damage to the explanatory power of the model when it comes to understanding processes of compliance.

Thus, while in some cases the presence of a logic of consequences or Type I socialisation might be sufficient, and Checkel does affirm that the three types should be seen as nominal categories instead of a full progressive hierarchy (Checkel, 2005, pp. 813–815), in general, it can be said that there must be persuasion to some extent and thus, that these processes must be better specified and brought to the forefront. This is especially true for the persuasion mechanisms that culminate in Type II socialisation since this is related to criticisms of the lack of consideration of the commitment/compliance gap and the movement between phases 3 to 5 in the spiral model. According to Checkel, we should not be satisfied with a 'thinner' level of socialisation. We will raise this point when discussing additions to the spiral model.

The scope conditions of the hybrid model

The aforementioned socialisation processes and logics of action do not work in a vacuum. To understand how they have been developing and how diffusion has progressed we must clarify the scope conditions present in each of these states. The scope conditions, according to the hybrid theory, consist of the following:

- *Domestic incentives*: the degree of empowerment domestic actors in politics and society have to demand reform and institutional change (Börzel & Risse, 2012, p. 11).
- Considering whether states have *consolidated or limited statehood*. For consolidated states, lack of compliance mainly occurs when such states refuse to implement norms. On the other hand, for states with limited statehood, this gap in compliance could also be attributed to lack of state capacity (Börzel & Risse, 2012, pp. 11–12).
- Considering whether states have *democratic or authoritarian regimes*. Democratisation processes usually bring improvements in human rights, and democratic countries are considered to be more likely to implement such norms than authoritarian regimes (Börzel & Risse, 2012, p. 12).
- Considering whether *rule implementation within states is centralised or decentralised*. The degree of centralisation makes a difference and thus, we cannot just assume the all states are unitary actors. Greater compliance tends to be connected with norms being administered by central authorities, since these organs can be more easily monitored and held accountable. Implementation by decentralised actors, however, requires more negotiation,

which makes compliance more difficult to secure (Risse & Ropp, 2013, pp. 18–19).

- The state's ***material vulnerability***, since states that are materially powerful will be strongest against external economic pressure (Risse & Ropp, 2013, p. 20).
- The state's ***social vulnerability***, since it may be easier to use 'shaming' techniques against democratic states that actually care about their international reputation, than against an authoritarian state, which would not be as sensitive to such reputational loss (Risse & Ropp, 2013, pp. 20–21).
- ***Overt diffusion***, which is the diffusion as a result of the 'overt diplomacy', or the physical presence of the EU through its local delegations in third states and international organisations (Manners, 2002, p. 245).

Mechanisms of diffusion and modes of action

Under such scope conditions, we can observe the work of mechanisms of diffusion and modes of social action, aiming to encourage norm compliance. Through analysing different material cases, it is possible to identify which would be the most efficient mechanisms of diffusion to be applied in each specific situation, and perhaps suggest which should be used to improve compliance in other instances.

The hybrid theory based on the spiral model identifies the following different types of mechanisms and their respective modes of action, dividing them into direct or indirect mechanisms. The direct mechanisms are:

- Incentive structures aiming for change that are manifested in the form of sanctions (negative incentives) and rewards (positive incentives).
- Capacity-building, which means the education, training and building up of administrative capacities necessary to enforce human rights, especially in target states with limited statehood (Risse & Ropp, 2013, pp. 13–16).
- Socialisation, connected to the logic of appropriateness, means that rather than maximising their self-interest, actors act by meeting social expectations in each situation. They are 'talking the talk' through complex learning and habitualisation.
- Persuasion and discourse, usually combined with negative and positive incentives.

In addition, we have indirect mechanisms, in the form of competition, lesson drawing and mimicry (Börzel & Risse, 2012, pp. 5–10), which reinforce the importance of domestic incentives and the capability of domestic actors to demand reforms themselves. They are defined as follows:

- Competition is a passive reception of ideas or solutions, which involves speedy change in behaviour by the actors as they compete over meeting certain performance criteria (which in this case is set by the EU).

- Lesson drawing is similar to competition, but it is said to be set off when actors are faced with a political or economic problem which needs institutional change to be solved, and they then look around for suitable institutional solutions.
- Mimicry (or normative emulation) occurs when actors emulate others for normative reasons, such as to increase their legitimacy.

These specifications of direct and indirect mechanisms help us to understand how international norms can be diffused and how domestic conditions can be different in the context of different case studies. Together with the aforementioned scope conditions and combined with the following five stages of the spiral model, these mechanisms form a hybrid framework which possesses significant explanatory power with regard to varied processes of norm diffusion.

The five phases of the spiral model of norm diffusion

With socialisation processes, scope conditions, and mechanisms of diffusion and modes of action in mind, we can proceed to the core of the spiral model, which is its explanation of how the previous socialisation processes work together during a set of five different phases of accepting and implementing international norms. As introduced simply in Figure 2.1, the five phases of the spiral model can be better defined as follows:

1. Repression (phase 1): this consists of attempts by political regimes to prevent any opposition groups from bringing human rights norms to light.
2. Denial (phase 2): clearly related to the boomerang effect, this is triggered when transnational groups manage to start an advocacy process using the

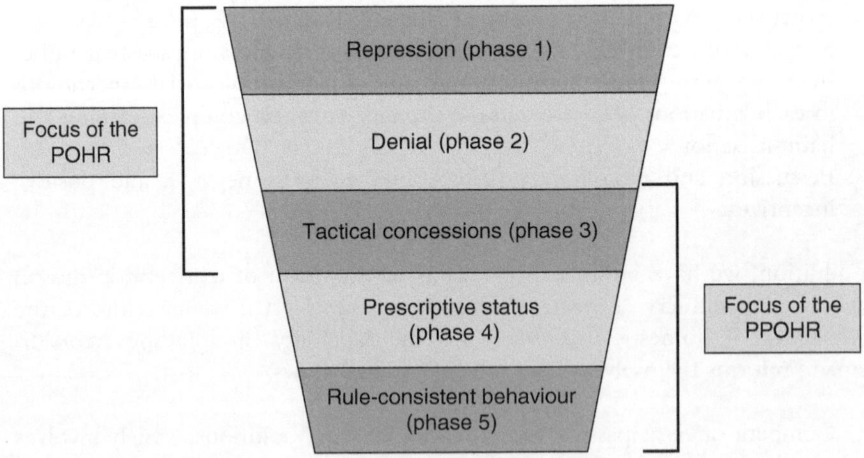

Figure 2.1 The five phases of the spiral model.

information they have on rights violations, which is acquired from domestic groups. As these national actors cannot fight for themselves, the lobbying from international organisations and from other nations is crucial to start a reaction from the abusing government, even if it is just to deny any wrongdoing. This phase is the one that kick starts discursive engagement and the process of international socialisation.

3. Tactical concessions (phase 3): the violating state starts using concessions to try to mitigate pressure from the international community. This empowers domestic advocacy groups and increases their mobilisation. However, this is risky, since the state could react to this movement in two opposing ways, either by complying with norms or repressing the actors fighting for them.
4. Prescriptive status (phase 4): this is the moment when the state discourse shifts, culminating with it beginning to recognise global governance norms through a defined set of state actions, practices and policies.
5. Rule-consistent behaviour (phase 5): the state shows clear behavioural change and sustained compliance with international norms, through actual implementation of prescribed norms both at the domestic and the international level.

We have now presented the main theoretical framework of the spiral model and explained how it can be used to analyse individual norm diffusion cases. However, although the basic contents of the model have remained constant through the years, some aspects of the model can be adapted, to reflect changes in international society, but also theoretical evolution. It is important to note how the model has interacted with other theories, and how it has itself developed from being applied in diverse case studies. It is necessary to discuss both support for and criticism of the model in the next section.

Support for and criticism of the spiral model: improving our analysis of norm diffusion

The spiral model remains a highly useful framework for understanding and improving processes of human rights norm diffusion, often appearing in related research and constantly being applied in a variety of case studies. Material cases, like that of Indonesia (Clarke, 2013, pp. 125–144) and of other states analysed through a comparative case study method (Risse & Ropp, 2013, p. 7), have proven that value. The successful application of the model in such cases also allowed the authors to affirm that the spiral model framework has 'a good deal of explanatory power for most of the individual cases' and that it could be used to generalise the different phases of human rights change 'across different types of political regimes, socio-economic systems, and cultural regions' (Risse & Ropp, 2013, p. 7).

Furthermore, regardless of economic, political, historical and social changes in international society, the spiral-shaped mutual interaction between states, international society and domestic society was also able to remain the strong core of the theory throughout the years. The Cold War conditions that were the background for the original formulation of the spiral model clearly did not apply anymore, and information on socialising mechanisms, mechanisms of diffusion and scope conditions needed to be updated. The range of rights-violating actors also needed to be broadened. However, the model has continued to be a useful way of understanding and improving the processes involved in the implementation of human rights norms, and has significant potential for adaptation in order to analyse diffusion of the SDGs.

Nevertheless, constructive criticism is always warranted to keep improving the spiral model. Some authors suggest that the model has a hidden ideological agenda and that there is a teleological dimension to the concept; it has been suggested that the model is 'teleological', 'deterministic', 'overly optimistic' and 'linear, even tautological' (Jetschke & Liese, 2013, p. 33). The model makes the mistake of taking a core group of developed democracies as states that would always respect human rights and that would make others respect them the same way (Risse, Ropp & Sikkink, 1999, p. 9). However, it ignored the fact that this first group could itself include norm-violating actors, which would also seek to use counter-strategies to avoid pressure with regard to their own human rights violations (Jetschke & Liese, 2013, p. 28). Too much credit was given to democracies, which resulted in an underestimation of both the divisions existent within democratic civil societies and of the lack of mobilisation of democratic states for human rights protection. Additional problems include difficulties with the measurement and operationalisation of key variables, cases of clashes between the empirical evidence and the application of the model and inadequate treatment of situations where competing norms were involved (Jetschke & Liese, 2013, pp. 26–42; Risse, Ropp & Sikkink, 1999, p. 8). Plus, as previously mentioned, a reconsideration of the importance of limited statehood changed the narrow assumption that only fully functioning states would be analysed, and without this prejudicial consideration towards the importance of institutional capacity, limited statehood cases began to be properly acknowledged.

While the basis of the theory has stayed the same, its focus has clearly changed. Initially, the theory aimed to understand how states might progress from *repression* (phase 1) to the level of *tactical concessions* (phase 3). This focus on explaining why states committed to international human rights made sense when juxtaposed with the way international society dealt with human rights-related issues at the time. However, it soon became clear that most countries could reach phase 3, and the focus of the theory shifted to understanding why states seemed to have so much difficulty in reaching the stages after that. In other words, it is now necessary to understand how states might make the move from *tactical concessions* (phase 3) to *rule-consistent behaviour* (phase 5). More than just achieving *commitment*, states need to overcome the stagnation they face when they reach *prescriptive status* (phase 4) in order to reach full *compliance* and engage in *rule-consistent behaviour*. It is key to move from a situation where 'actors accept international human rights as valid and binding for themselves' to one where 'sustained behaviour and domestic practices that conform to the international human rights norms' are a reality (Risse & Ropp, 2013, pp. 9–10).

Another key issue for the spiral model is the fact that it has a lot of difficulty explaining how states move from commitment to compliance, or more specifically, that there is an under specification of the processes that occur between phases 3 to 5. This is intrinsically related to the overestimation of the approach of leading democracies towards human rights protection, and requires a reconsideration of the causal mechanisms and background processes that were the focus of the first three phases, as they are not so effective in its last two phases (Jetschke & Liese, 2013, pp. 30–32). The model could definitely be improved with clearer distinctions being made between its later phases, and by having better guidelines for matching states with the phases they find themselves in. However, this issue could also be used instead to strengthen the theory, by allowing researchers to use it to identify gaps in commitment/compliance and to point out the problems in implementation processes in different countries. This issue will also be highly relevant when we apply the spiral model to diffusion of SDG norms, because the SDGs' initiative is so closely connected to compliance with a series of clearly stated prior targets. States have committed to reaching the targets, but to what extent could there be an SDG commitment/compliance gap?

The under-theorisation of cases where states could not move beyond the phase of *prescriptive status* and reach the level of sustained *rule-consistent behaviour* is another criticism that follows closely from that identified above. There is an under specification of the processes and scope conditions by which and under which states as well as private actors could evolve from commitment to compliance (Risse, Ropp & Sikkink, 1999, p. 11). To reach that point of rule-consistent behaviour, there must be continuous mobilisation and pressure from the international community in a top-down flow, together with the same kind of action from domestic organisations, in a bottom-up fashion (Risse, Ropp & Sikkink, 1999, p. 33). As the cases analysed by the model have shown, full compliance does not stem naturally from simple treaty ratification. Thus, there needs to be more focus on what conditions are needed to reach phase 5, and on how strong this pressure must be (Jetschke & Liese, 2013, p. 32). Lastly, this focus on the later phases could also help deal with some authors' warnings about the model not paying enough attention to social, political and economic nuances that influence the domestic impact of transnational advocacy, which evolved into an overestimation of the effectiveness of such actors and their actions. While the interaction between domestic and international actors is the basis of the theory, this cannot be understood in a vacuum, counting on states to be consistently proactive towards implementing SDGs after reaching the phase of *prescriptive status* and beyond. Thus, many factors could make a state regress or progress between these phases.

Authors have been attempting to address these problems of the model in order to improve it. For example, questions concerning the model's approach to domestic cultural expression, legal plurality, local customs and norms and to the importance of domestic courts have been raised (Jetschke & Liese, 2013, p. 42) and mitigated by the introduction of aspects from other relevant theories. In the next section, we will identify examples of how the spiral model can be even more useful when supplemented with other works related to norm implementation.

Strengthening the spiral model: adding theories of types of socialisation, norm localisation and norm contestation to improve the framework

Theoretical approaches should evolve constantly and the spiral model is no exception. Integration of the model with other theories is undoubtedly important for its improvement and does not detract from the usefulness of the model in itself. With particular regard to further specification and exploration of the processes that move states from phase 3 to 5 and to the difficulties in adapting internationally accepted values to domestic societies, this section will introduce some works that could help broaden the range and the impact of the spiral model.

Differentiating socialisation and persuasion

When talking about the gap between phases 3 to 5, we must look at the way this can be connected with different types of socialisation. In this chapter, we have already presented the key elements of Checkel's theory and explained the issues related to the under specification of the processes happening in these last phases. Considering these issues, we suggest a framework to looks deeper into phases 3 to 5 and to understand the movement, or rather the lack of movement happening there. This framework includes the insight from Checkel's definition of socialisation and persuasion, that the presence of either of these types of socialisation (Type I/socialisation or Type II/persuasion) could affect how the actors move between the phases.

Here, we first suggest that a differentiation should be made in phases 3 and 4. In phase 3, we have instrumental concessions made by actors based on calculations of benefit and/or just so they can stall criticism from others. On the other hand, we have legitimacy-based opposition, which happens when actors base their opposition to a norm through valid reasoning, perhaps by raising the need to prioritise the implementation of other SDG targets or by bringing up specific cultural and traditional justifications. As an extension of that, the division continues in phase 4, specifying situations where states act after being truly persuaded or by just following a prevalent social script. Respectively, we can divide this into 'sincere' ratification and 'tactical' ratification. This division could help explain situations where phase 4 is actually closer to being just an extension of phase 3, *tactical concession*, which would consequently affect the possibility for a state to move into phase 5.

Next, we suggest dividing phase 5 into three separate stages of norm implementation: partial implementation, substantial implementation and comprehensive implementation. This would help us classify different case studies and to consider more precisely which modes of action and mechanisms of diffusion would be more effective in each specific situation. These two tentative additions to the spiral model allows us to put a magnifying glass on the last three phases of the model and to think about how actors have been interacting in those situations, by looking at them through an even more robust framework. By doing so, we believe it will be possible to gain deeper understanding concerning the commitment/compliance gap.

Acharya's theory of norm localisation

Connected to the concepts of socialisation and persuasion, the localisation of international norms plays a huge role in the process of reaching the phase of *rule-consistent behaviour*, since states are the ones actually bringing international norms and rules to life in their domestic societies and legal structures. Acharya's theory of norm localisation is highly useful to enhance the effectiveness of compliance by individual nations, especially because it focuses on how principles understood as universal should not be forced upon, but instead adapted according to different cultures and customs. He defines localisation as 'the active construction (through discourse, framing, grafting, and cultural selection) of foreign ideas by local actors, which results in the former developing significant congruence with local beliefs and practices' (Acharya, 2004, p. 245), clearly prioritising respectful dialogue between local beliefs and foreign norms. By respecting both the role of local actors and of foreign actors in this dialogue and aiming for true persuasion, the theory manages to help us see the spiral model of norm diffusion as a balanced framework, without prioritising either transnational agents or local actors. This might also be helpful to understanding the processes operating towards achieving norm compliance, which happens in the *tactical concessions*, *prescriptive status* and *rule-consistent behaviour* stages.

Theories of norm contestation and the work of Jacqui True

Another possible area of improvement for the spiral model comes from theories of norm contestation. Jacqui True is one of the authors that questions the constructivist approach to the social construction of power, and criticises the excessive focus on the state as the most relevant actor in the diffusion of norms, to the detriment of other domestic and international subjects. According to her, norms are not fixed rules, but are plural and dynamic in their content and in the degree to which they are internalised. The content of norms themselves can change, and sometimes different norms might complement, and sometimes they might compete with each other. Norms are also not power-neutral and thus, implementing them without paying attention to this point might create new patterns of domination and marginalisation for minority groups. Finally, it must always be remembered that norms do not stand above power but result from global power relations and thus, are highly likely to reproduce them when being implemented domestically (True, 2013, p. 76). In conclusion, what we can take from this approach is that while understanding normative change is important, looking at what kind of change is being made and actively bringing about normative change that is positive to marginalised groups is possibly even more important. Overcoming the status quo and breaking with the process of normalisation is another way of making sure the conformity to damaging ideas and power relations are not being forced during the process of norm diffusion (True, 2013, pp. 73–77). International norms themselves are dynamic and sometimes combine and sometimes compete, and should be understood as such when being adopted and implemented (Krook & True, 2012, p. 104).

Direct, indirect and locally-mediated diffusion

In this section we also want to explain three important concepts for the understanding of norm diffusion theory; direct and indirect norm diffusion, and locally-mediated diffusion. Börzel and Risse make an important distinction between the first two types of diffusion mechanisms:

> First, ideas, policies, and institutions might diffuse through direct influence mechanisms. An agent of diffusion actively promotes certain policies or institutional models in her interactions with a receiving actor or group of actors. Second, diffusion also occurs through indirect mechanisms, namely emulation. Here, the action starts at the receiving end. Actors need to solve a problem or to overcome a crisis and look around for "best practices" and institutional solutions that serve their needs (logic of consequences).
>
> (Börzel & Risse, 2012, p. 5)

It is always important to ask ourselves who are the norm senders in any particular case, i.e. those engaged in direct norm diffusion. And also to ask whether actors in the target state, such as governments or pro-human rights non-governmental organisations (NGOs), are engaged in *emulation*, either normative or instrumental. For Börzel and Risse, processes of socialisation 'often result in complex learning by which actors redefine their interests and identities' (2012, p. 7). In some cases, this can mean that domestic actors are socialised directly by an external actor such as the United Nations (UN) or the EU. Sometimes, however, domestic dynamics replace international dynamics. Börzel and Risse anticipate this possibility. For them:

> Socialisation also relies on domestic actors, but the ways in which domestic actors facilitate reforms are different. Norm entrepreneurs such as epistemic communities or advocacy networks socialise domestic actors into new norms and rules of appropriateness through persuasion and social learning, and they redefine their interests and identities accordingly.
>
> (Börzel & Risse, 2012, pp. 7–8)

This account accurately describes what happened in several of the case studies in this book. For example, in Bacon and Usayapant's case study of Thailand and decent work (Chapter 10) the EU engaged in *Capacity-building* by funding the International Labour Organization (ILO) and several domestic NGOs with expertise in human rights law. The ILO and the NGO experts in turn worked on the ground in the local target state to engage in socialisation and persuasion of the Thai government. It is clear that the EU-funded efforts of the ILO and the NGO experts was an important Capacity-building effort that increased their socialisation and persuasion capabilities. Risse and Ropp (2013, p. 16) identify Capacity-building as 'creating the preconditions so that logics of appropriateness can apply', and that is exactly what happened in this case. What this also therefore suggests is that, building on Börzel and Risse's framework, we need to specify a third category of diffusion, that of 'mediated local diffusion', this takes place:

> where an external norm sender such as the UN or EU successfully builds the capacity of local non-state actors (through financial assistance, knowledge transfer, etc.) enabling them to act as direct diffusers of the human rights norm in question, in the local domestic context of the target state.
>
> (Bacon & Nakamura, 2021)

In this case, the external norm sender was the EU, and the local norm entrepreneurs carrying the norm within the target state were the ILO and the local Thai human rights experts. In this particular case, from an external actor or EU perspective, the diffusion has become indirect, because this is now being carried out by local intermediaries. These local non-state actors are themselves engaging in direct diffusion, but the EU is now working through intermediaries and proxies, local norm entrepreneurs or norm carriers in the target state. This process of 'mediated local diffusion' can be a very important factor in norm diffusion. One other criticism of the spiral model is that although the model is highly dependent on the interaction between external norm senders and local proxies, the way in which this happens is actually very under specified in the model. In several of the case studies in this volume, contributors identify the external norm senders and agents of mediated local diffusion.

The spiral model as a powerful tool of norm diffusion and norm compliance

In this chapter, we presented the basic theoretical elements of a hybrid theory of norm diffusion based on the spiral model, introduced some of the constructive criticism directed at it and explained how such criticism can be used as a stimulus to apply other complementary theories to the model, thereby improving the framework and expanding possibilities for application. We focused on how, although the model offers a powerful explanation of the movement of actors from diffusion to commitment, it has also faced issues explaining the processes that take us from commitment to compliance. We must focus our efforts on rethinking the implementation gap issue and in suggesting ways to conceptualise and facilitate states reaching the phase of compliant, *rule-consistent behaviour.*

We cannot be satisfied with symbolic state commitment to international goals or treaties, even more when this commitment is based only on the application of a logic of consequences or appropriateness. Aiming for deep and enduring norm compliance, we must understand how to promote productive dialogue between states and non-state actors concerning SDG norms, and how to facilitate domestic adoption and perhaps adaptation of these norms in the most beneficial way for the groups they are meant to protect. There is a need to analyse how states, civil societies, and national and transnational organisations have been acting in different material cases, and then to use conclusions from these analyses to examine the extent to which conscious acts of persuasion have taken place and have culminated in true norm internalisation.

In conclusion, as a theory of norm diffusion, the spiral model offers a powerful explanation of the gap between the formulation and articulation of the SDG norms, the solemn public commitments that states make about implementing the SDGs and their actual material implementation of SDG norms in domestic society. The model can serve as a tool to help researchers find ways of bridging the gap between commitment and compliance. The spiral model's emphasis on and strength in analysing the commitment/compliance gap in the human rights domain will prove especially useful in our investigation of any possible commitment/compliance gap with regard to the SDGs. The first step towards this is, however, understanding criticisms of the model and complementing it with other theories according to the different cases in question. Next, there must be an analysis of the extent to which particular norms (on education, health and decent work, etc.) have been domestically diffused by means of norm localisation, through mutual dialogue between international institutions like the EU, the UN and its specific organs or other transnational actors, and specific states experiencing difficulties with norm compliance. In this way, we can gain a more comprehensive and nuanced understanding of processes that span from initial norm diffusion to successful and continuous norm implementation.

References

Acharya, A. (2004). How ideas spread: Whose norms matter? Norm localization and institutional change in Asian regionalism. *International Organization*, *58*(2), 239–275.

Bacon, P., & Nakamura, H. (2021). Diffusing the abolitionist norm in Japan: EU 'Death Penalty Diplomacy' and the gap between rhetoric and reality in EU–Japan relations. *Journal of Common Market Studies*, *59*(5), 1230–1246. https://doi.org/10.1111/jcms.13177

Börzel, T. A., & Risse, T. (2012). From Europeanization to diffusion: Introduction. *West European Politics*, *35*(1), 1–19.

Checkel, J. T. (2005). International institutions and socialization in Europe: Introduction and framework. *International Organization*, *59*(4), 801–826.

Clarke, A. M. (2013). Chapter 7 – The normative context of human rights criticism: Treaty ratification and UN mechanisms. In T. Risse, S. C. Ropp, & K. Sikkink (Eds.), *The persistent power of human rights: From commitment to compliance* (pp. 125–144). Cambridge University Press.

Jetschke, A., & Liese, A. (2013). Chapter 2 – The power of human rights a decade after: From euphoria to contestation? In T. Risse, S. C. Ropp, & K. Sikkink (Eds.), *The persistent power of human rights: From commitment to compliance* (pp. 26–42). Cambridge University Press.

Keck, M. E., & Sikkink, K. (1998). *Activists beyond borders: Advocacy networks in international politics.* Cornell University Press.

Keck, M. E., & Sikkink, K. (1999). Transnational advocacy networks in international and regional politics. *International Social Science Journal, 51*(159), 89–101.

Krasner, S. D. (1999). *Sovereignty: Organized hypocrisy.* Princeton University Press.

Krook, M. L., & True, J. (2012). Rethinking the life cycles of international norms: The United Nations and the global promotion of gender equality. *European Journal of International Relations, 18*(1), 103–127.

Manners, I. (2002). Normative Power Europe: A contradiction in terms? *JCMS: Journal of Common Market Studies (JCMS), 40*, 235–258. https://doi.org/10.1111/1468-5965.00353

Risse, T., & Ropp, S. C. (2013). Chapter 1 – Introduction and overview. In T. Risse, S. C. Ropp, & K. Sikkink (Eds.), *The persistent power of human rights: From commitment to compliance* (pp. 3–25). Cambridge University Press.

Risse, T., Ropp, S. C., & Sikkink, K. (1999). *The power of human rights: International norms and domestic change.* Cambridge University Press.

Risse, T., Ropp, S., & Sikkink, K. (Eds.). (2013). *The persistent power of human rights: From commitment to compliance.* Cambridge: Cambridge University Press.

Risse, T., & Sikkink, K. (2013). Chapter 15 – Conclusions. In T. Risse, S. C. Ropp, & K. Sikkink (Eds.), *The persistent power of human rights: From commitment to compliance* (pp. 275–295). Cambridge University Press.

True, J. (2013). Chapter 4 – Feminist problems with international norms. In J. A. Tickner & L. Sjoberg (Eds.), *Feminism and international relations: Conversations about the past, present and future* (pp. 73–88). Routledge.

Section 2

Ensuring healthy lives and promoting well-being (SDG 3)

3 Diffusion of UHC through global health diplomacy

Yasushi Katsuma

Introduction

This chapter discusses norm diffusion related to Sustainable Development Goal (SDG) 3: ensuring healthy lives and promoting well-being for all at all ages. Among the targets set within SDG 3, the author focuses on Target 3.8: universal health coverage (UHC). UHC is increasingly accepted internationally as a strategic health policy to realise 'health for all' (HFA) or SDG 3. The origins of the current policy focus on UHC are analysed from the perspective of norm diffusion. The author aims to explain: (1) how the right to health was translated into the HFA vision; (2) how the HFA vision became integrated into the Millennium Development Goals (MDGs), and then into the SDGs, especially Target 3.8 (UHC); (3) how international organisations and conferences, such as the World Health Organization (WHO), the United Nations (UN), the Group of 7 or 8 (G7 or G8) Summit and the Group of 20 (G20) Summit, have been providing their members with arenas for global health diplomacy to promote UHC.

Through the process of explaining the relationship between the right to health, HFA and UHC, the author argues that norm diffusion took place in a multi-disciplinary manner (see Table 3.1). The concept of the right to health was deliberated by human rights scholars. HFA was initially proposed by health experts, but it was later incorporated into international development goals. To achieve HFA, a few strategic health policies were proposed by health scholars, including primary health care (PHC) and UHC.

The right to health

This section reviews how the right to health has been internationally agreed as a human right at the WHO and at the UN. The *Constitution of the World Health Organization*, an intergovernmental agreement to establish the WHO, was adopted at the International Health Conference held in New York from 19 June to 22 July 1946. The *WHO Constitution*, signed by the representatives of 61 states on 22 July 1946, entered into force on 7 April 1948. The WHO, with its headquarters in Geneva, was established in 1948 as an intergovernmental organisation

DOI: 10.4324/9781003205951-5

Table 3.1 Norms and their disciplinary areas

Norms	*Goals and targets*	*Disciplinary areas*
The right to health	Progressive realisation	Human rights
Health for all (HFA)	Health for all by 2000 (Goals 4, 5 and 6 of the MDGs by 2015) Goal 3 of the SDGs by 2030	Development
Universal health coverage (UHC)	Target 3.8 of the SDG 3 by 2030	Health

Source: Author

with its own *Constitution*, as well as its own member states. However, at the same time, it was also designated as a specialised agency of the UN, within the terms of Article 57 of the *Charter of the United Nations.* With the agreement between the UN and the WHO, approved at the UN General Assembly on 15 November 1947 and then by the WHO on 10 July 1948, it was expected that the WHO would coordinate their work with the UN.

Realisation of the right to health is considered as one of the core missions of the WHO. In the preamble of the *WHO Constitution* (1946), it is stated that 'The enjoyment of the highest attainable standard of health is one of the fundamental rights of every human being without distinction of race, religion, political belief, economic or social condition'. This norm was then brought to the UN. The *Universal Declaration of Human Rights* (UDHR), adopted at the UN General Assembly in New York in 1948, states in its article 25 that 'Everyone has the right to a standard of living adequate for the health and well-being of himself and of his family, including food, clothing, housing and medical care and necessary social services...'. As an outcome of the efforts to codify the UDHR into legally binding human rights treaties, the *International Covenant on Economic, Social and Cultural Rights* (ICESCR) was adopted at the UN General Assembly in 1966, and then opened for signature, ratification and accession by the member states. It entered into force on 3 January 1976, in accordance with its article 27. Article 12 of the ICESCR states that 'The states' parties to the present covenant recognise the right of everyone to the enjoyment of the highest attainable standard of physical and mental health'. As of January 2022, there are 171 states party to the ICESCR. It may be said that 'the right to health of everyone to the enjoyment of the highest attainable standard of physical and mental health' is explicitly accepted as a legally binding norm by almost 90% of the countries in the world, while the UN is made up of 193 member states. The signatory states bear a duty to domestically implement the internationally agreed ICESCR, including the right to health, in their respective countries, while their people are considered as rights-holders.

In April 2002, the Special Rapporteur on the right of everyone to the enjoyment of the highest attainable standard of physical and mental health was established by the then Commission on Human Rights (UN Commission on

Human Rights, 2002). After the Human Rights Council was established in 2006, replacing the Commission on Human Rights, the mandate of the Special Rapporteur was extended in 2007, and most recently renewed in 2019 (UN Human Rights Council, 2019). The mandate of the Special Rapporteur was established to:

(1) Gather, request, receive and exchange information.
(2) Foster dialogue on possible cooperation with relevant actors, including the WHO and the UN.
(3) Report on the realisation of the right to health throughout the world.
(4) Address specific cases of alleged violations of the right to health.

The Special Rapporteur on the right to physical and mental health has been engaging in dialogue with the WHO for the purpose of expressing their common understanding on the right to health (UN High Commissioner for Human Rights & WHO, 2008).

'Health for all' and primary health care

This section discusses how the right to health was translated into the HFA vision. The right to health is part of the economic, social and cultural rights that need to be progressively realised (UN High Commissioner for Human Rights, 2008). The signatory states of the ICESCR have an obligation to take appropriate measures towards the full realisation of the right to health to the maximum of their available resources in their countries. However, there is recognition that the right to health can be hampered by a lack of domestic resources. This reference to 'resource availability' leads to the need of many low-income countries to seek development cooperation from high-income countries.

At the thirtieth World Health Assembly (WHA) convened by the WHO Secretariat in Geneva in 1977, the WHO member states agreed on a vision that all the people of the world should attain a level of health that would permit them to lead a socially and economically productive life by the year 2000. This international development norm is popularly known as 'health for all (HFA) by the year 2000'. The WHO serves as an intergovernmental organisation to promote multilateral cooperation for health development, providing technical assistance to low-income member countries. At the same time, high-income countries have been expected to provide bilateral development assistance, not only technical assistance but also grant aid for health to low-income countries, for the purpose of achieving HFA globally by 2000.

The right to health is a human rights norm, in which people are treated as rights-holders and states as the duty-bearer. Emphasis is put on the obligation of each state to take appropriate measures to realise the right to health for everyone in his/her country. On the other hand, HFA is a development norm that encourages international cooperation for health, so that low-income countries suffering from resource scarcity can receive development assistance from intergovernmental organisations and high-income countries. In this context, this interdisciplinary norm diffusion from human rights to development areas is significant, as health financing is indispensable for the progressive realisation of the right to health.

To achieve HFA by 2000, particularly among low-income countries, a strategic focus was chosen within the health sector. In 1978, an international conference was held in Almaty, where the Declaration of Alma-Ata on PHC was unanimously adopted. In the wake of these events, at the thirty-second WHA in 1979, the 'Global Strategy for Health for All' was launched, in which PHC was endorsed (WHO, 1981).

The concept of PHC has been redefined repeatedly since 1978, and there are several variants. One of the most recent international consensuses reached by the major intergovernmental organisations, that is, the WHO and the United Nations Children's Fund (UNICEF), is the following:

> *PHC is a whole-of-society approach to health that aims at ensuring the highest possible level of health and well-being and their equitable distribution by focusing on people's needs and as early as possible along the continuum from health promotion and disease prevention to treatment, rehabilitation and palliative care, and as close as feasible to people's everyday environment.*
>
> (WHO & UNICEF, 2018)

After World War II, the UN and its specialised agencies started supporting many Asian and African countries that had become independent from their colonial rulers. Both in health and education, such support was extended to the tertiary level, either rehabilitating or establishing national hospitals and universities. Therefore, the Declaration of Alma-Ata on PHC in 1978 was a paradigm shift of focus from the tertiary to the primary level, ensuring that all people have access to essential health services in their community (see Figure 3.1). Similarly, in education, the World Declaration on Education for All was adopted in Jomtien, Thailand in 1990, shifting the focus from tertiary to primary or a basic level of education.

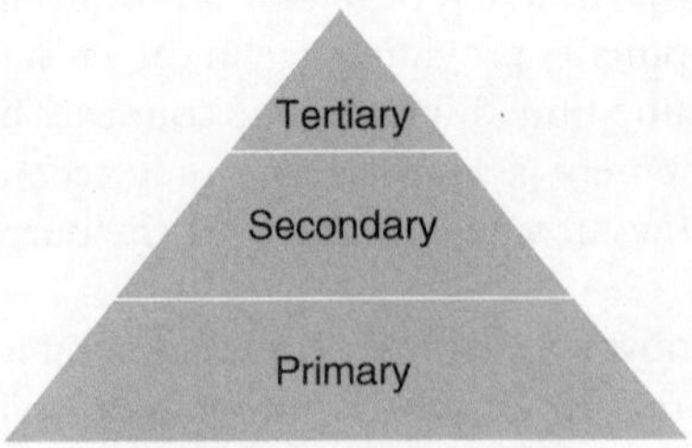

Figure 3.1 Three levels of delivery.
Source: Author.

The concept of PHC consists of three synergistic components (WHO, 2021):

1. Comprehensive integrated health services that embrace primary care as well as public health goods and functions as central pieces.
2. Multisectoral policies and actions to address the upstream and wider determinants of health.
3. Engaging and empowering individuals, families and communities for increased social participation and enhanced self-care and self-reliance in health.

The original concept of PHC was challenged in the 1980s. There were at least three reasons. The first criticism came from within the PHC circle. It was argued that the original PHC was too comprehensive to be achieved realistically, particularly in the context of low-income countries. There was a call for 'selective PHC' with a focus on specific diseases (Walsh & Warren, 1979).

Second, high-income countries that provided development assistance for health were more willing to support measurable interventions, such as immunisations. At the Development Assistance Committee (DAC) of the Organisation for Economic Cooperation and Development (OECD), the topic of evaluating official development assistance (ODA) had started to be put on the agenda since the early 1970s. The high-income countries that were members of the DAC became more interested in measurable health indicators, such as immunisation coverage, as the demand for accountability increased.

Third, some communicable diseases have also become threats to high-income countries. When the WHO declared the objective of global eradication of smallpox in May 1980, there was some sense of optimism. However, after HIV/AIDS was discovered in 1981, and transmitted among people in high-income countries, there was a growing interest in infection prevention and control (IPC), calling for health security.

'Health for all' in international development goals: from the MDGs to the SDGs

This section explains how the HFA vision became integrated into the MDGs, and then into the SDGs, especially Target 3.8 (UHC). The MDGs were not part of the Millennium Declaration adopted at the Millennium Summit of the UN in 2000. The framework of the MDGs was prepared later, as a programme of action to carry out section 3 'Development and Poverty Eradication' of the Millennium Declaration. In this context, the MDGs' framework was prepared as a composite of the international goals agreed earlier.

HFA is not explicitly expressed in the Millennium Declaration. The HFA vision is fragmented in the MDGs, as there are three health goals, without an overarching vision (see Table 3.2). MDG 4 can be traced back to the child survival goals committed to in the World Declaration on the Survival, Protection

Table 3.2 Health goals in the MDGs and the SDGs

MDGs by 2015	Goal 4: Reduce child mortality
	Goal 5: Improved maternal health
	Goal 6: Combat HIV/AIDS, malaria and other diseases
SDGs by 2030	Goal 3: Ensure healthy lives and promote well-being for all at all ages

Source: Author

and Development of Children (A/45/625), adopted at the World Summit for Children held in New York in 1990. Similarly, MDG 5 can be traced back to the Programme of Action (A/CONF.171/13/Rev.1) adopted at the International Conference on Population and Development held in Cairo in 1994.

MDG 6 became an independent goal, due to an increasing interest in combating communicable diseases and the eventual establishment of the Global Fund to Fight AIDS, Tuberculosis and Malaria (GFATM) in 2002. The Okinawa Infectious Disease Initiative, launched at the G8 Summit in Kyushu and Okinawa in 2000, led to strengthened global efforts to combat not only HIV/AIDS, tuberculosis and malaria, but also polio, parasitic and other neglected tropical diseases. The dialogues at the 2000 G8 Summit prompted the establishment of the GFATM, as well as corresponding disease-specific programmes, which are directly linked to MDG 6.

In MDG 6, malaria was explicitly mentioned, in addition to HIV/AIDS, showing solidarity with sub-Saharan African countries suffering from the disease. The Roll Back Malaria (RBM) initiative, launched by the WHO, UNICEF, the United Nations Development Programme (UNDP) and the World Bank in 1998, has been helping strengthen public–private partnerships to reduce malaria episodes in the world, especially in Africa. The goal of the RBM partnership is to reduce the burden of malaria by forming an alliance of a wide range of partners, including malaria-endemic African countries, intergovernmental organisations, bilateral development agencies, non-governmental organisations (NGOs), foundations and private businesses, organisations of affected communities, and research and academic institutions. In response, in 2000, African heads of state convened an RBM Summit in Abuja to express their personal commitments to combat malaria.

At the third Tokyo International Conference on African Development (TICAD) in September 2003, malaria was discussed not only as a threat to African children and women but also as an obstacle to economic development in Africa. It became clear that the private sector played an important role in reducing the malaria burden. For example, the Olyset bednet, the first long-lasting insecticidal net (LLINs) approved by the WHO, was identified as an effective tool to prevent malaria infection at night.

Although the health goals within the MDGs seemed fragmented, without an overarching vision of HFA, there was an increasing interest in strengthening health systems in low-income countries. This renewed attention to health systems' strengthening (HSS) may be explained by four factors.

First, it became clear that MDG 4 (child health) and MDG 5 (maternal health) were not on track to be achieved by 2015, while some tremendous progress was reported in relation to MDG 6 with a focus on specific diseases, thanks to the GFATM. Although annual deaths among children under five dipped below 10 million in 2006, child mortality rates remained unacceptably high (UN, 2008). Similarly, the high risk of dying in pregnancy or childbirth continued unabated in many countries in sub-Saharan Africa and South Asia. Therefore, it was increasingly recognised that MDG 4 and MDG 5 could not be achieved without the HSS.

Second, in 2008, as the thirtieth anniversary of the 1978 Alma-Ata Declaration was celebrated, the concept of PHC was revisited and reinterpreted at the WHA where a document titled 'Primary health care, including health system strengthening' was adopted (WHO, 2009). The WHO proposed that countries should make health systems and health development decisions guided by four interlinked policy directions: universal coverage, people-centred services, healthy public policies and leadership (WHO, 2008).

Third, eight years after the G8 Summit in Kyushu and Okinawa, Japan again hosted the G8 Summit in 2008, this time in Toyako, Hokkaido, in which global health was identified as one of the priorities on the agenda. In his speech on global health and Japan's foreign policy, then Japanese Foreign Minister Masahiko Koumura stated that 'human security is a concept that is very relevant to cooperation in the 21st century. …we not only focus on the health of individuals and protect them, but also strive to empower individuals and communities through health system strengthening' (Koumura, 2007). At the G8 Summit, there was a shift of focus from communicable diseases to the HSS.

Fourth, in 2007, the International Health Partnership (IHP+) was launched. The IHP+ was a partnership of low-income countries, high-income countries and intergovernmental development organisations that signed an IHP+ Global Compact. The IHP+ partners were committed to improving coordination and harmonisation within the health sector by uniting around a single health strategy.

In this context, on 12 December 2012, the resolution on global health and foreign policy (A/RES/67/81) made a recommendation to include UHC in the discussions on the post-2015 development agenda, that is, the SDGs. The health goal of the SDGs (SDG 3), 'Ensure healthy lives and promote well-being for all at all ages' (See Table 3.2) is an overarching vision that resembles HFA, overcoming the fragmentation of health goals within the MDGs. In the framework of SDG 3, there are several targets (see Table 3.3), but the focus in this chapter will be Target 3.8: the UHC.

Target 3.8 has two indicators (see Table 3.4). Indicator 3.8.1 is the coverage of essential health services, while Indicator 3.8.2 is the proportion of the population with large household expenditures on health as a share of total household expenditure or income. There have been coordinated efforts to monitor progress toward UHC in each country, collecting data on the indicators (WHO & World Bank, 2021).

Table 3.3 Targets within SDG 3

Target 3.1	By 2030, reduce the global maternal mortality ratio to less than 70 per 100,000 live births
Target 3.2	By 2030, end preventable deaths of newborns and children under 5 years of age, with all countries aiming to reduce neonatal mortality to at least as low as 12 per 1,000 live births and under-5 mortality to at least as low as 25 per 1,000 live births
Target 3.3	By 2030, end the epidemics of AIDS, tuberculosis, malaria and neglected tropical diseases and combat hepatitis, water-borne diseases and other communicable diseases
Target 3.4	By 2030, reduce by one third premature mortality from non-communicable diseases through prevention and treatment and promote mental health and well-being
Target 3.5	Strengthen the prevention and treatment of substance abuse, including narcotic drug abuse and harmful use of alcohol
Target 3.6	By 2030, halve the number of global deaths and injuries from road traffic accidents
Target 3.7	By 2030, ensure universal access to sexual and reproductive health-care services, including for family planning, information and education, and the integration of reproductive health into national strategies and programmes
Target 3.8	Achieve universal health coverage, including financial risk protection, access to quality essential health-care services and access to safe, effective, quality and affordable essential medicines and vaccines for all
Target 3.9	By 2030, substantially reduce the number of deaths and illnesses from hazardous chemicals and air, water and soil pollution and contamination
Target 3.a	Strengthen the implementation of the World Health Organization Framework Convention on tobacco control in all countries, as appropriate
Target 3.b	Support the research and development of vaccines and medicines for the communicable and non-communicable diseases that primarily affect developing countries, provide access to affordable essential medicines and vaccines, in accordance with the Doha Declaration on the Trade-Related Aspects of Intellectual Property Rights (TRIPS) Agreement and Public Health, which affirms the right of developing countries to use the full provisions in the Agreement on Trade-Related Aspects of Intellectual Property Rights regarding flexibilities to protect public health, and, in particular, provide access to medicines for all
Target 3.c	Substantially increase health financing and the recruitment, development, training and retention of the health workforce in developing countries, especially in least developed countries and small island developing states
Target 3.d	Strengthen the capacity of all countries, in particular developing countries, for early warning, risk reduction and management of national and global health risks

Source: UN, Department of Economic and Social Affairs
Available at: https://sdgs.un.org/goals/goal3

Table 3.4 Target 3.8 and its indicators

Target 3.8	Achieve universal health coverage, including financial risk protection, access to quality essential health-care services and access to safe, effective, quality and affordable essential medicines and vaccines for all	
	Indicator 3.8.1	Coverage of essential health services (defined as the average coverage of essential services based on tracer interventions that include reproductive, maternal, newborn and child health, infectious diseases, non-communicable diseases and service capacity and access, among the general and the most disadvantaged population)
	Indicator 3.8.2	Proportion of population with large household expenditures on health as a share of total household expenditure or income

Source: UN, Department of Economic and Social Affairs
Available at: https://sdgs.un.org/goals/goal3

The IHP+ responded to this shift from the MDGs to the SDGs by discussing how best the partnership could contribute to SDG 3. In early 2016, the IHP+ Steering Committee and signatory partners agreed to expand the scope of IHP+ to include the HSS towards the achievement of UHC. It was also agreed to broaden the base of the partnership as the SDGs are relevant for all countries, while the MDGs were for low-income countries only. It was envisaged that the new partnership would broaden the scope to focus on the HSS and domestic spending in all countries.

In September 2016, the Director-General of the WHO formally announced the establishment of the 'International Health Partnership for UHC 2030' at a High-Level Meeting to End AIDS during the UN General Assembly in New York. This transformed the IHP+ into the UHC2030. Its mission is to create a movement for accelerating equitable and sustainable progress towards UHC. After UHC was included in the SDGs as Target 3.8 in 2015, Japan hosted the first UHC forum with the World Bank, the WHO and UNICEF among others in Tokyo on 13–14 December 2017, for the purpose of further mainstreaming UHC on the global agenda. The co-organisers adopted the 'Tokyo Declaration on Universal Health Coverage' (2017), calling for greater commitment to strengthen global momentum towards UHC, to accelerate country-led processes towards UHC and to nurture innovation for UHC.

Interestingly, PHC is not explicitly mentioned among the targets of SDG 3, probably due to a lack of consensus on the definition of PHC at that time, in the wake of the debate between 'comprehensive' PHC and 'selective' PHC. However, in 2018, after 40 years since the Declaration of Alma-Ata, the Global Conference on Primary Health Care was held in Astana, Kazakhstan. The 'Declaration of Astana' (2018) states that PHC is a cornerstone of a sustainable health system for UHC and health-related SDGs.

2019 Osaka G20 Summit and UN High-Level Meeting on UHC

This section demonstrates how international organisations and conferences, such as the WHO, the UN and the Summit, have been providing their members with arenas for global health diplomacy to promote UHC. In this section, the G20 Summit in 2019 is analysed as a case to show norm diffusion of UHC from health ministers to finance ministers. At the end, the UN High-Level Meeting (UN HLM) on UHC in 2019 will be presented as a political commitment made by the heads of state and government. The heads of state and government of the G20 met in Osaka on 28–29 June in 2019, and then adopted the 'G20 Osaka Leaders' Declaration' (G20, 2019a), in which global health was one of the major issues addressed. In paragraph 30 of the declaration, the first paragraph in the section 'Global Health,' summarises the consensus reached among G20 leaders on UHC. As an outcome of the 2019 G20 Osaka Summit, the consensus on UHC is significant for the following three reasons (Katsuma, 2019).

First, before the heads of state and government met, G20 finance and health ministers were convened to organise a joint session for the first time on 6 June 2019, and then endorsed the 'G20 Shared Understanding on the Importance of UHC Financing in Developing Countries' (G20, 2019b). The finance ministers of powerful economies agreed that investing in health at an early stage of development is important for sustainable and inclusive growth. For supporting this argument, the World Bank provided evidence (World Bank, 2019). Then, G20 finance and health ministers encouraged low-income countries to mobilise their domestic resources for UHC. The G20 Health Ministers' Meeting, held in Okayama in October 2019, followed up on the agreement.

Second, Japan, as the host of the 2019 G20 Osaka Summit, took a whole-of-society approach in strengthening partnerships and engaged in policy dialogues with various G20 Engagement Groups. Although the G20 Summit was an intergovernmental process, many NGOs, particularly G20 Engagement Groups, were given opportunities to provide the host government with policy recommendations. For example, the Civil 20 (C20) published the 'C20 Policy Pack 2019' (C20, 2019), containing a policy paper on global health prepared jointly by many civil society organisations, in April 2019. The C20 Global Health Working Group organised a roundtable in Tokyo on 19 April, inviting Japanese government officials from the Ministry of Health, Labour and Welfare, the Ministry of Foreign Affairs and the Ministry of Finance, as well as some members of the Think 20 (T20) Health Working Group. A C20 policy paper on global health was presented, and views on UHC, healthy and active ageing, and health security were exchanged among the participants.

T20 is a research and policy advice network for the G20, consisting of several task forces. Its Task Force 1 focused on the 2030 Agenda for Sustainable Development, and then published 11 policy briefs. The T20 Working Group on UHC produced one of the policy briefs entitled 'Deliberate next steps toward a new globalism for universal health coverage' (Bloom et al., 2019) in March 2019. The policy brief consisted of four proposals: (1) leaving no one behind; (2) prioritising reliable domestic financing and cost-effective best buys; (3) harnessing innovation and access to technology judiciously; and (4) supporting common monitoring mechanisms, mutual learning platforms and coordinated international cooperation for UHC. A workshop was organised in Tokyo on 19 February 2019, where Japanese government officials were invited to receive the policy brief and exchange ideas on the recommendations.

In addition to the above official G20 Engagement Groups, two interesting private initiatives were taken to advocate for UHC. One is the Health Professionals Meeting (H20) organised by the World Medical Association (WMA) and the Japan Medical Association (JMA) in Tokyo on 13–14 June 2019, in which the 'Memorandum of Tokyo on UHC and the Medical Profession' (WMA & JMA, 2019) was adopted. The other is the Biopharmaceutical CEOs Roundtable (BCR) organised by the International Federation of Pharmaceutical Manufacturers and Associations (IFPMA) in Tokyo on 3–4 June 2019. The IFPMA prepared a joint statement signed by pharmaceutical manufacturers in Japan, the US and Europe (IFPMA, 2019), and presented it to Prime Minister Shinzo Abe in anticipation of Japan's leadership in accelerating progress towards UHC, in resolving unmet medical needs and in transforming to a new health-care system utilising various medical data.

Third, G20 heads of state and government recalled the commitment to the 2030 Agenda for Sustainable Development and the SDGs made by all member states of the UN in 2015, and then identified the urgent need to formulate a global health action plan so that SDG 3 and its Target 3.8 (UHC) could be achieved by all stakeholders in a harmonised manner.

A few months after the heads of state and government adopted the 'G20 Osaka Leaders' Declaration' in June 2019, the UN HLM on UHC was held in New York in September. The theme of the HLM-UHC was 'Universal Health Coverage: Moving together to build a healthier world'. As an outcome, the 'Political Declaration of the High-Level Meeting on Universal Health Coverage' (A/RES/74/2) was adopted. In response to the need for a global action plan, expressed by the G20 head of states and government at the Osaka G20 Summit, the WHO presented a global health action plan (WHO, 2019). It was a milestone event to mobilise the highest political support to package the entire health agenda under the umbrella of UHC.

Conclusion

In this chapter, first, norm diffusion toward UHC was analysed. The author presented Table 3.1, and then showed that there has been interdisciplinary norm diffusion from the right to health to HFA and then to UHC. The human rights norm of the right to health was translated into the development norm of HFA because of the needs of low-income countries for development cooperation from high-income countries. Then, the development norm of HFA was integrated into the health norm of UHC representing a strategic health policy to achieve HFA or SDG 3.

Table 3.5 Action areas and diplomatic arenas for UHC

Action areas for UHC	*Main actors*	*Diplomatic arenas*
UHC as a health policy	Health Ministers	WHO
UHC as a social investment	Finance Ministers; Health Ministers	G7, G20, World Bank
UHC as a political priority	Heads of State and Government; Foreign Ministers	UN HLM on UHC

Source: Author

Second, the author showed the diffusion of the UHC norm from health to finance, and then to politics through global health diplomacy (see Table 3.5). At the WHA convened by the WHO, health ministers of the member states agreed on the importance of UHC, as well as PHC, as a critical health policy to achieve HFA toward the realisation of the right to health. For financing UHC, it is also important that finance ministers endorse UHC as a good social investment for development. In this chapter, we used the 2019 G20 Osaka Summit as a case study to demonstrate this. Finally, at the UN HLM on UHC, heads of state and government adopted the 'Political Declaration' so that domestic resources were mobilised, and NGOs invited to participate, taking a whole-of-society approach in each country.

References

Bloom, G., Katsuma, Y., Rao, K. D., Makimoto, S., & Leung, G. M. (2019). *Deliberate next steps toward a new globalism for universal health coverage (UHC)*. https://t20japan.org/wp-content/uploads/2019/03/t20-japan-tf1-1-deliberate-next-steps-toward-new-globalism-for-uhc.pdf

C20. (2019). *C20 policy pack 2019*. https://civil-20.org/2019/wp-content/uploads/2019/08/C20-POLICY-PACK-2019-web2.pdf

Declaration of Astana. (2018). *Global conference on primary health care* (WHO/HIS/SDS/2018.61). www.who.int/docs/default-source/primary-health/declaration/gcphc-declaration.pdf

G20. (2019a). *G20 Osaka leader' declaration*. www.mofa.go.jp/policy/economy/g20_summit/osaka19/en/documents/final_g20_osaka_leaders_declaration.html

G20. (2019b). *G20 shared understanding on the importance of UHC financing in developing countries: Towards sustainable and inclusive growth*. www.mof.go.jp/english/policy/international_policy/convention/g20/annex8_1.pdf

International Federation of Pharmaceutical Manufacturers & Associations (IFPMA). (2019). *Mimeo*. www.phrma-jp.org/wordpress/wp-content/uploads/2019/07/BCRJointStatement_EN.pdf

Katsuma, Y. (2019). Global health diplomacy to promote universal health coverage at the 2019 Osaka G20 Summit. *AJISS-Commentary*, *275*. www2.jiia.or.jp/en_commentary/201909/27-1.html

Koumura, M. (2007). Global health and Japan's foreign policy. *The Lancet*, *26*. https://doi.org/10.1016/S0140-6736(07)61726-7

Tokyo Declaration on Universal Health Coverage. (2017). *Universal Health Coverage Forum 2017*. www.who.int/universal_health_coverage/tokyo-decleration-uhc.pdf

UN. (2008). *The Millennium Development Goals Report, 2008*. United Nations.

UN Commission on Human Rights. (2002). *The right of everyone to the enjoyment of the highest attainable standard of physical and mental health: Commission on Human Rights resolution 2002/31* (E/CN.4/RES/2002/31). United Nations.

UN, Department of Economic and Social Affairs. Available at: https://sdgs.un.org/goals/goal3

UN High Commissioner for Human Rights. (2008). *Frequently asked questions on economic, social and cultural rights* (Fact Sheet No.33). United Nations.

UN High Commissioner for Human Rights & WHO. (2008). *The right to health* (Fact sheet No.31). United Nations.

UN Human Rights Council. (2019). *Resolution adopted by the Human Rights Council on 26 September 2019* (A/HRC/RES/42/16). United Nations.

Walsh, J. A., & Warren, K. S. (1979). Selective primary health care: An interim strategy for disease control in developing countries. *The New England Journal of Medicine, 301*, 967–974. https://doi.org/10.1056/NEJM197911013011804

WHO. (1981). *Global strategy for health for all by the year 2000*. WHO.

WHO. (2008). *World health report 2008 – Primary health care: Now more than ever*. WHO.

WHO. (2009). *Primary health care, including health system strengthening*. 124th session, World Health Assembly, January 26.

WHO. (2019). *Stronger collaboration, better health: Global action plan for healthy lives and well-being for all*. WHO.

WHO. (2021). *Primary health care: Key facts*. www.who.int/news-room/fact-sheets/detail/primary-health-care

WHO & UNICEF. (2018). *A vision for primary health care in the 21st century: Towards UHC and the SDGs*. WHO.

WHO & World Bank. (2021). *Tracking universal health coverage: 2021 global monitoring report*. WHO.

World Bank. (2019). *High-performance financing for Universal Health Coverage: Driving sustainable, inclusive growth in the 21st century* (G20 Finance Ministers and Central Bank Governors Meeting version). World Bank Group. www.mof.go.jp/english/policy/international_policy/convention/g20/annex8_2.pdf

World Medical Association (WMA) & Japan Medical Association (JMA). (2019). *Memorandum of Tokyo on UHC and the Medical Profession*. www.med.or.jp/dl-med/wma/h20e.pdf

4 Diffusion of SRHR and local constraints

The Philippines

Elena Avramovska

Introduction

In the Sustainable Development Goals (SDGs), sexual and reproductive health is framed as a human right. The prominence the SDGs give to this set of rights can be traced back to the landmark International Conference on Population and Development (ICPD) in Cairo in 1994. The ICPD opened roads for building an international framework on reproductive health rights, and the subsequent Beijing Platform for Action marked a normative shift from 'population control' to placing human rights at the core of population debates (Chandra-Mouli et al., 2015). In addition, the programme for action demanded the inclusion of gender equality and women's empowerment, and the needs of young people and adolescents (Haslegrave, 2013). Despite these milestones, the full inclusion of sexual and reproductive health into development has not always been steady. Finding consensus on the inclusion of sexual rights was not possible, nor were governments able to reach an agreement on full access to safe abortion (Haslegrave, 2013). Furthermore, since the ICPD, different religious organisations and right-wing governments have made international coalitions that continue to contest progress on gender equality rights (Bob, 2012; Buss, 2000 Chappell, 2006; Collantes, 2017).

Contestation pertaining to sexual and reproductive health rights (SRHR) has also manifested in the context of the Millennium Development Goals (MDGs). The backlash against SRHR resulted in the avoidance of using the term 'reproductive health', intended to replace the term 'maternal health' (Berro Pizzarossa, 2018). In 2005, universal access to reproductive health was brought back into the MDG framework (Haslegrave, 2013). In contrast, the 2030 Agenda for Sustainable Development, similar to the preceding ICPD and the Beijing Platform, makes more specific references to human rights instruments (Berro Pizzarossa, 2018). The protection of sexual and reproductive health is currently reflected in two of the SDG targets: SDG 3.7 and SDG 5.6. The 2030 Agenda for Sustainable Development pledges to ensure universal access to sexual and reproductive health-care services, including family planning, information and education, as well as to integrate reproductive health into national strategies and programmes.

DOI: 10.4324/9781003205951-6

The following chapter examines how these international accords were implemented in the context of a specific case: the Philippines. It studies the evolution of the Philippine policy framework on sexual and reproductive health and the efforts by various governments to bring this policy domain into conformity with international frameworks, such as the SDGs. Focussing on sexual and reproductive health in the context of the Philippines is important as this policy domain embodies an outlier. In contrast to the notable progress in other legislative spheres on gender equality, such as violence against women and economic and political participation, in the domain of sexual and reproductive health, the country has remained a laggard (David et al., 2018). Abortion has been criminalised for over a century and access to contraceptives has remained highly restricted (Ruiz-Austria, 2004). What this chapter illustrates is the fact that many of the reasons why the Philippines maintained a restrictive legal framework concerning sexual and reproductive health can be understood by looking into the historic trajectory of specific legislation in this domain. Hence, this chapter focuses on the most substantive piece of legislation concerning sexual and reproductive health, *The Responsible Parenthood and Reproductive Health Act of 2012* (known as the RH Law). The many hurdles this bill had to overcome until its passing into law, as well as its contested nature after its adoption, are illustrative of the persistent difficulties governments have in legislating in this policy area.

While norm diffusion literature often assumes that states are unwilling to comply with certain human rights norms, rather than being incapable of doing so (e.g. Börzel & Risse, 2012), this chapter shows the reverse. The cumbersome trajectory of the RH Law illustrates how various governments attempted to make legislative progress in the area of sexual and reproductive health yet were stifled by a coalition led by the Catholic Church of the Philippines. Similarly, while norm diffusion scholarship, in particular in terms of the spiral model, makes a general assumption that civil society actors are either benign or supportive of international human rights norms, this chapter paints a different picture. It shows how various conservative civil society actors, in a coalition with the Catholic Church, acted as 'norm spoilers' with regards to sexual and reproductive health (Sanders, 2018). In this context, the chapter argues that the success of this coalition can be explained by the vast power resources the Catholic Church holds. To understand why it was able to amass these power resources, one needs to look at the role of 'limited statehood' (Börzel & Risse, 2012, 2016). To illuminate this, the chapter adopts a historical lens and discusses how the development of the Philippine state was closely tied to the Catholic Church. Given that historically, the Philippine state formed as a layer on top of a pre-existing institutional network operated by the church, it often failed to gain similar levels of legitimacy and social trust. The specific episode surrounding the RH Law illustrates how the Catholic Church could translate its high degree of legitimacy into political clout, which it then used to disrupt legislative processes in the domain of sexual and reproductive health.

Thus, the chapter proceeds as follows. Firstly, it starts with a theoretical debate on norm diffusion and introduces the idea of 'limited statehood' and its implications for understanding failures with norm compliance. Secondly, by adopting a historical perspective, it explains how the limited consolidation of the Philippine state in its formative years kept the balance of power between church and state in favour of the church and enabled it to become a forceful veto player in the domain of sexual and reproductive health politics. Finally, the chapter traces the contestations pertaining to the attempts of translating international covenants on SRHR into domestic legislation.

Norm diffusion and areas of limited statehood

The following section discusses the conditions under which states might not comply with international norms and introduces the concept of limited statehood. Before engaging in a discussion of specific conditions that lead to the failure of norm compliance, it needs to be delineated how the concept of 'norm compliance' differs from 'norm commitment', two concepts that are often conflated (for a more detailed discussion see Chapter 2). In line with the definitions posed by Börzel and Risse (2012, p. 7), actors are 'committed' to international norm frameworks when they accept them as valid and binding. In practice, this implies the signing and ratification of international human rights accords. On the other hand, compliance with international norms signifies continued conduct and domestic practices that correspond to international human rights norms. Norm compliance is also known as 'rule-consistent' behaviour (Börzel & Risse, 2012). As discussed in more detail in Chapter 2 with regards to the specific elements of the spiral model, such rule-consistent behaviour is normally preceded by states giving human rights norms a 'prescriptive status' (Risse, Ropp & Sikkink, 2013). This phase of the spiral model is characterised by implementing a variety of state actions, such as translating international covenants of human rights into domestic legislation. The distinction between these concepts is important as the account of the Philippines presents a case in which norm commitment and norm compliance strongly diverged. As this chapter shows, while the country showed strong commitments to international covenants on SRHR, we observe only a 'partial prescriptive status' when it comes to adjusting the national legislation to these norms. Ultimately, this led to incomplete norm compliance with regards to sexual and reproductive health.

Different mechanisms leading to norm compliance have been identified across the literature, such as coercion, changing incentives, and persuasion and discourse (e.g. Checkel, 2001; Risse et al., 2013; Tallberg, 2002). However, scholars still struggle with understanding the varying success of these mechanisms across cases. In this context, Börzel and Risse (2012) advise us to examine the more general scope conditions under which these mechanisms unfold, such as the degree of state centralisation or the type of political regime. When it comes to scope conditions, only recently have scholars started to consider the question of state consolidation. In some early norm diffusion theories (e.g. Risse et al., 1999), it was assumed that states are unwilling, rather than incapable or constrained in their ability to comply with international human rights norms. By taking consolidated statehood for granted, they assumed that states have a full monopoly over the means of violence and the ability to implement rules, an assumption that proved unattainable in many states. Rectifying this, Börzel and Risse (2012, p. 7) in their updated norm diffusion theory, underlined the importance of distinguishing between consolidated and limited statehood. They define limited statehood as 'parts of a country's territory or policy areas where central state authorities cannot effectively implement or enforce central decisions or even lack the monopoly over the means of violence' (p. 2; see also Risse, 2011)). Most scholars have studied these areas of limited statehood in terms of territorial limitations as more than 70% of all countries in the world contain areas that are not under full control of the central state (Stollenwerk, 2018).

Less attention has been given to the aspect of limited statehood in the context of policymaking (for exceptions see Ellersiek, 2018; Holzscheiter, 2018). Limited statehood in terms of policymaking occurs when the state technically has the capacity to reach a territory, yet it competes with a powerful competitor organisation within this area. This form of limited statehood is, thus, less about technical capacity but about legitimacy (e.g. Gilley, 2009; Levi et al., 2009; Schmelzle & Stollenwerk, 2018). Competitor organisations, whether these are economic, religious or even criminal, are here understood as organisations that enjoy higher levels of legitimacy within a specific cohort of the population or a given territory (Risse & Stollenwerk, 2018). In contrast to the legal authority of modern nation-states, non-state organisations can draw their legitimacy from tradition or long-established customs and social structures, the presence of charismatic leadership or the more effective provision of goods and services (Weber, 2008(1919)).

With regards to the Philippines, the chapter will use the concept of limited statehood to explain how the Catholic Church became a powerful player in the domain of sexual and reproductive health. By adopting a historical perspective, it discusses how, in many ways, the Philippine state consolidation was hindered, especially in its formative years. The difficulty for the Philippine state to consolidate has to be partly understood through the vast pre-existing institutional network of the Catholic Church and its role in providing substantial governing functions. As this chapter shows, the church has continuously substituted the state in the provision of education, health and welfare services (Grzymala-Busse & Slater, 2018). Through this, it gained immense legitimacy and political leverage. Although some of these functions diminished over the years, the church used its political clout to remain a dominant actor in the domain of sexual and reproductive health, both as a moral authority and a veto player in legislative politics. The next sections discuss these processes in more detail.

Limited statehood and SRHR in the Philippines

This chapter uses the concept of limited statehood to explain how the Catholic Church acquired a profound influence in the policy domain of sexual and reproductive health in the Philippines. Looking into history explains how the Catholic

Church gained the necessary legitimacy to function as a veto player (Tsebelis, 2011) in this legislative area.

The evolution of the Philippine state is closely intertwined with the role of the Catholic Church. In the Philippines, there is a strong fusion of national and religious identities (Grzymala-Busse & Slater, 2018). The Catholic Church arrived in the Philippines as a Spanish colonial import and preceded any notion of a nation across the Asian archipelago. Before the Spanish colonisation (1565–1898), the Philippine islands had not been united under a single political power (Grzymala-Busse & Slater, 2018). The Catholic friars became the central authority figures in the country and their first mission was to Christianise the population (Schumacher, 1979; Shirley, 2004). Without a separation of church and state, the Catholic Church swiftly penetrated all spheres of life and slowly became a bedrock of morality and national identity (Moreno, 2008, p. 32). Even after the replacement of Spain as a colonial occupier by the United States in 1898, the fabric of Philippine society remained closely intertwined with Catholicism. While the United States introduced a separation of church and state as well as various political and institutional reforms, it did not challenge the societal authority of the church. The church continued to replace the weak state in the provision of goods and services, such as education, health care and even natural disaster relief, especially in areas distant from the capital (Grzymala-Busse & Slater, 2018). Furthermore, even after Philippine independence from the United States in 1946, there was no secular nation-building process that could have offered a counterweight to the long-established fusion of religious and national identities (Grzymala-Busse & Slater, 2018). Hence, by taking over the functions of the state, the Catholic Church acquired strong legitimacy and social trust, which enabled it to extend its power prerogatives from community life to political institutions.

However, the provision of goods and services was not the only source of legitimacy for the Catholic Church. As discussed in the next section, the church's political authority was additionally heightened in the context of the People's Power Revolution that ousted Ferdinand Marcos. By standing on the right side of history as the main organiser of the revolution, the church once again bolstered its standing as a human rights defender (Boudreau, 2009). While Philippine politics, had been and remains until today, defined by vast inequalities, corruption and elitism, the church managed to create an image of standing above the political as a morally superior entity and later on translated this legitimacy into political power (Grzymala-Busse & Slater, 2018). In particular, it used its political authority to meddle in legislative processes in the area of sexual and reproductive health. The trajectory of the sexual and reproductive health policies in the Philippines, in particular with regards to the enactment of the RH Law, exemplify these arguments in the following section.

The trajectory of sexual and reproductive health policies in the Philippines

The following section examines the evolution of the Philippine policy framework on sexual and reproductive health and the efforts by several governments to bring this policy domain into conformity with international accords. In particular, it illustrates how, at different points in history, the attempts to legislate in this domain were impeded by the Catholic Church.

As mentioned, before the ICPD in 1994, the provision of reproductive health services did not have a human rights dimension, but it was framed as an issue of population management. Similar developments also occurred in the Philippines. Already under the authoritarian rule of President Ferdinand Marcos (1965–1986), his administration was the first to introduce programmes on family planning which were aimed at regulating the size of the population (Collantes, 2017). Their National Population Programme promoted information and services on family planning, and by doing so, touched upon a domain previously solely held in the hands of the church (Abinales & Amoroso, 2005). These programmes sparked a wide condemnation by the Catholic bishops. In their extensively disseminated pastoral letters,[1] the bishops firmly positioned themselves as being opposed to the use of any modern contraceptive methods. This was the start of a long crusade against any legal regulation in the domain of sexual and reproductive health.

However, the programmes on family planning introduced by Marcos ceased once his dictatorship ended and Corazon 'Cory' Aquino took over the presidency in 1986. Cory Aquino came to power with the help of the People's Power Revolution, which was led by the Catholic Church and a variety of civil society organisations (Abinales & Amoroso, 2005; Boudreau, 2009), including several feminist and women's organisations. The start of her presidency, marked by the drafting of a new constitution, opened avenues for the Catholic Church to meddle in legislative processes in the years to come. The interests of the church were reflected in a variety of constitutional provisions, such as non-taxation of church property and the introduction of religious instruction in public schools (Collantes, 2017). Yet, the strongest legislative gains for the church occurred in the sphere of sexual and reproductive health. Although abortion had been criminalised for centuries, its ban was elevated to the constitutional level with a provision that guaranteed the 'right to life of the unborn' (Melgar et al., 2018). In addition, the constitution reiterated that divorce would remain prohibited by stating that 'marriage, as an inviolable institution, [was] the foundation of the family and shall be protected by the state' (Philippine Constitution, 1987, Article XV, section 2). However, while the Catholic hierarchy opposed legislative progress with regards to sexual and reproductive health, the democratic transition brought a variety of laws on gender equality in various domains due to the pressure of women's and gender organisations. These included policies on violence against women, female political participation and gender budgeting, making the Philippines a leader in these legislative domains in the region and beyond (e.g. David et al., 2018).

Despite the success in other domains on gender equality, struggles to legislate in the area of sexual and reproductive health continued in the following years. The election of Fidel Ramos (1992–1998), the only former Protestant President, brought new attempts to provide contraceptive service to the large population. These attempts were however swiftly stifled. Soon after taking office, Ramos, as part of his economic reforms, introduced a programme for the promotion of 'freedom of choice' and the use of modern contraceptives. The Catholic bishops responded to this campaign by 'declaring a war' on his policies (Youngblood, 1998, p. 12). The strained relations between Ramos and the Catholic Church further deteriorated with regards to the Philippines' role at the ICPD in Cairo in 1994. In anticipation of the Conference, Cardinal Sin, who was a central figure in the People's Power Revolution in 1986, stepped into the debate claiming that Ramos' programmes were set to 'destroy the family'. In addition, the bishops organised large-scale mobilisations and protests ahead of the event and published new pastoral letters asking Catholics to subvert the governmental proposals. Resulting from this mounting pressure, Ramos replaced two of the representatives scheduled to attend the conference with religious authorities. Furthermore, his administration, together with the Catholic Church, agreed on a joint statement that asserted that the country would stay univocally opposed to abortion, despite abortion being illegal in the Philippines (Youngblood, 1998).

However, a few years later, in 1998, the Department of Health (DOH) adopted a new framework on sexual and reproductive health. In line with the agreed recommendations at the ICPD, the framework aimed at shifting the debate on access to sexual and reproductive health services from being an issue of population management to being a human right. The new programme also aimed at resuming a reproductive health strategy on the national level (Melgar et al., 2018). Yet such attempts remained futile in the next decade. A large coalition headed by the Catholic Church continued to hamper legislation in this domain. The strength of the coalition became particularly evident when looking at the events that preceded the enactment of the Reproductive Health Law in 2012. This will be discussed in more detail in the following section.

Reproductive Health Law of 2012

The following section examines the events preceding the enactment of *The Responsible Parenthood and Reproductive Health Act of 2012*, which became known as the RH Law. As discussed in more detail in the following, the RH Law was enacted after a longer-than-a-decade legislative battle with a conservative coalition led by the Catholic Church. The RH Law was the first of its kind at the national level, as it invokes respect for human rights and non-discrimination. The bill's declaration of principles states the following:

> The state recognizes and guarantees the human rights of all persons that include the right to equality and equity, the right to development, the right to reproductive health, the right to education, and the right to choose and make decisions for themselves. The state shall ensure universal access to reproductive health, services, information, and education.
>
> (House Bill No. 4110)

While the enactment of the legislation was undoubtedly a big success for those who long campaigned for it, its trajectory was arduous, and it fell short of its original intent. For instance, in its final version, the bill mandated that married individuals required spousal consent before having basic reproductive health services, as well as that health practitioners were allowed to deny married couples reproductive health assistance based on their religious beliefs (Melgar & Carrera-Pacete, 2016).

Even in the aftermath of its enactment, the Catholic hierarchy, yet again, demonstrated its stronghold in the domain of sexual and reproductive health. A coalition led by the Catholic Church challenged the law's constitutionality in front of the Supreme Court, which ruled that some of its 'controversial' provisions were unconstitutional. As a result, access to contraceptives for adolescents became further restricted, spousal consent for receiving reproductive health became mandatory and the court broadened the meaning of 'conscientious objection' pertaining to the provision of reproductive health services (Melgar & Carrera-Pacete, 2016). Furthermore, some constraints occurred with regards to its implementation and the de facto availability of contraceptives. After the filing of another petition, the Supreme Court ruled that before the state purchases and distributes them, the Food and Drug Administration (FDA) must certify that they are not an abortifacient, defined as 'any drug or device that induces abortion, or the destruction of the fetus inside the mother's womb' (Republic Act No. 10354). Furthermore, governmental hospitals and local government health institutions were not permitted to purchase or acquire emergency contraceptive pills (Hilbay, 2016).

Challenges before the Supreme Court were only the final strikes the coalition led by the Catholic Church took against this piece of legislation. Attempts at undermining it went as far back as its first draft proposal, which in itself had been a response to a trend of undermining sexual and reproductive freedoms. The first version of the RH Bill was filed in 2001 after a series of decisions that further restricted the already limited access to 'family planning' services across the country. One of these was the banning of family planning services by pro-life executives in the City of Manila and some other local governments (2000–2010). Another was the FDA delisting of the emergency contraceptive pill. Furthermore, the education department stopped a pilot project on adolescent sexual education (2009) and the DOH started using only 'natural family planning' methods (2003–2010) (Melgar et al., 2018, p. 9). Another event that motivated the filing of the RH Bill originated at an international level. In 1999, the United Nations Population Fund (UNFPA) organised the ICPD+5 Conference aimed at revising the implementation of the ICPD Plan of Action. The conference motivated the Philippine delegates to start working on a new reproductive health bill, centred on human rights in line with international frameworks on sexual and reproductive health (Melgar et al., 2018). The filing of the bill sparked a long legal odyssey in the years to come.

The nature of this legal odyssey was unprecedented as it involved a multitude of actors who joined one of two large coalitions: one in favour of the proposed legislation and one opposed to it. Most of the advocacy activities of the coalition in favour of the RH Bill were headed by a grand non-governmental organisation (NGO) consortium composed of various NGOs who worked on gender equality and sexual and reproductive health. Many of these organisations were long-standing advocates for gender equality in the Philippines (Ocampo, 2014). The RH Bill was also strongly and publicly supported by various government agencies, such as the DOH, the Department of Social Welfare and Development (DSWD) and the Philippine Commission on Women (PCW). In addition, different Christian denominations and the Islamic Clerics of the Autonomous Regime of Islamic Mindanao publicly supported it, as did numerous academics and public figures. It also enjoyed the support of the public, with 71% agreeing to its content, according to the Social Weather Survey of 2008. Most importantly, the proposed legislation was supported by the then President Benigno Aquino III, who became the first-ever Philippine head of state to publicly endorse a piece of legislation that went against the insistence of the Catholic Church for the use of 'natural only' methods of contraception. Aquino's endorsement sparked a fierce reaction and mobilisation by the coalition that opposed the passing of the law.

The opposition to the enactment of the bill was composed of actors with different profiles, including several pro-life organisations, such as 'Couples for Christ' and 'Human Life International'. However, the main protagonist of the so-called 'anti-RH Bill coalition' was the highest body of the Catholic Church: the Catholic Bishops Conference of the Philippines (CBCP). The CBCP had been a central actor in the organisation of the People's Power Revolution in the late 1980s and enjoyed a high 'moral' standing in Philippine society (Bautista, 2010). As a leader of the coalition against the RH Bill, the CBCP took a forceful role and moved the disputes pertaining to the RH Bill from the political institutions and the media to the lay communities. Within its vast institutional network, the church's hierarchy mobilised citizens all across the country and organised large campaigns against the proposed legislation (Ocampo, 2014, p. 14). It continuously instructed citizens not to vote for any politicians who supported the proposed bill (e.g. Collantes, 2017). Furthermore, some religious authorities reprimanded their members for supporting the RH Bill and the CBCP even threatened to deny them religious services (Cornelio & Raffin, 2009; Radford Ruether, 2008). While such strategies might not have impacted legislative processes in other countries, in the Philippines, they proved to be a successful way of hampering the enactment process (Ocampo, 2014).

When seen through the prism of the spiral model of norm diffusion, we could argue that in the Philippines, the norms on sexual and reproductive health reached a 'partial prescriptive status'. As exemplified through the enactment of the RH Law, various governments attempted to shift the discourse on SRHR as well as to change the domestic legislation in line with international norms. However, these processes have only been partially successful. The actual implementation of the prescribed norms has remained incomplete, as the state's ability to continuously sustain its rule-consistent behaviour with regards to sexual and reproductive health continued to be challenged.

Conclusion

This chapter aimed at examining how international accords on sexual and reproductive health, such as the SDGs, were implemented in the context of the Philippines. It proceeded from the observation that the lack of consistent progress in the domain of sexual and reproductive health stands in stark contrast to the other gender policy areas of the Asian archipelago. The chapter demonstrated how, despite the country showing strong commitments to sexual and reproductive health norms, the actual compliance with these prescribed norms has been incomplete. To examine this discrepancy, the chapter looked closely into the evolution of the most substantive piece of relevant legislation, *The Responsible Parenthood and Reproductive Health Act of 2012*, the chapter shows how a powerful coalition headed by the Catholic Church obstructed governments in their attempts at comprehensively legislating in the domain of sexual and reproductive health. Looking at the reasons for the political clout that the church had in opposing this bill, it introduces the concept of limited statehood. It shows how the church's political power originated in the high degree of legitimacy it had gained throughout history. Functioning as a competitor organisation to the state, when it comes to the provision of goods and services and by having had a unique role during the democratic transition of the country, the church enjoyed a strong moral authority. The case study of the RH Law shows how the church managed to translate this authority into raw political power, which it used to stifle comprehensive legislation in the domain of sexual and reproductive health.

Note

1 Catholic Bishops Conference of the Philippines (CBCP). 1973. *Pastoral Letter of the Catholic Hierarchy of the Philippines on the Population Problem and Family Life.*

References

Abinales, P. N., & Amoroso, D. J. (2005). *State and society in the Philippines.* Rowman & Littlefield Publishers.

Bautista, J. (2010). Living piously in a culture of death: The Catholic church and the state in the Philippines. *Asia Research Institute Working Paper No. 130.*

Berro Pizzarossa, L. (2018). Here to stay: The evolution of sexual and reproductive health and rights in international human rights law. *Laws, 7*(3), 29.

Bob, C. (2012). *The global right wing and the clash of world politics.* Cambridge University Press.

Börzel, T., & Risse, T. (2012). Human rights: The new agenda. *Transworld. The Transatlantic Relationship and the Future Global Governance, 07.* www.iai.it/sites/default/files/TW_WP_07.pdf

Börzel, T. A., & Risse, T. (2016). Dysfunctional state institutions, trust, and governance in areas of limited statehood. *Regulation & Governance*, *10*(2), 149–160.

Boudreau, V. (2009). *Resisting dictatorship: Repression and protest in Southeast Asia*. Cambridge University Press.

Buss, D. (2000). Racing populations, sexing environments: The challenges of a feminist politics in international law. *Legal Studies*, *20*(4), 463–484.

Chandra-Mouli, V., Svanemyr, J., Amin, A., Fogstad, H., Say, L., Girard, F., & Temmerman, M. (2015). Twenty years after International Conference on Population and Development: Where are we with adolescent sexual and reproductive health and rights? *Journal of Adolescent Health*, *56*(1, Supplement), S1–S6. https://doi.org/10.1016/j.jadohealth.2014.09.015

Chappell, L. (2006). Contesting women's rights: Charting the emergence of a transnational conservative counter-network. *Global Society*, *20*(4), 491–520.

Checkel, J. T. (2001). Why comply? Social learning and European identity change. *International Organization*, *55*(3), 553–588.

Collantes, C. F. (2017). *Reproductive dilemmas in metro Manila: Faith, intimacies and globalization*. Springer.

Cornelio, J. S., & Raffin, A. (2009). The Catholic church and education as sources of institutional panic in the Philippines. *Asian Journal of Social Science*, *37*(5), 778–798.

David, C. C., Albert, J. R. G., & Vizmanos. J. F. V. (2018). *Sustainable Development Goal 5: How does the Philippines fare on gender equality?* (Discussion Paper Series No. 2017-45 [revised]). Philippine Institute for Development Studies.

Ellersiek, A. (2018). Education. In T. Risse, T. A. Börzel, & A. Draude (Eds.), The Oxford handbook of governance and limited statehood (1st ed., pp. 479–497). Oxford University Press.

Gilley, B. (2009). *The right to rule: How states win and lose legitimacy*. Columbia University Press.

Grzymala-Busse, A., & Slater, D. (2018). Making Godly nations: Church-state pathways in Poland and the Philippines. *Comparative Politics*, *50*(4), 545–564.

Haslegrave, M. (2013). Ensuring the inclusion of sexual and reproductive health and rights under a sustainable development goal on health in the post-2015 human rights framework for development. *Reproductive Health Matters*, *21*(42), 61–73. https://doi.org/10.1016/S0968-8080(13)42742-8

Hilbay, F. (2016). Reproductive health and the conservative strategy of access denial: Comments on Alfi v. Garin. *Philippine Law Journal*, *90*, 734–752.

Holzscheiter, A. (2018). Health. In T. Risse, T. A. Börzel, & A. Draude (Eds.), The Oxford handbook of governance and limited statehood (pp. 438–458). Oxford University Press.

Levi, M., Sacks, A., & Tyler, T. (2009). Conceptualizing legitimacy, measuring legitimating beliefs. *American Behavioral Scientist*, *53*(3), 354–375.

Melgar, J. L. D., & Carrera-Pacete, J. (2016). *Understanding Catholic fundamentalism in the Philippines: How conservative religious teachings on women, family, and contraception are wielded to impede the Reproductive Health Law and other reproductive health policies: National report, Philippines: Building new constituencies for women's sexual and reproductive health and rights (SRHR): Interlinkages between religion and SRHR*. Likhaan Center for Women's Health.

Melgar, J. L. D., Melgar, A. R., Festin, M. P. R., Hoopes, A. J., & Chandra-Mouli, V. (2018). Assessment of country policies affecting reproductive health for adolescents in the Philippines. *Reproductive Health*, *15*(1), 205. https://doi.org/10.1186/s12978-018-0638-9

Moreno, A. F. (2008). *Church, state, and civil society in post-authoritarian Philippines: Narratives of engaged citizenship*. Ateneo de Manila University Press.

Ocampo, J. N. (2014). Structure and agency in contentious reform: Reproductive health policy in the Philippines. In Fabella et al. (Eds.), *Room for manoeuvre: Social sector policy reform in the Philippine* (pp. 119–153). The Asia Foundation.

Radford Ruether, R. (2008). Women, reproductive rights and the Catholic church. *Feminist Theology, 16*(2), 184–193.

Risse, T. (2011). *Governance without a state? Policies and politics in areas of limited statehood*. Columbia University Press.

Risse, T., Ropp, S. C., & Sikkink, K. (1999). *The power of human rights: International norms and domestic change*. Cambridge University Press.

Risse, T., Ropp, S. C., & Sikkink, K. (2013). *The persistent power of human rights: From commitment to compliance* (Vol. 126). Cambridge University Press.

Risse, T., & Stollenwerk, E. (2018). Legitimacy in areas of limited statehood. *Annual Review of Political Science, 21*, 403–418.

Ruiz Austria, C. S. (2004). The church, the state and women's bodies in the context of religious fundamentalism in the Philippines. *Reproductive Health Matters, 12*(24), 96–103.

Sanders, R. (2018). Norm spoiling: Undermining the international women's rights agenda. *International Affairs, 94*(2), 271–291.

Schmelzle, C., & Stollenwerk, E. (2018). *Virtuous or vicious circle? Governance effectiveness and legitimacy in areas of limited statehood*. Taylor & Francis.

Schumacher, J. N. (1979). *Readings in Philippine church history*. Loyola School of Theology, Ateneo de Manila University.

Shirley, S. (2004). *Guided by God: The legacy of the Catholic church in Philippine politics*. Cavendish Square Publishing.

Stollenwerk, E. (2018). Measuring governance and limited statehood. In T. Risse, T. A. Börzel, & A. Draude (Eds.), *The Oxford handbook of governance and limited statehood*. (pp. 106–127). Oxford University Press.

Tallberg, J. (2002). Paths to compliance: Enforcement, management, and the European Union. *International Organization, 56*(3), 609–643.

Tsebelis, G. (2011). *Veto players*. Princeton University Press.

Weber, M. (2008). Politics as a vocation. In J. Drejmanis (Eds.), *Max Weber's complete writings on academic and political vocations*. Algora Publishing.

Youngblood, R. L. (1998). President Ramos, the church, and population policy in the Philippines. *Asian Affairs: An American Review, 25*(1), 3–19. https://doi.org/10.1080/00927678.1998.10771180

5 Sexuality education in Thailand

Contestation and reconciliation

Mina Chiba

Introduction

As part of the Sustainable Development Goal (SDG) on ensuring healthy living for all (Goal 3), school-based sexuality education is considered a key measure for achieving the target of ending the AIDS epidemic (Target 3.3) and promoting sexual and reproductive health and rights (SRHR). Specifically, SDG Target 3.7 calls for ensuring 'universal access to sexual and reproductive health-care services, including for family planning, information and education', which is reinforced by Target 5.6 on ensuring 'universal access to sexual and reproductive health and reproductive rights'. Among the various approaches to sexuality education, the United Nations' (UN) agencies had emphasised the importance of comprehensive sexuality education (CSE) even before the SDGs were formulated. For instance, the World Health Organization (WHO) issued guidelines for the prevention of teenage pregnancy in developing countries and encouraged government ministries, non-governmental organisations (NGOs) and donor agencies to promote wider implementation of CSE (WHO, 2011). Accordingly, several states have collaborated to develop regional frameworks to promote CSE within their territories, as seen in the 2013 Eastern and Southern African ministerial commitment to deliver CSE and sexual and reproductive health services for adolescents and young people.

What are the characteristics of CSE as an approach to sexuality education? CSE is defined as 'a curriculum-based process of teaching and learning about the cognitive, emotional, physical and social aspects of sexuality', which primarily aims to 'equip children and young people with knowledge, skills, attitudes and values that will empower them to realise their health, well-being and dignity' (UNESCO, 2018a). Its unique characteristics lie in providing scientifically accurate information regarding sexual and reproductive health, developing critical thinking skills, promoting gender equality and taking a human rights-based approach to sexuality education. While CSE recognises abstinence as an important method for young people to prevent HIV infections and unintended pregnancy, it emphasises their right to choose when and with whom they engage in sexual relationships (UNESCO, 2018b). Thus, CSE informs young people on ways to access various forms of contraceptives and how to use them.

DOI: 10.4324/9781003205951-7

There is growing evidence of the positive impact of CSE in reducing young people's risky behaviours related to HIV infection and teenage pregnancy (Fonner et al., 2014; Kirby, 2011; UNESCO, 2009). As a place for offering CSE, schools are considered the best possibility for reaching out to many of the young people currently in need of CSE, as the education enrolment rate is dramatically increasing worldwide (UNESCO, 2014). However, in the Asia-Pacific region, the degree of resource allocation and implementation of CSE has varied significantly across states (International Planned Parenthood Federation, 2019). This limited implementation is closely related to the unique characteristics of CSE, which are often seen as contradictory to existing sociocultural norms. Thailand is one among many states struggling to promote school-based CSE through its national policies. Although the Thai government recognises the need for school-based CSE and mandates schools to provide sexuality education, CSE has not been incorporated into the educational curriculum as a compulsory stand-alone subject. Consequently, the degree of CSE's implementation has varied widely among schools.

This chapter aims to elucidate the norm diffusion process of school-based CSE within Thailand by answering: how did the various stakeholders react to the call for promoting CSE in Thailand; who contested or accepted the CSE-related norm and why; how has CSE been diffused and what kind of role did these stakeholders play in this process? Accordingly, the remainder of this chapter proceeds by exploring the policy development context for the domestic promotion of school-based CSE in Thailand. Second, it highlights the implementation of CSE and investigates the reasons for contestation among the school-level actors in Thailand. Third, it analyses a national-scale project implemented by an international NGO in collaboration with Thailand's ministries, which aimed at promoting CSE throughout the country. Based on a study of the successful schools from this project, it outlines key strategies to widen the implementation of CSE at the school level. Finally, this chapter concludes by discussing the implications of Thailand's case for the norm diffusion of school-based CSE.

The study is based on document analysis of government reports and secondary literature as well as interviews with key informants including former officers of Thailand's ministries and staff of international organisations. The case study focused on schools that participated in the Teenpath Project, which was implemented by the Program for Appropriate Technology in Health (PATH) during 2003–2014 and deployed to 1,833 schools in 43 provinces all over Thailand. The schools selected for this study were secondary schools located in rural areas in the north-eastern region that had successfully incorporated CSE into their school curriculum. In these schools, most of the students' parents were farmers and the students' religion was predominantly Buddhism. The case study involved conducting in-depth one-to-one interviews with school principals and teachers, as well as group interviews with students and parents.

Policy development of school-based CSE in Thailand

This section explores how the norm of school-based CSE was diffused at the ministerial level in Thailand by tracing the historical development of related policies since the 1990s. It does this by revealing the characteristics of the concerned actors and domestic incentives to promote CSE in the country.

Massive public information and education on HIV/AIDS in the 1990s

Since the first HIV case was reported in Bangkok in 1984, the incidence of this infection has rapidly increased in Thailand. In particular, the national HIV prevalence among brothel-based female sex workers had reached 30% by the mid-1990s (Chariyalertsak et al., 2008). In 1991, Thailand's government regarded HIV/AIDS prevention and control as a national priority and adopted a series of progressive policies to achieve this goal. For instance, to address the HIV/AIDS epidemic among commercial sex workers and their clients, the government launched the '100% Condom Campaign' to promote universal condom usage in the sex industry. Simultaneously, under the initiative of cabinet member Mechai Viravaidya, education on HIV prevention was provided through the mass media, such as TV and radio, and in workplaces and schools. Many of the materials used for HIV prevention education were developed by the Ministry of Public Health (MoPH) and the Population and Development Association (PDA), which is an NGO led by Mr. Viravaidya himself (Lyttleton, 1996).

Between 1992 and 1997, the main players coordinating and formulating policies for the HIV/AIDS programme were the MoPH and the NGO community, whereas the Ministry of Education (MoE) was involved in the provision of HIV/AIDS education by launching peer education programmes and annual essay competitions among school students (Phoolchaeron, 2006). In 1993, the MoE issued teaching manuals for HIV/AIDS education, encouraging primary and secondary schools to spread knowledge about this issue (Kasai & Ohsawa, 1999). However, according to the key interviewees for this study,[1] school-based HIV/AIDS education was not prioritised in Thailand's HIV/AIDS policies at the time. A former MoPH officer said, 'because adolescents were believed to have a low risk of infection from HIV, they were not considered to be the main target of HIV/AIDS education'. Additionally, 'the role of schools was not considered to be very important' (Interviewed in December 2014). A former MoE officer added that 'although peer education was promoted at schools, in reality, HIV/AIDS education was mainly provided by external institutions, such as NGOs and hospitals' (Interviewed in December 2014).

Thailand's HIV/AIDS policies during the 1990s are well known for their success in curbing the spread of HIV infections related to commercial sex work. According to sentinel surveillance data, HIV prevalence among brothel-based female sex workers declined from above 30% to below 10% during 1994–2004 (Chariyalertsak et al., 2008). Nevertheless, this study's key interviewees were somewhat critical about the content of the HIV/AIDS education and media campaigns during this period. For instance, they perceived that education overemphasised the risk of HIV transmission and focused too much on prohibitive matters based on people's fears. An NGO staff interviewee believed that such education was far from the intent of CSE and instead contributed towards discouraging people from using condoms in relationships outside the sex industry by negatively associating condoms with HIV and commercial sex.

Promotion of school-based sexuality education from the 2000s

As part of the global movement to address the HIV/AIDS epidemic, the United Nations General Assembly Special Session (UNGASS) on HIV/AIDS issued a Declaration of Commitment on HIV/AIDS in 2001. This was not a legally binding document but urged governments to act together to end the AIDS epidemic. The declaration clarified what the governments should do and emphasised the need to reduce HIV prevalence among young people (aged 15–24 years). The signatory countries were requested to submit a report to the Joint United Nations Programme on HIV/AIDS (UNAIDS) to monitor their implementation following the declaration. Thailand successfully submitted a UNGASS report every two years, demonstrating its interest in promoting CSE in the report. In the 2006 UNGASS Country Progress Report on Thailand, the National AIDS Prevention and Alleviation Committee (NAPAC) stated that the prevalence of HIV infections had expanded to young people in Thailand and highlighted that HIV/AIDS education was being promoted through its national policy on HIV/AIDS (NAPAC, 2006). Subsequently, in the 2010 UNGASS Report, the NAPAC emphasised the need for school-based CSE because of the increasing rate of HIV infections, sexually transmitted infections (STIs) and pregnancy among adolescents in the country (NAPAC, 2010).

Although the UNGASS reports recognised the need for CSE targeting adolescents, Thailand was still facing policy improvement challenges regarding the institutionalisation of CSE in its school system (NAPAC, 2010). The 2010 UNGASS Report implied that there was tension between the MoPH and the MoE over CSE's implementation. While sexuality education had been officially incorporated into the national curriculum (Basic Education Curriculum 2001) as a part of health and physical education, its content overemphasised the biomedical aspects of sexuality (UNESCO, 2014). Therefore, according to the NAPAC, the MoPH had studied and developed the content of sexuality education to be more comprehensive and submitted their ideas to the MoE in order to integrate it into the health education curriculum (NAPAC, 2010). However, the MoE administrators and teachers had negative attitudes towards accepting the need for CSE, illustrated by the MoE's reluctance to incorporate CSE into the core curriculum (NAPAC, 2010). Interestingly, Thai Buddhist authorities were reported to be supportive of sexuality education from the early stages (Smith et al., 2003).

With the adoption of the Basic Education Core Curriculum 2008, teaching CSE was emphasised in Thailand for the first time (UNESCO, 2014). The contents of sexuality education included more diverse topics and covered the socio-emotional aspects of sexuality, such as life skills' development, sexual health and gender equality. However, the MoE did not include CSE as a compulsory stand-alone course in this curriculum or as part of the Ordinary National Education Test (O-Net), which is equivalent to a graduation exam. In Thailand's education system, which authorises schools to formulate a large part of their curricula, this positioning of CSE contributed towards only a limited implementation of CSE in schools. The degree of CSE's implementation continued to be insufficient and was mostly dependent on the motivation of individual schools and teachers (UNESCO, 2014).

Meanwhile, civil society advocated for accelerating the implementation of CSE in the formal and non-formal educational systems by referring to the 'adolescent's right to accurate and practical information about sex through CSE' (NAPAC, 2010, p. 54). For instance, the international NGO, PATH, conducted the Teenpath Project during 2003–2014. This project aimed at introducing CSE into the formal curriculum of secondary and vocational schools by developing a CSE curriculum and training teachers, managers and educational supervisors. The project also encouraged schools to foster youth leaders and networks to promote CSE through the establishment of a youth club, namely a CSE club, to develop student peer educators. The project was implemented in collaboration with the MoPH and the MoE and was funded by the Global Fund to Fight AIDS, Tuberculosis and Malaria (Global Fund). However, this CSE curriculum was used only as guide and whether and how this curriculum was taught depended on teachers and schools (NAPAC, 2010). The project staff perceived that one of the major constraints limiting its reach was the MoE's contrasting vision and commitment to CSE with its education philosophy focusing mostly on academic excellence (UNESCO, 2014).

Discussions on the institutionalisation of school-based CSE started gaining traction, mostly in the context of teenage pregnancy prevention in Thailand with the increase in awareness of this problem. For instance, in 2010, BBC News reported that thousands of foetuses sent from illegal abortion clinics were found on the grounds of a Bangkok Buddhist temple, which helped raise public awareness of the problem in this country. Officially, the UNFPA (2014) stated that Thailand's adolescent birth ratio was alarming in 2012 compared to neighbouring countries. Accordingly, various policies and development plans stressed the need for school-based CSE during this period. Some of these included the 2012–2016 National Child and Youth Development Plan, the 2014–2016 National AIDS Prevention and Control Policy and Strategy and the 2015–2026 Teenage Pregnancy Prevention and Alleviation Strategy, supervised by the MoPH. In 2016, continuous efforts of the MoPH to promote school-based CSE resulted in the enactment of the Prevention and Solution of the Adolescent Pregnancy Problem Act. This law mandated schools to implement sexuality education, as written in Section 6: 'An educational establishment shall undertake the prevention and solution of the adolescent pregnancy problem as follows: (1) to provide teaching and learning on sexuality studies which is appropriate to age of pupils or students …'. Following this enactment, a national committee on teenage pregnancy chaired by the Prime Minister was formed, which served to supervise the development of ministerial regulations of all concerned ministries, including the MoE.

Implementation of CSE in schools in Thailand

Despite domestic policies to promote school-based CSE, the implementation of CSE in schools remains limited in Thailand. UNICEF and MoE (2017) reported that only 51.3% of the surveyed teachers from secondary education in Thailand responded that CSE is treated as a stand-alone course in their schools. The biological aspects and the negative consequences of sexual intercourse are heavily emphasised in many schools (Boonmongkon et al., 2019). One of the main factors for this limited implementation is the negative attitude of teachers and parents towards CSE. For instance, many school principals believe that sexuality education should promote sexual mores based on traditional Thai culture; for example, students should not have sexual relationships at their age, and that they should behave in accordance with their gender roles (UNICEF & MoE, 2017). Similarly, many teachers believe that premarital sexual relationships are immoral and teaching about sexuality promotes teenage sexual intercourse (Vuttanont et al., 2006). In addition, teachers feel embarrassed and incapable of talking about sexuality because of its taboo nature in Thai society (Kay et al., 2010; Thammaraksa et al., 2014).

According to UNICEF and MoE (2017), most parents with children in secondary education are aware of the risk of increasing teenage pregnancy and support school-based sexuality education. However, another study reported that parents with children aged 15–18 years believe that their children were too young to be educated about sexual intercourse fearing that 'sex education might encourage experimentation with sex' (Sridawruang et al., 2010, p. 440). Additionally, some parents strongly believed that their children would follow parental instructions and not undertake risky behaviour, contrary to the fact (Fongkaew et al., 2012). Synchronising with the MoE's vision, Thai school administrators and teachers tend to place higher focus on students' academic excellence (UNESCO, 2014). In Thailand's school system, where students' O-Net scores are the standards to measure the success of education, subjects included in this exam, such as mathematics and the Thai language, tend to be prioritised (UNICEF & MoE, 2017). Therefore, in some schools, school principals do not pay attention to CSE or acknowledge its importance (UNICEF & MoE, 2017).

The results of the case study with three schools partly corresponded to the above reasons for contestation and negative attitudes of teachers and parents towards CSE. In the studied schools, the majority of teachers and parents did not support CSE when it was introduced, whereas some teachers were self-motivated to provide CSE because of their strong awareness of the problem of student pregnancy and HIV/AIDS. When these schools initiated CSE, the school principals were criticised by the teachers and parents, who indignantly asked whether they supported students' sexual intercourse. This result suggests that there was a popular misconception that CSE aims to teach students about sexual intercourse and encourages teenagers to become sexually active. In addition, it was found that teachers' contestation was driven by the fear of cultural taboos and their discomfort in talking about sexuality. For instance, one teacher interviewee explained that the teachers in opposition at her school said that 'talking about sexual matters is embarrassing, and these matters are not something to talk about in public. They should be hidden and not taught'. Teachers who were assigned to teach CSE were reluctant to participate in the CSE training because they felt that the training would be 'an obscene training' and the content would contradict their beliefs based on Thai culture. In this context, only one female teacher out of nine teacher interviewees referred to religion saying, 'I was wondering if he [school principal] thought we don't have any religious beliefs' (Chiba, 2021, para 37). On the other hand, prioritisation of academic excellence was not the main reason for parents' and teachers' contestation of CSE. This may be because these schools were located in rural areas, and they had only limited expectations for students gaining tertiary education. The results demonstrated that in Thailand's schools, the lack of acceptance of the norms of CSE is common among teachers and parents because of perceived conflicts with existing Thai sociocultural norms and the popular misconception of CSE. Without clear education policies prioritising CSE among other school subjects, teachers' neglect in teaching CSE is an expected occurrence.

Norm diffusion of CSE at the school level

Currently in Thailand, where the degree of CSE implementation is highly dependent on the enthusiasm of schools and teachers, what are the key factors affecting the wider implementation of CSE at the school level? This section attempts to answer this question through a case study of the three schools from the Teenpath Project, which successfully formulated CSE into their school curriculum. Through semi-structured interviews with school principals and teachers in charge of CSE and group interviews with students and parents, factors that contributed to its success were identified as follows.

These successful schools demonstrated effective leadership among school principals, which was a key factor for initiating and continuing CSE despite contestation from teachers and parents. The school principals were well aware of the problem of student pregnancy and HIV/AIDS in their personal experience and had a strong will to solve this problem from the beginning of the project. One teacher interviewee commented that 'the principal had a clear vision, and she was not scared of opposition'. Principals in these schools were commonly very decisive and enthusiastic about encouraging teachers to participate in CSE training. Simultaneously, they supported the teachers assigned to teach CSE (hereafter CSE teachers) in various ways. For instance, one CSE teacher explained how the principal dealt with claims from parents against CSE and commented that 'our school principal protected us from the contrary wind'. Meanwhile, school principals did not show an oppressive attitude towards teachers in opposition. One teacher commented that his school principal just wanted those in opposition to 'learn about CSE gradually' in 'a positive way'. As this comment suggests, the school principals did not attempt to forcefully change teachers' opinions but sought to promote a proper understanding of CSE.

Capacity-building of CSE teachers and the principal's communication with teachers and parents prior to CSE initiation were important foundations for the success of its implementation. In particular, the CSE training provided by PATH contributed to reducing teachers' discomfort in teaching CSE by introducing new teaching methods. For instance, one female teacher who was hesitant to teach CSE said:

> The instructor of PATH talked interestingly about topics that were not recognised in Thai society, and I have learned a new teaching technique. [...] I used to be stubborn but now I can talk about that without feeling embarrassed.
>
> (CSE Teacher N, Female in her 50s)

However, briefing sessions prior to the CSE contributed to promoting teachers' and parents' understanding of CSE only to a limited extent. Although these sessions provided explanations for the need and content of CSE, they did not instantly change most people's opinions towards CSE. It is significant that CSE became widely accepted only after its positive outcomes were recognised. These outcomes include students' favourable responses and positive learning attitude towards the CSE class and a decrease in the student pregnancy rate. One of the school principals described how people's understanding that CSE's purpose was to promote student health proliferated over time:

> Since we started the [CSE] class, I have shown its positive results. By implementing CSE, I had the results claim that "you were against it [CSE], but you were wrong" and that "we are not telling our students to have sexual intercourse". Since then, fewer parents have opposed it, and they have come to agree with it. [The idea of supporting CSE] has spread to the community.
>
> (School principal A, in his 50s)

Teachers believed that the students' attitude towards CSE also influenced other teachers' opinions. According to them, those teachers in opposition were surprised at students' positive learning attitudes in the CSE class and started wondering why students liked this class so much. The teachers who saw the students enjoy the CSE class highly evaluated its learning process and found the class helpful for the students. Experiencing that CSE gradually had gained support from teachers and parents, one CSE teacher commented that 'students are like mirrors' and added 'even if we do not say that we are doing something good, other teachers came to understand it'. This comment suggests that the norm diffusion of CSE occurs with people's subjective recognition of its positive outcomes.

At the end of the Teenpath Project funded by the Global Fund, it was found that CSE teachers and students belonging to the CSE club in these schools were transformed into norm entrepreneurs, and diffusers of the CSE norm. The interviewed teachers, who were reluctant to participate in the CSE training at the beginning of the project, demonstrated that they were now proud of teaching CSE and felt that they were helping students through doing 'the right thing'. Some of these teachers were leading the CSE clubs and fostering student peer educators. Their primary motivation to promote CSE was the prevention of students' HIV infection and unexpected pregnancy. The student peer educators enjoyed teaching CSE to other students and people in their communities. Their motivation to promote CSE was also derived from the will to help their friends avoid such difficulties. However, it is interesting that some of the peer educators also referred to changing existing social norms related to sexuality in this context. For instance, one male student stated that he is motivated about making society more open to talk about sexuality. He explained how this topic was taboo in his community and that this social norm created hardship for adolescents when consulting with adults on sexuality-related issues. Interviewed parents were also positive about schools providing CSE and emphasised the importance for students to obtain accurate information to prevent unexpected pregnancy. The parents perceived that forbidding their children to have sexual relationships or shunning away from sexual information is no longer possible due to the spread of the Internet. They preferred their children not to have sexual intercourse but accepted that it was necessary to equip children with knowledge and skills to use contraceptives to avoid risk.

Discussion and conclusion

The case of Thailand's promotion of school-based CSE illuminates the challenges faced by the state in diffusing the norm of CSE domestically while addressing opposition. In accordance with the international frameworks to promote CSE, Thailand's government has developed national policies to accelerate domestic implementation with much struggle. However, this policy development has not yet resulted in the full implementation of CSE in schools. At the ministerial level, school-based CSE was promoted predominantly from a public health perspective in Thailand. The domestic incentives to promote CSE were strongly derived from the proliferation of risky sexual behaviour among young people in terms of HIV infection and teenage pregnancy. Thailand's MoPH and its public health policies are known to be innovative, effective and pragmatic, as represented by the successful '100% Condom Campaign' in the 1990s. Therefore, it was rational for the MoPH to promote CSE to prevent HIV/AIDS and teenage pregnancy, as this education was proven to be effective in achieving this purpose. However, Thailand's MoE was not very enthusiastic about incorporating CSE into the education curriculum because of its educational philosophy of focusing on 'academic excellence' and the fact that health education has not been its primary interest. Because the MoPH and the NGO community were historically the main players in the coordination and policy formulation of the HIV/AIDS programme in Thailand, the MoE perhaps considered addressing health issues to be outside of its mandate.

At the school level, teachers' and parents' contestation was one of the major impediments to the diffusion of CSE. The reasons for the contestation were closely related to the perceived conflicts with existing sociocultural norms in Thailand. Interestingly, similar to the ministerial level, the major incentive to accept the norm of CSE was to solve the problem of adolescent health at the school level. However, teachers and parents hardly viewed the significance of CSE in promoting the adolescents' rights to access information on sexual and reproductive health. The case studies of the schools suggested that the key to diffusing CSE at the school level was to enhance teachers' and parents' subjective recognition of the positive outcomes of CSE. In addition, students indirectly contributed to the diffusion by demonstrating their strong interest in and need for CSE through positive responses. As parents and teachers have a strong interest in their children's benefits, witnessing the benefits that students gained from CSE possibly helped in convincing them of its value.

This case study of Thailand can be regarded as an example of 'locally mediated diffusion' (Bacon & Nakamura, 2021) discussed by Souza and Bacon in Chapter 2. The external norm senders of CSE, such as UN agencies, the Global Fund and international NGOs played roles of direct and indirect diffusers of the CSE norm in Thailand through advocacy of adolescents' SRHR, development of a CSE curriculum and human resources, and support and implementation of the project to promote school-based CSE. Through interaction with these organisations, the local agents of norm diffusion, predominantly the MoPH at the ministerial level, were convinced of the benefits of CSE and engaged in persuasion and socialisation of other local agents, such as the MoE and schools. It is considered that the MoPH was indispensable in local norm diffusion particularly contributing to the MoE's instrumental adaptation of promoting school-based CSE through the creation of domestic pressure. At the community level, school principals and CSE teachers, including those who used to be sceptical about the value of CSE, were persuaded and in turn acted as norm entrepreneurs, who socialised other teachers and parents into the CSE norms. During this process, student peer educators were also mentored to become norm diffusers. Parents in the schools with such active local norm diffusers were eventually persuaded of the merits of CSE through subjective recognition of its positive outcomes and understanding the needs of CSE for adolescents' pregnancy prevention.

When considering diffusion of the CSE norm, it is important to be aware that there are several different SRHR related norms bundled in this educational approach. These norms may include: 1. the right to access scientifically accurate information regarding sexual and reproductive health; 2. the right to choose when and with whom adolescents engage in sexual relationships. Most of the local norm diffusers highlighted in this study were concerned about the sexually-related risks of adolescent health whether HIV infection or pregnancy. Their primary interests lay in how CSE could be useful to solving these problems. Therefore, as represented by the parental perspectives, some of the local actors seemed to be eventually persuaded of the first norm of promoting CSE in connection with adolescent health promotion. However, they only instrumentally adopted, or possibly neglected the second norm. We can interpret this as evidence that the principles and ideas of CSE were partially diffused in the community in accordance with local agents' interests and existing sociocultural norms. This situation in Thailand corresponds to Acharya's theory of norm localisation (2004), suggesting how foreign ideas undergo cultural selection and are actively reconstructed by actors within the target state.

Despite the valuable observations from the Thai case, this case study has some limitations in providing generalisable implications for the norm diffusion of CSE. For instance, this case study does not account for societies or regions where religious norms are the main reasons for contestation. In Thailand, some school principals and teachers suggested the possibility of a correlation between Buddhist norms and their negative attitudes, particularly towards the adolescent right to choose when and with whom they engage in sexual relationships; however, this study did not find religious beliefs to be the main reason for contestation of CSE either at the ministerial or school levels. Thailand's case is different from many countries where CSE seems to conflict with religious norms. For instance, Smith et al. (2003) reported that the ministry official of Brunei responded, 'sex education ... in its liberal sense is not taught in any of the topics in the science syllabus' because '[u]nlawful and immoral sex practices including premarital sex are all forbidden (haram) in Islam' (Smith et al., 2003, p. 10). Regarding the conflicts between the notion of CSE and existing sociocultural and religious norms, the meaning of 'culturally appropriate CSE' and its relationship with SRHR should be further discussed. Diffusion of school-based CSE is a complex process, particularly where this norm is perceived to contradict the existing sociocultural norms. To achieve SDG Targets 3.7 and 5.6, further efforts are needed in the international community to understand the architecture and dynamics of domestic actors involved in this norm diffusion. Further studies should also consider the potential of school-level actors, such as teachers, parents and students, in influencing ministerial decisions on policy development and determining the degree of implementation in schools. Furthermore, more knowledge should be accumulated on how CSE can survive contestation at the community level.

Note

1 This study's key interviewees include a former MoPH officer, former MoE officers, NGO staff (The Path2Health Foundation officers) and a UNICEF Regional Office for East Asia and the Pacific (EAPRO) officer based in Thailand. All interviewees provided informed consent before participating in the interviews.

References

Acharya, A. (2004). How ideas spread: Whose norms matter? Norm localization and institutional change in Asian regionalism. *International Organization*, *58*(2), 239–275.

Bacon, P., & Nakamura, H. (2021). Diffusing the abolitionist norm in Japan: EU 'Death Penalty Diplomacy' and the gap between rhetoric and reality in EU–Japan relations. *Journal of Common Market Studies*, *59*(5), 1230–1246. https://doi.org/10.1111/jcms.13177

Boonmongkon, P., Shrestha, M., Samoh, N., Kanchawee, K., Peerawarunun, P., Promnart, P., Ojanen, T., & Guadamuz, T. E. (2019). Comprehensive sexuality education in Thailand? A nationwide assessment of sexuality education implementation in Thai public secondary schools. *Sex Health*, *16*(3), 263–273. https://doi.org/10.1071/SH18121

Chariyalertsak, S., Aramrattana, A., & Celentano, D. D. (2008). The HIV/AIDS epidemic in Thailand: The first two decades. In D. D. Celentano & C. Beyrer (Eds.), *Public health aspects of HIV/AIDS in low and middle income countries* (pp. 401–432). Springer Science+Business Media. https://doi.org/10.1007/978-0-387-72711-0

Chiba, M. (2021). Promotion of school-based comprehensive sexuality education: Building support from teachers and parents in Thailand. *Development in Practice*. https://doi.org/10.1080/09614524.2021.1981249

Fongkaew, W., Cupp, P. K., Miller, B. A., Atwood, K. A., Chamratrithirong, A., Rhucharoenpornpanich, O., Rosati, M. J., Chookhare, W., & Byrnes, H. F. (2012). Do Thai parents really know about the sexual risk taking of their children? A qualitative study in Bangkok. *Nursing & Health Sciences*, *14*(3), 391–397. https://doi.org/10.1111/j.1442-2018.2012.00703.x

Fonner, V. A., Armstrong, K. S., Kennedy, C. E., O'Reilly, K. R., & Sweat, M. D. (2014). School based sex education and HIV prevention in low- and middle-income countries: A systematic review and meta-analysis. *PLOS One*, *9*(3). https://doi.org/10.1371/journal.pone.0089692

International Planned Parenthood Federation East & South East Asia and Oceania Region (IPPF ESEAOR). (2019). *Comprehensive sexuality education in Asia and the Pacific region* (Regional review 2019 background report). Retrieved August 20, 2021, from https://drive.google.com/drive/folders/1oGjMIO8QSNYxaTI6z7kl2oW_e0-9-Wvv

Kasai, N., & Ohsawa, S. (1999). Tai ni okeru gakkouhokenkyouiku karikyuramu to AIDS kyouiku no kousei ni kansuru kenkyu [Study on school health education curriculum and AIDS education in Thailand]. *Gakkou hoken kenkyu* [Japanese Journal of School Health], *41*, 138–152.

Kay, N. S., Jones, M. R., & Jantaraweragul, S. (2010). Teaching sex education in Thailand. *ICHPER-SD Journal of Research*, *5*(2), 10–16.

Kirby, D. (2011). *The impact of sex education on the sexual behaviour of young people*. www.un.org/en/development/desa/population/publications/pdf/expert/2011-12_Kirby_Expert-Paper.pdf

Lyttleton, C. (1996). Messages of distinction: The HIV/AIDS media campaign in Thailand. *Medical Anthropology*, *16*(4), 363–389. https://doi.org/10.1080/01459740.1994.9966122

National AIDS Prevention and Alleviation Committee (NAPAC). (2006). *UNGASS country progress report Thailand: Reporting period January – December 2004*. https://data.unaids.org/pub/report/2006/2006_country_progress_report_thailand_en.pdf

National AIDS Prevention and Alleviation Committee (NAPAC). (2010). *UNGASS country progress report Thailand: Reporting period* January 2008 – December 2009. www.tncathai.org/data/data13.pdf

Phoolchareon, W. (2006). Thailand. In T. Yamamoto & S. Itoh (Eds.), *Fighting a rising tide: The response to AIDS in East Asia* (pp. 247–265). Japan Center for International Exchange.

Smith, G., Kippax, S., Aggleton, P., & Tyrer, P. (2003). HIV/AIDS school-based education in selected Asia-Pacific Countries. *Sex Education*, *3*(1), 3–21. https://doi.org/10.1080/1468181032000052126

Sridawruang, C., Pfeil, M., & Crozier, K. (2010). Why Thai parents do not discuss sex with their children: A qualitative study. *Nursing & Health Sciences*, *12*(4), 437–443. https://doi.org/10.1111/j.1442-2018.2010.00556.x

Thammaraksa, P., Powwattana, A., Lagampan, S., & Thaingtham, W. (2014). Helping teachers conduct sex education in secondary schools in Thailand: Overcoming culturally sensitive barriers to sex education. *Asian Nursing Research*, *8*(2), 99–104. https://doi.org/10.1016/j.anr.2014.04.001

UNESCO. (2009). *International technical guidance on sexuality education: An evidence-informed approach for schools, teachers and health educators.* www.unfpa.org/sites/default/files/pub-pdf/ITGSE.pdf

UNESCO. (2014). *Comprehensive sexuality education: The challenges and opportunities of scaling-up*. https://unesdoc.unesco.org/ark:/48223/pf0000227781

UNESCO. (2018a). *Why comprehensive sexuality education is important.* Retrieved August 21, 2021 from https://en.unesco.org/news/why-comprehensive-sexuality-education-important

UNESCO. (2018b). *International technical guidance on sexuality education: An evidence-informed approach.* UNESCO. https://unesdoc.unesco.org/ark:/48223/pf0000260770

UNFPA. (2014). *The state of Thailand's population report 2013: Motherhood in childhood, facing the challenge of adolescent pregnancy*. https://thailand.unfpa.org/sites/default/files/pub-pdf/State%20of%20Thailand%20Population%20report%202013-MotherhoodinChildhood_en.pdf

UNICEF & Ministry of Education Thailand. (2017). *Review of comprehensive sexuality education in Thailand.* www.unicef.org/thailand/sites/unicef.org.thailand/files/2018-08/comprehensive_sexuality_education%20EN.pdf

Vuttanont, U., Greenhalgh, T., Griffin, M., & Boynton, P. (2006). 'Smart boys' and 'Sweet girls', Sex education needs in Thai teenagers: A mixed-method study. *The Lancet*, *368*(9552), 2068–2080. https://doi.org/10.1016/S0140-6736(06)69836-X

World Health Organization (WHO). (2011). *WHO guidelines on preventing early pregnancy and poor reproductive health outcomes among adolescents in developing countries.* http://apps.who.int/iris/bitstream/handle/10665/44691/9789241502214_eng.pdf;jsessionid=EBA9C3952F0219D8BC5C878C1A918150?sequence=1

Section 3

Ensuring inclusive and equitable quality education (SDG 4)

6 Reformulation of inclusive education

Cambodia

Makiko Hayashi

Introduction

The diffusion of inclusive education as one of the educational policies of the Government of Cambodia has shown rapid acceleration within the post-2015 agenda, and with particular relevance to Sustainable Development Goal (SDG) 4. The policy-oriented strategy of SDG 4 stressed 'ensur(ing) inclusive and equitable quality education and promot(ing) lifelong learning opportunities for all' (United Nations, 2015) as the vision and one of the objectives of the 'Policy on Inclusive Education' in the country since its approval in June 2018 (MoEYS, 2018). Nevertheless, the Salamanca Statement adopted in 1994 and the Convention on the Rights of Persons with Disabilities, adopted in 2006 have both been key drivers of the concept of inclusive education, primarily at the intention level.

This chapter is divided into five sections. The first section examines the normative framework of inclusive education as developed and discussed globally, as part of educational development. The second section illuminates the present situation for inclusion and education based on numerical data on children left behind from Education for All (EFA), or namely out-of-school children and youth. The third section investigates the existing legal and non-legal normative framework, together with the institutional framework behind how the norm of inclusive education is diffused and delivered. It is then followed by further analysis in section four, on the reformulation of the norm through contestation, mainly arising from actors involved at the classroom level. As a result, the analysis delves into how delivery of inclusive education is transformed and internalised through those contestations. Preferably, the end result of such classroom experiences is the need to stress ways to change the delivery of inclusive education content and method, as an effective mode of action for actual implementation. Lastly, the fifth section concludes by discussing implications for Cambodia's present and prospective adaptation of inclusive education towards the target year of 2030.

DOI: 10.4324/9781003205951-9

Historical background and global definitions of inclusive education

Tracing the historical background and definitions from the study of the concept of inclusion, encompassing the notion of embracing diversity, '(t)he aim of inclusive education is to eliminate social exclusion that is a consequence of attitudes and responses to diversity in race, social class, ethnicity, religion, gender and ability' (Ainscow & Miles, 2008, p. 16). Historically speaking, children with special needs were generally excluded from the educational system itself before the 1960s and the 1970s (Balescut & Eklindh, 2006). Physical and social barriers excluded and denied these persons from society and prevented them from participating within the educational system.

A gradual shift from a human rights perspective in the 1960s and 1970s led to initial efforts consisting of specialised programmes, institutions and specialist educators, which all functioned outside the mainstream education system. And eventually, dissatisfaction with special education led to a new approach, namely special needs' education, which emphasised integration. Integrated education was a system limited to children with disabilities (CWDs), locating them physically within ordinary schools, but in specialised classrooms with trained teachers, or sharing several hours of the same class with non-disabled children in ordinary schools. However, the Salamanca Statement in 1994 offered significant impetus to the notion of inclusion. This statement suggested radical changes to the form of integration, which signified a brand-new concept of accepting a diverse range of special needs or excluded groups not only limited to those with disabilities (UNESCO, 1994).

The present definition of inclusive education itself remains ambiguous when exploring the definitions used and practiced by various countries worldwide. For instance, some countries still tend to use the term inclusion targeting only CWDs, whereas other countries use inclusive EFA children with special needs. Despite this confusion, inclusion has two fundamental objectives and roles, as highlighted in the principles of the 1994 statement, distinguishing itself from both integrated and special education systems. First, inclusive educational settings should accommodate the addressed needs beyond disability, for instance of girls, children from ethnic minorities, rural areas, poor families and even multiple disadvantages to promote their schooling opportunities and also to improve and enrich their quality of education. Second, and specifically speaking, enrichment of education also refers to non-cognitive skills related to behavioural change and attitudes of children without special needs, a positive stimulus and influence to combat discriminatory attitudes towards children with special needs.

Data on and for inclusion and education in Cambodia

In order to measure the up-to-date situation of children and youth who are still left behind from EFA, a few representative indicators of education are utilised.

These indicators are crucial to measure how far the most disadvantaged are falling behind from equitable and quality education.

Data on inclusion and education

As shown in Table 6.1, equitable access to education from the primary level through the secondary level presents a challenge in leaving no one behind the educational agenda. The out-of-school rate at the primary education level totals 9% for boys and 10% for girls, while this rate totals 12% for males and 14% for females at the lower secondary education level (UNICEF, 2019). One of the biggest obstacles confronted by many countries in the process of meeting the Millennium Development Goals (MDGs) was the inclusion of the last 5% and 10% of the population left behind the EFA agenda. The proportion of the population of children and youth in Cambodia described above falls exactly into the category of those still excluded from the right to education. This huge challenge is carried over from the MDGs agenda into the SDGs. Furthermore, as pointed out by Rix et al. (2013) and Utsumi (2016) as cited in the report of the NGO Education Partnership (2018, p. 12), 'most of CWDs (children with disabilities) are not attending school, but those who have attended are very likely to drop out. And, most frequently dropping out at grade 1'.

In terms of tackling the right to quality education, completion rates through primary to upper secondary education levels, as well as learning outcomes, are considered additional bottlenecks. Specifically, completion rates decline by roughly a half for both males (41%) and females (39%) for lower secondary

Table 6.1 Data on/for inclusion and education in Cambodia

Equitable access	Out-of-school rate (2012–2018)	* **Primary education: 9% (male), 10% (female)** * Lower secondary education: 12% (male), 14% (female) * Upper secondary education: NA
Completion	Completion rate (2012–2018)	* Primary education: 68% (male), 79% (female) * **Lower secondary education: 41% (male), 39% (female)** * **Upper secondary education: 20% (male), 20% (female)**
Learning	Learning outcomes (2012–2018)	* Youth literacy rate: 92% (male), 93% (female) * Minimum proficiency level (end of primary): 61% (reading), NA (math) * **Minimum proficiency level (end of lower secondary): 38% (reading), 17% (math)**
Budget	Public expenditure on education (2010–2018)	* As % of GDP: 1.9% * As % of government budget: 8.8%

Source: adapted from UNICEF (2019) and UNESCO (2020)

education from the primary level. Moreover, this rate decreases by another half at 20% for both males and females for upper secondary education. The low completion rates at the overall secondary education level are connected to the low attainment of a minimum proficiency level at the end of the lower secondary level, 38% for reading and 17% for mathematics (UNICEF, 2019).

Data for inclusion and education

The numerical data and evidence provided here in the description and in the table (see Table 6.1) strictly reflect the various challenges addressed in SDG 4 that Cambodia is facing. For instance, in the Incheon Strategy 'Make the Right Real' and Framework for Action, it puts forward the vision of Education 2030 for sustainable development regardless of sex, age, colour, race, ethnic minority, language, religion, political view, birth or disability to ensure inclusion and that no one is left behind (United Nations, 2012). Furthermore, SDG 4.1 'ensure(s) that all girls and boys complete free, equitable and quality primary and secondary education leading to relevant and effective learning outcomes', and together with SDG 4.5, '(it) impl(ies) the elimination of gender disparities in education and ensures equal access to all levels of education and vocational training for the vulnerable, including persons with disabilities, indigenous peoples, and children in vulnerable situations'. In addition, SDG 4.a articulates the importance of 'build(ing) and upgrad(ing) education facilities that are child, disability and gender sensitive and provide safe, non-violent, inclusive, and effective learning environments for all'.

Diffusion as intended and delivered

As intended: the legal and non-legal normative framework of inclusive education

Cambodia ratified the two major human rights covenants, the International Covenant on Economic, Social and Cultural Rights (ICESCR) and the International Covenant on Civil and Political Rights (ICCPR) (see Table 6.2), along with major United Nations conventions such as the Convention on the Rights of the Child in 1992. In addition, examining the other key player of diffusion as intended, the Government of Cambodia signed the Convention of the Rights of Persons with Disabilities on 1 October 2007, followed by its ratification on 20 December 2012. After the signing of this convention, a number of legal instruments were created so that the existing mechanisms could prepare the country for actual implementation.

For instance, the Cambodian Disabled People's Organization made extensive efforts in pushing the government to ratify the convention, and produced a position paper to urge the government to pass the Law on the Protection and Promotion of the Rights of Persons with Disabilities, leading to its adoption in 2009, only two years after the signature of the convention (MoEYS, 2009a).

Table 6.2 Cambodia's signature and ratification of international instruments on human rights

International Instruments on Human Rights	*Signature/Ratification*
1. The International Covenant on Economic, Social and Cultural Rights (ICESCR)	1980/1992 (accession)
2. The International Covenant on Civil and Political Rights (ICCPR)	1980/1992
3. The Convention on the Elimination of All Forms of Discrimination against Women (CEDAW)	1980/1992
4. The Convention on the Rights of the Child (CRC)	NA/1992 (accession)
5. The Convention on the Elimination of All Forms of Racial Discrimination (ICERD)	1966/1983
6. The Convention against Torture and Other Cruel, Inhuman, or Degrading Treatment or Punishment (CAT)	NA/1992
7. Convention for the Protection of All Persons from Enforced Disappearance (CED)	NA/2013 (accession)
8. The Convention on the Rights of Persons with Disabilities (CRPD)	2007/2012

Source: adapted from OHCHR (2020)

In this same year, the Prakas Inter Ministerial on the Criteria for Definitions of Disability Classification was adopted (MoEYS, 2009b). Together with efforts of the Cambodia's Disabled People's Organization, the Disability Action Council was designated as the national coordination and advisory mechanism on disability issues and housed within the Ministry of Social Affairs, Veteran and Youth Rehabilitation (Huy, 2017). The rapid actions of the Cambodian Disabled People's Organization, Cambodia Disabled People's International and the Disability Action Council played a crucial role in pushing the Cambodian government to build this stronger legal framework.

Further to these rapid movements, it is noteworthy to highlight the language used in the National Constitution of Cambodia (Kingdom of Cambodia, 1993), the National Education Law of Cambodia adopted in 2007 and the Law on the Protection and Promotion of the Rights of Persons with Disabilities of 2009 (MoEYS, 2007, 2009a). The National Constitution states that, '(t)he State shall provide free primary secondary education to all citizens in public schools', while the National Education Law makes it explicit in Article 39 that, '(d)isabled learners who are not able to learn with able learners, even with facilitation, have the right to receive special education in separate special classes at community schools in their locality'. While Article 27 of the Law on the Protection and Promotion of the Rights of Persons with Disabilities adopted in 2009 implies full inclusion of all students with disabilities as follows, '… all students with disabilities have the right to enrollment in public and private educational establishments', Article 28 of this same law declares that 'the State shall develop policies and strategies which promote inclusive education to the utmost extent and only after that to establish special classes to respond to the needs of students with disabilities'. What is interesting to note here is that while the National Education Law was not specific to inclusive education, as it admitted the right to receive education in separate special classes, in the Law on the Protection and Promotion of the Rights of Persons with Disabilities, it changes its language dramatically as it responds to special classes and to the needs of students with disabilities only after the promotion of inclusive education.

In terms of the non-legal framework, it is clear-cut and obvious how the diffusion of inclusive education policies as intended gained significant momentum within the Education 2030 agenda. Before the year 2015, a national social protection policy framework was formulated, creating a number of policies on those with single or multiple disabilities from particular social groups. For example, Policy on Gender Mainstreaming in Education, Policy on Scholarship Programmes, Policy on School Feeding Programmes and Policy on Children with Disabilities, which were approved in 2008. However, in keeping with the SDG 4 policy-oriented framework, comprehensive policies on inclusive education have also been developed in recent years. They include: the Policy on Inclusive Education approved in 2018; the National Disability Strategic Plan (2014–2018); the Education Strategic Plans of 2014–2018 and 2019–2023; the Cambodia SDG 4 2030 Roadmap; and the Rectangular Strategy, Phases I, II and III. The Policy on Inclusive Education from 2018 has been important, with its roots in the Policy on Children with Disabilities developed in 2008. Not only does this new Policy on Inclusive Education re-emphasise educational rights for CWDs, a clearer vision towards 'ensuring inclusive and equitable quality education …for all' is affirmed.

As delivered: the institutional framework of inclusive education

Moving further from diffusion as intended to diffusion as delivered, it becomes pivotal to look at transformative changes made at the institutional level and in the administrative framework, together with the budgetary dimension. Firstly at the institutional level (see Table 6.3), the Ministry of Education, Youth and Sport has, since 2015, comprised seven Directorates-General, having started with six in 1998. The Directorate General of Policy and Planning was added, implying that policy and planning are positioned as essential elements within the government framework. Another major transformation observed as part of the administrative framework is the increase in the number of departments of the Directorates-General of Education, from six departments in 1998 to ten in 2015. The four added departments are: the Curriculum Development Department; the Teacher Training Department; the Department of Vocational Orientation; and the Special Education Department.

Regarding the Special Education Department, before 2015 it was placed under the Primary Education Department as the Special Education Office. With administrative promotion and under its current status, the Special Education Department is allocated a budget to operate a number of additional

Table 6.3 Institutional framework of inclusive education within the Ministry of Education, Youth and Sport

Ministry of Education, Youth and Sport of the Government of Cambodia	
• **Directorate General of Education**	✓ **Departments under the DGE** ✓ Early Childhood Education Department
• Directorate General of Policy and Planning	✓ Primary Education Department
• Directorate General of Sports	✓ General Secondary Education Department
• Directorate General of Youth	✓ Non-Formal Education Department
• Directorate General of Higher Education	✓ School Health Department
• Directorate General of Administration	✓ **Curriculum Development Department**
• Finance Inspectorate General	✓ **Teacher Training Department**
	✓ **Department of Vocational Orientation**
	✓ **Special Education Department**
	✓ Publishing and Distribution House

Source: Hayashi (2020)

establishments, a huge step being the foundation of the National Institute of Special Education and the establishment of five special schools for the deaf and the blind, originally managed nationwide by an international local non-governmental organisation (NGO), to be operated fully under the government as public schools. The recent establishment of the National Institute of Special Education emphasises teacher training and teacher training for special education, with the first round of initiatives to prioritise and focus on braille and sign language education and training. As such, through the lens of budgetary allocation, the structure of the Ministry of Education, Youth and Sport is at present witnessing many transformational changes with the Education 2030 agenda in mind. There has been a change, from being solely an administrative framework for the diffusion of inclusive education policy, to actual delivery and implementation.

There is indisputable progress and accelerated movements are in place to comply with numerous international human rights norms. However, the environment surrounding inclusive education encompasses a variety of ministerial functions not only related to the Ministry of Education, Youth and Sport, but the Ministry of Social Affairs and Youth and Rehabilitation. A few fundamental questions are raised. What is the role of the Ministry of Education, Youth and

Sport in terms of inclusive education diffusion as intended and delivered? Where is the focal point for coordination within the Ministry of Social Affairs and Youth and Rehabilitation? And, are the independent monitoring mechanisms of the Convention on the Rights of Persons with Disabilities existent and functioning?

Reformulation and norm diffusion through contestation

This section analyses how the concept of inclusive education at the delivery stage is constantly reformulated partly through the 'cascade model' of teacher education and training. At this particular stage of delivery and diffusion, norm reformulation starts to become apparent. This section scrutinises why the inclusive education norm is not diffused (accepted, adapted and internalised) as originally intended, which can be explored and largely explained by contestations expressed by norm receivers.

Firstly, inhibiting factors for the implementation of inclusive education can include tensions arising between the supply and demand sides of inclusive education. As reported in the 2020 Global Education Monitoring Report, '(i)n Cambodia, despite teachers' strong support for child-centered pedagogy… (they) questioned the feasibility of applying child-centered pedagogy in a context of overcrowded classrooms, scarce teaching resources and overambitious curricula' (UNESCO, 2020, p. 136, 148). The author undertook field research involving semi-structured open-ended interviews from 2013 to 2014 on the outskirts of Phnom Penh, and in Kandal and Kampot provinces involving 88 interviewees (Hayashi, 2015; Hayashi & Edwards, 2015). Many of the interviewees expressed similar reservations to those reported in the 2020 Global Education Monitoring Report. For instance, 'the class arrangement… I arrange that in one class I allow only three disabled students to study with non-disabled students. And the purpose is in order to reduce the burden to the teachers in teaching the disabled students' (school director P). The author's research corroborates the findings reported in the 2020 Global Education Monitoring Report, that teachers tend to have positive attitudes towards inclusion, but also doubts about its feasibility.

Secondly, teachers' perceptions of the possibility of inclusion of students with disabilities depended on the type of disability to be accommodated. At least half of the respondents considered inclusion of students with learning, physical, visual and hearing impairments 'very possible' or 'possible'. However, less than 20% felt the same in the case of students who were blind or deaf, had intellectual disabilities or had severe and multiple disabilities (Kartika & Kuroda, 2019, as cited in UNESCO, 2020). Furthermore, a statement by a student without a disability claims that,

> (I)t is better to separate the blind and deaf students in another class, because then they can learn more better with the special teachers…(s)ome of the deaf students fool around during class time and some of us cannot concentrate much.
>
> (student without a disability T)

From what has been explored from statements and reports made on a global scale, there are some crucial obstacles, hardships and difficulties being faced, which are expressed through contestations by both norm receivers and norm diffusers in implementing and delivering inclusive education. The acting supply and demand sides of inclusive education in this part are the teachers at stake. Through a defined set of government actions, practice and policies, teachers including school principals are the first receivers of inclusive education norms. It is a fact, as also stipulated in the 2020 Global Education Monitoring Report, that teachers are supportive of inclusion and in most cases, teachers have positive attitudes towards this principle. Yet, it cannot be denied that teachers' are not fully in agreement with what is actually delivered in terms of the acceptance, adaptation and internalisation of inclusive education. At the same time, it goes without questioning that teachers play an important intermediary role, both as inclusive education norm receivers and also as inclusive education norm diffusers of good practice for learners, both with and without disabilities. In this context, we can say that as norm receivers, teachers have been socialised to accept the general idea of inclusive education. However, as norm diffusers, teachers have in fact favoured a more practical approach, and localised the content of the inclusive education norm to match the realities of limited resources on the ground.

It is important to re-emphasise and highlight the intermediary role of teachers on both the supply and demand sides of inclusive education norms. At present, there is still inadequate quality pre-service and in-service teacher training in the country. Teacher education and training must include extensive modules on education for learners with special needs, together with ensuring a definitive follow-up with teachers on their skills to teach learners with special education needs (UNESCO, 2020). This importantly relates to teacher's self-confidence, and as an end result, the behavioural acceptance of inclusive education policies of teachers will much likely leave room and space for actual positive transformation in terms of executing good delivery and practice at the classroom level. In addition to provision of adequate teacher training and education, 'inclusion' and 'inclusive education' as principles and definitions remain quite vague for teachers at the practical level. The reason behind this vagueness is partially related to what will be explored in the last section of this chapter, yet in most cases, inclusive education is understood as the provision of special education, ensuring the right to education for learners with disabilities or special education needs. This also includes classrooms which provide education in the form of integrated classrooms in public schools. In other words, the distinctions and connections between understandings of 'inclusive education' and 'special education' remain unclear.

Finally, there is also a common and cross-cutting issue across the globe, but also within the context of Cambodia. This is the tension for teachers between the emphasis on inclusion and the need to make traditional exams successful (Forlin, 2010, as cited in Hayashi, 2019). This raises the question and the challenge of how inclusive education norms, when delivered as good action and practice, incorporate *both* 'inclusive and equitable quality learning outcomes' (SDG 4) for all learners, those with and without disabilities and special education needs. Is there ultimately a tension between the norm of inclusive education, and the norm of quality learning outcomes? Findings from the 2020 Global Education Monitoring Report and my personal fieldwork suggest that this could be the case. The issue of learning assessments is another critical thematic arena to successfully diffuse inclusive education norms with positive acceptance, practical adaptation and internalisation, not only for teachers as norm receivers and diffusers, but also for learners at the classroom level as receivers of inclusive education.

Conclusion and implications

By tracing the historical development of inclusive education as discussed on a global scale, and the Salamanca Statement of 1994 being the turning point to facilitate the normative diffusion of inclusive education, it is noteworthy to compare this international and historical movement with that of Cambodia's case. As illustrated in Figure 6.1, persons with disabilities faced social exclusion in the past, with exclusion having its roots in conflict, cultural and traditional beliefs, denying their rights to educational opportunities. However, these practices of social exclusion met with resistance from grassroots movements at both the international and national levels through the power of the idea of human rights. Persons with disabilities have persistently raised international and national concerns on the provision of their right to education in the form of various types of education including special education, integrated education or what is partially understood as inclusive education.

However, in most cases, educational provision did not meet the requirements necessary to implement and practice special education and integrated education due to a lack of teachers, equipment, tools and all other resources indispensable for special education. Much of this educational provision has long been provided through donor aid of international NGOs and organisations. Yet, teacher training

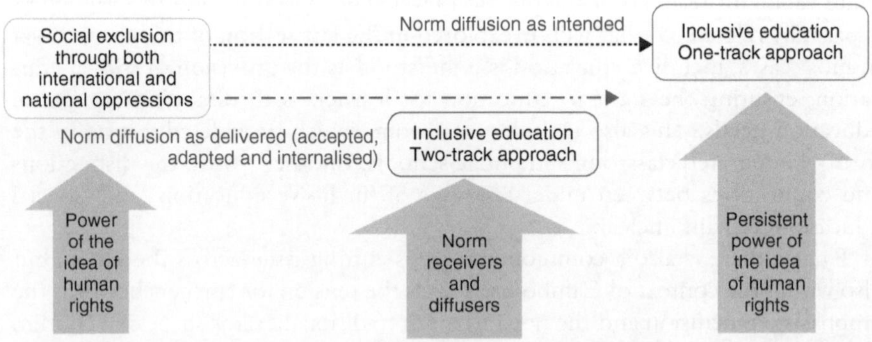

Figure 6.1 The 'two approaches' to Cambodia's inclusive education.
Source: created by the author.

on special education has clearly remained insufficient within the national teacher training institute covering teachers nationwide. Teacher education and training were provided through local NGOs targeting a limited number of teachers. Moreover, training and workshops for public school teachers teaching learners with disabilities were offered for a limited period of time, usually once or lasting for only a few days, which apparently proves insufficient.

In parallel with the struggle to practice and implement educational provision for learners with disabilities, the norm diffusion of inclusive education has continued to follow the international path in terms of intention at the policy level. The author identifies this movement of inclusive education norm diffusion as the 'one-track approach,' basically following the definition and interpretation set forth initially in the Salamanca Statement of 1994, together with Article 24 of the Convention on the Rights of Persons with Disabilities. As specified in the National Law on the Protection and Promotion of the Rights of Persons with Disabilities of 2009, the Government of Cambodia has positioned itself to align closely with the inclusive education policy as intended, leaving discussions on the role of special education entirely within the umbrella framework of the one-track approach. Needless to say, one cannot deny the influence of donor aid in this field of education, yet the call for an inclusive educational approach for learners with disabilities and special needs seems to be an apparent expression of the way forward for Cambodia's future, with inclusive education by intention.

However, this is not the end of the story of Cambodia's diffusion of inclusive education norms. It was made explicit that this norm diffusion is not being delivered and is not being accepted, adopted and internalised in the way it was intended at both the international and national policy levels. As an alternative, norm receivers and diffusers in this context refer to the intermediary role played by the teachers who are currently accepting, adopting and internalising inclusive education norms, firstly through special education. In contrast to what the author has called the one-track approach to inclusive education, the present status of Cambodia's internalisation of inclusive education norms lies in its strong recognition of the need to follow a 'two-track approach' to inclusive education. One could say that although teachers have been positively socialised into accepting the idea of inclusive education at a general level, in terms of delivery on the ground, teachers have localised the content of this norm and adapted their practice to reflect the reality of limited resources by adopting a two-track approach. This implies that the contestations as expressed by teachers and other norm receivers and diffusers of inclusive education demand resolution in the form of further investment in the development and use of special education resources, including teacher education and training on the special education curriculum and textbooks.

Although inclusive education as intended is not the norm or the practice in Cambodia at present, partially inclusive practices are positively implemented. Yet at the same time, positive practices also encounter contestation at the classroom level. The way to effectively tackle the challenging issues at hand is to advance installation of special education resources, which can help create a path towards a one-track approach in the future, even though there is currently a de facto two-track approach to inclusive education on the ground. It is necessary to combine medium-term aspirations for the achievement of inclusivity with a short-term perspective, which is realistic about Cambodia's adaptation and internalisation of inclusive education.

References

Ainscow, M., & Miles. S. (2008). Making education for all inclusive: Where next? *Prospects, 38*(1), 15–34. https://doi.org/10.1007/s11125-008-9055-0

Balescut, J., & Eklindh, K. (2006). *Historical perspective on education for persons with disabilities* (Background paper for EFA Global Monitoring Report 2006 Literacy for Life). UNESCO.

Hayashi, M. (2015). *Disparities within policy on equity and inclusion across educational concepts and social groups at both international and national contexts: A trade-off between needs and realities in Cambodia* (PhD Dissertation, Waseda University). Waseda University Repository. http://hdl.handle.net/2065/51282

Hayashi, M., & Edwards Jr., D. B. (2015). Policy intention versus policy implementation: Disparities in equity and diversity in inclusive education in Cambodia. In Y. Kitamura et al. (Eds.), *The political economy of schooling in Cambodia: Issues of quality and equity* (pp. 81–102). Palgrave Macmillan. https://doi.org/10.1057/9781137456007

Hayashi, M. (2019). *Final draft of the regional paper on 'Inclusion and equity in education in the Asia-Pacific region'.* UNESCO Asia and Pacific Regional Bureau for Education [Unpublished manuscript].

Hayashi, M. (2020). *Dynamics of skills formation through inclusive education of primary school children without disabilities in Cambodia* (Work supported by JSPS KAKENHI Grant Number JP16K17427) [Unpublished manuscript].

Huy, K. (2017). Understanding CRPD implementation in Cambodia. In D. L. Cogburn & T. Kempin Reuter (Eds.), *Making disability rights real in Southeast Asia: Implementing the UN Convention on the Rights of Persons with Disabilities in ASEAN* (pp. 129–142). Lexington Books.

Kingdom of Cambodia. (1993). *The Constitution of the Kingdom of Cambodia.* Phnom Penh, Cambodia.

Ministry of Education, Youth and Sport (MoEYS). (2007). *Education law.* Phnom Penh, Cambodia.

Ministry of Education, Youth and Sport (MoEYS). (2009a). *Law on the protection and the promotion of the rights of persons with disabilities.* Phnom Penh, Cambodia.

Ministry of Education, Youth and Sport (MoEYS). (2009b). *Prakas inter ministerial on the criteria definitions of disability classification.* Phnom Penh, Cambodia.

Ministry of Education, Youth and Sport (MoEYS). (2018). *Policy on inclusive education.* Phnom Penh, Cambodia.

NGO Education Partnership. (2018). *An assessment of children with disabilities in accessing primary education in Cambodia: Understanding challenges, opportunities, and ways forward.* www.academia.edu/44451845/An_Assessment_of_Children_with_Disabilities_in_Accessing_Primary_Education_in_Cambodia

OHCHR. (2020). *Ratification status for Cambodia.* Retrieved June 1, 2020, from https://tbinternet.ohchr.org/_layouts/15/TreatyBodyExternal/Treaty.aspx?CountryID=29&Lang=EN.

UNESCO. (1994). *The Salamanca World Conference on Special Needs Education: Access and quality.* UNESCO & The Ministry of Education and Science, Spain. https://unesdoc.unesco.org/ark:/48223/pf0000110753

UNESCO. (2020). *Global education monitoring report 2020: Inclusion and education: all means all.* https://unesdoc.unesco.org/ark:/48223/pf0000373718

UNICEF. (2019). *The State of the World's Children 2019.* www.unicef.org/sites/default/files/2019-12/SOWC-2019.pdf

United Nations. (2012). *Incheon strategy to "Make the Right Real" for persons with disabilities in Asia and the Pacific.* www.unescap.org/sites/default/d8files/knowledge-products/Incheon%20Strategy%20%28English%29.pdf

United Nations. (2015). *The 17 goals: Sustainable development.* Retrieved July 28, 2021, from https://sdgs.un.org/goals.

7 Diffusion of inclusive education in Malawi

Jun Kawaguchi and Kazuo Kuroda

Introduction

This paper examines the process of diffusion of 'inclusive education' as an educational policy norm from the regional to the national level and subsequent reception at the local level. Inclusion is one of the key terms in Sustainable Development Goals (SDGs) for all 17 goals while Goal 4, which focuses on education, aims to 'ensure *inclusive* and equitable quality education and promote lifelong learning opportunities for all'.

Qualitative and quantitative field data collected in Malawi are used to conduct two stages of analysis. The first stage analyses policy documents and interviews with officials from the Ministry of Education to clarify the process of adoption of inclusive education into educational policy. In stage two, class observations and results of a parent survey illuminate how inclusive education policies have been received in schools and communities. Data from these three categories of actors, 'government officials', 'teachers' and 'parents' yielded a wide variety of viewpoints, even within the same category. Thus, efforts were made to collect as much data as possible in an attempt to capture the diverse voices of the respondents.

Malawi is a landlocked country in central Southeast Africa with a per capita GDP of roughly 394USD (World Bank, 2021). As of 2010, external funds from 47 international aid agencies accounted for approximately 39% of state finance (JICA, 2011), heightening the influence of international policy trends on national policy, educational or otherwise. Further, Malawi is known for its responsible and transparent use of aid funding. Thus, while one would expect inclusive education to be easily integrated into Malawian society, this research finds that this is not the case. Instead, adoption, implementation and reception of inclusive education in Malawi is inconsistent, with deepening resistance observed at each layer of society.

Adoption of inclusive education policy in Malawi: from the regional to the national level

While many Southeast African countries have adopted inclusive education in their education policies, Malawi was one of the first to do so. This section elucidates

DOI: 10.4324/9781003205951-10

the process of adoption and implementation of inclusive education policy in Malawi by reviewing relevant policy documents.

Inclusive education in policy documents

Inclusive education policies in many countries have stemmed from measures aiming to support socially disadvantaged children and students, many of whom are disabled. In what follows, policies on education for persons with disabilities are reviewed to establish the context within which inclusive education emerged.

With the declaration of the Salamanca Statement in 1994 and subsequent Grant Aid Policy for Basic Education, student enrolment in Malawi skyrocketed. Yet while enrolment continued to increase, the problem of out-of-school children soon became apparent, particularly with the so-called 'last 5%, 10%' of students with special needs. The Government of Malawi Policy Investment Framework 2001 stated that by 2012, all inequalities within schools would be eliminated and measures would be taken to support students with special needs (Ministry of Education, 2001).

In 2004, the National Policy on People with Disabilities was established, recognising the need for access to basic social services for people with disabilities and marking the first such policy introduced on a nationwide scale (Ministry of Education, 2004). In 2006, the first policy guaranteeing the rights of all people with disabilities was established, and in 2007 the 'Convention on the Rights of People with Disabilities' was signed.[1] As the convention was adopted by the United Nations in December 2006, Malawi was one of the first countries to sign it. In the same year, the government declared its adoption of 'inclusive education' in the National Policy on Special Needs Education (Ministry of Education, 2007), signalling an early policy shift from special and integrated education to inclusive education.

While special education involves the separation (or removal) of special needs children from general education classes, inclusive education aims to embrace all students and address their particular learning needs within the same physical space. Although integrated education is often confused with inclusive education due to its focus on bringing all students together to learn in the same space, they are in fact vastly different concepts. While integrated education aims to mainstream special needs children into general education classes, inclusive education seeks system-wide change by leveraging the unique characteristics of each school to design learning that meets student needs.

With inclusive education featured as a central concept in the 2007 National Policy on Special Needs Education, system-wide change should be a prominent theme in the policy. However, this is not the case. While the policy claims that the necessary public funds will be allocated to each relevant agency (Ministry of Education, 2007), no explicit mention is made of system-wide change. Further, in the 2008–2017 National Strategic Plan for Education, the narrative again shifted, this time to 'special needs education' and the 'Special Needs Education

Guideline' was published the same year. Special needs education was developed with special education as its foundation and is a concept distinct from inclusive education. In 2016, inclusive education returned to centre stage with the publication of the 'Inclusive Education Strategy 2017–2021'. However, the document is heavily conceptual, stating lofty goals with no financial backing or concrete implementation strategies.

These policy documents reveal that there has been no uniform policy vision toward education for students with special needs since the first mention of 'inclusive education' in 2007. Rather, multiple policy changes have occurred rapidly over a short period. Mr. M.Y. (50), formerly in charge of education for children with disabilities at the Malawi Ministry of Education, explains:

> Project proposals by aid agencies in the education sector are tied to aid money, so it's difficult to express opposition to them (within the Ministry). Usually, whenever a new policy is introduced, potential negative impacts are analysed, but in the education sector, there is a tendency for proposals to be viewed favourably.

Indeed, at first glance it is difficult to detect any potential negative impacts of educational policy in comparison to environmental, economic or agricultural policy. Yet Malawi is a country in constant shortage of adequate supplies and facilities, a structural issue that makes it easy to fall into to the trap of 'take all I can get' thinking. The manifestation of such thinking was plain to see during tours of Malawian schools with classrooms lined with educational supplies and equipment from aid agencies. Numerous braille kits and typewriters from European and North American aid agencies and non-governmental organisations (NGOs) are evidence of special education aid.

Yet, frequent policy shifts have complicated long-term efforts to improve special education quality, such as teacher training. In the following section, we examine how inclusive education policy has been implemented against the backdrop of such persistent policy shifts.

Adoption and development of inclusive education policy

As evidenced in the preceding section, government policy toward education for students with special needs shifted continuously prior to the introduction of inclusive education policies. With numerous international aid agencies active in Malawi, policy tends to fall in line with the agendas of the international aid community. Yet while policy documents and ratification of conventions have been readily adopted, the implementation of such policies has been less straightforward. Malawi's chronic shortage of finances creates significant barriers to implementation. While policies introduced by international organisations are tied to funding, this funding is not continuous. Even if the implementation and development of related projects is carried out by international organisations, it is the responsibility of the recipient country to develop and carry out the project. In

Malawi, however, resource and budgetary constraints often hinder any long-term or continuous policy development.

Thus, a closer look at the implementation of inclusive education policy since its introduction in 2016 is warranted. We focus on two key issues fundamental to the implementation of inclusive education policy: teacher training and the status of special education. Firstly, the introduction of inclusive education policy necessarily entails the training of teachers qualified to teach inclusively. Currently in Malawi, Montfort College, a private teacher training institution, offers training to teach students with visual, hearing or intellectual disabilities. The teacher training college for primary school teachers, however, had no programmes related to inclusive education across its six schools as of 2020. Thus, inclusive education policy has been introduced without securing teachers qualified to teach inclusively. As illustrated above, project-level teacher training programmes, for example those implemented by international organisations, do exist in Malawi. However, such programmes are often ad hoc rather than established, mainstreamed programmes.

Special education schools in Malawi are classified into those for students with visual impairment and those for students with hearing impairment. Prior to 2016 there were two public schools each for students with visual and hearing impairment. Yet with the introduction of inclusive education policy, the visual impairment schools were shut down. At the same time, schools for the hearing impaired continued to flourish and by 2021 had grown to six schools. This reflects a fundamental difference in the way education for the visual and hearing impaired is approached in Malawi. In line with the philosophy of integrated education, visual impairment is not considered a formidable barrier to integrating special needs students into general education schools. However, many feel that students with hearing impairment cannot be taught in general education schools. This tendency to consider hearing impairment as more acute than visual impairment stems in part from Malawi's deep oral traditions that far outvalue written traditions.

Analysis of contextual factors: Malawi in Southeast Africa

In the previous sections we have shown that inclusive education policy was transferred from the regional to the national level. To better understand this process, this section examines the contextual factors contributing to such movement.

Perhaps the most prominent African regional education conference on inclusive education was held in Yaounde, Cameroon in September 2008. The Preparatory Conference of the African region for the forty-eighth session of the International Conference on Education entitled 'Inclusive Education: Major Issues and Priorities in Africa' brought together representatives from Ministries of Education across the African region to discuss all aspects of inclusive education, from policy to implementation. However, the conference yielded no resolutions or debate on defining inclusive education as a transformation of the education system as a whole, effectively ignoring the gains made through the Salamanca Statement and the United Nations Educational, Scientific and Cultural Organization (UNESCO) Inclusive Education Guidelines and further blurring the lines between inclusive and integrative education (UNESCO International Bureau of Education, 2008). With such misunderstanding and deliberate misinterpretation of policy apparent in the transfer from the global to the regional level, it is not hard to imagine further distortion in the translation from regional to national policy.

Further, the Salamanca Statement asserts that inclusive education is an effective way to fight discriminatory attitudes and create a society in which all people are accepted. Yet discrimination in society can pose an obstacle to the construction of an inclusive educational environment. In their study examining discrimination against people with disabilities in African societies, Abosi and Koay (2008) found that in many African societies, discrimination, prejudice and neglect stem from the belief that disability is a divine punishment. Inclusive education requires the transformation of attitudes and values of all educational stakeholders and confronting the prejudice and discrimination that exists in traditional society; upholding diversity and promoting tolerance and understanding are the foundations of inclusive education. For these ideals to be realised, it is essential for policy makers to understand the precise meaning of inclusive education, ensuring that the concept's core principles can be articulated in different policy contexts.

Despite such misinterpretations, inclusive education in educational policy has been on the rise in the region, particularly in Southeast Africa. Although driven by many factors, one reason for this expansion is the traditional cultural belief in 'Harambee'. Existing in parallel with the more discriminatory traditional beliefs as described above, 'Harambee' is the notion that 'If you find someone in need you should help them'. This concept captures the essence of 'inclusion' in the Malawian context, thwarting the claim that traditional culture and custom relieve the necessity for inclusive education.

We now turn to the factors driving Malawi's early adoption of inclusive education policies. It is first important to understand the structural background. As a country highly dependent on sustained international aid, Malawi is susceptible to the policy agendas of aid organisations. While not particular to the education sector, NGOs and international organisations have significant influence over Malawian policy. For example, in the 2010s an average of 90% of Malawi's national education budget was allocated to operating costs while only 10% went to development (JICA, 2011). This reflects a lack of government freedom to develop and implement its own policies and budgets, instead having to rely on policy that will secure funding.

Further, there is the influence of national character. The national credo, 'Never speak ill of a person in front of others', underlies the difficulty of expressing critical views. Thus, the adoption of educational policy with a focus on the short term likely stems at least in part from a culture of silence within the Ministry of Education itself. With no critical debate over educational policies, especially those tied to aid budgets, such policies tend to be adopted with little resistance or thought for the future.

When it comes to implementation of inclusive education policy, there is minimal funding to invest, resulting in inadequate preparation and poor implementation. Thus, rather than building on existing policies by reinforcing budgets, policies are merely replaced as new policies come with aid money attached.

Teacher and parent reception of inclusive education policy: from national to local

This section examines the expansion of inclusive education from the national to the local level, focusing on reception in schools and local communities. As mentioned above, the introduction of inclusive education was based on a series of rapid and short-term policy shifts, and policy implementation did not lead to actual inclusion. At least the concept of inclusive education was adopted in Malawi. Yet, the actual practice is very far from the internationally defined inclusive education. According to Souza and Bacon (Chapter 2), this situation can be described as a failure in transition from 'prescriptive status (phase 4)' to 'rule-consistent behaviour (phase 5)'.

Teacher evaluation of inclusive education policy

Within the local level, focus will first be put on schools to examine teacher reception of inclusive education policy. To this end, a questionnaire survey (n = 113*) and interviews of Malawian teachers were conducted.

Results of the questionnaire survey

The questionnaire survey asked respondents to compare the efficacy of special classes versus inclusive education based on the following four perspectives: 'human rights approach', 'access to school', 'contribution to society' and 'quality of education'. As shown in Figure 7.1 below, inclusive education was rated higher on all items. However, there was no significant difference in the quality of education between the two.

While the results shown in Figure 7.1 include all survey respondents, Figure 7.2 below shows the results for the subsection of teachers who specialise in special needs education. Compared to the results for all survey respondents, the difference in evaluation of special classes and inclusive education was smaller. In terms of 'quality of education', the ratings for special classes and inclusive education were reversed.

In other words, special education teachers perceive that inclusive education provides a lower quality of education than special class education. At the same time, however, it is also apparent that these teachers believe that inclusive education is effective in terms of human rights, politics and access.

In fact, when observing special needs education classes in Malawi, it is often the case that the quality of teaching is much higher than in general education

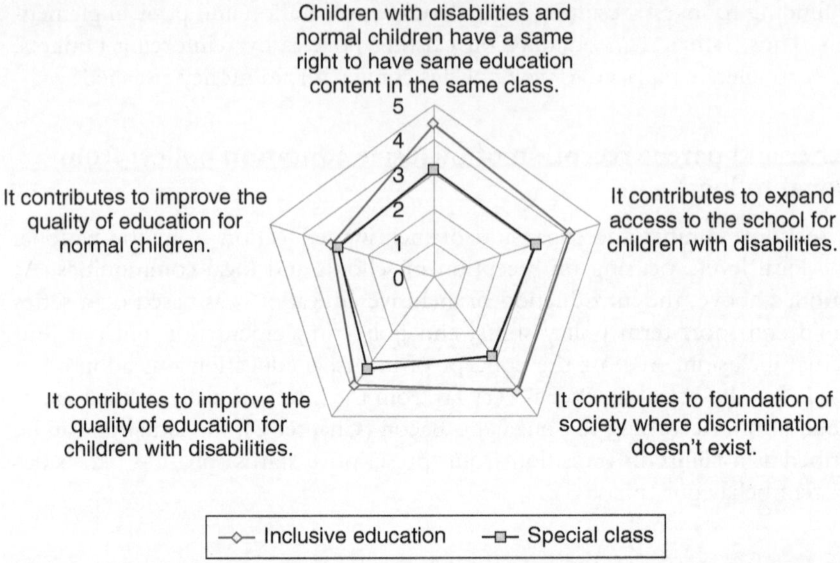

Figure 7.1 Teacher evaluation of special classes versus inclusive education based on four perspectives (human rights, politics, access and quality) [all respondents].

N = 113 *We collected 137 responses, but after cleaning the data, we could use 113 only. (5 Strongly agree, 4 Agree, 3 Fair, 2 Not agree, 1 Never agree).

Source: Kawaguchi and Kuroda (2013).

classes, which often serve large numbers of students. Even in classes with students with developmental disorders, teachers are able to control the class skilfully.

Results of interviews with teachers

The teachers interviewed ranged from lecturers at teacher training colleges to elementary school teachers, and a wide variety of opinions were heard. Through the interviews it became clear that there is a gap between the Ministry of Education staff and teachers in terms of perception and evaluation of inclusive education. The following opinion, expressed by a lecturer from a teacher training college, sums up the current situation:

> Currently, it is too early to promote inclusive education in regular classes in Malawi. Few schools have adequate facilities and teachers, and in most schools, even though they claim to be inclusive, children with disabilities simply sit in the regular classroom. In primary schools in Malawi today, EFA is ridiculed as Enclosure for All. It is true that inclusive education is the best policy for cramming children into schools.
>
> (Mr. D.M., lecturer, Montfort College, 40s)

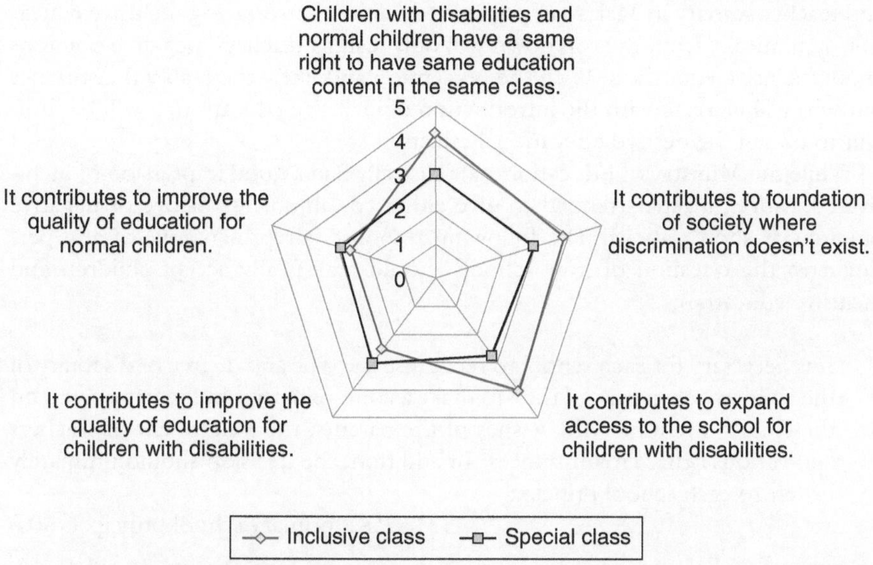

Figure 7.2 Teacher evaluation of special classes versus inclusive education based on four perspectives (human rights, politics, access and quality) [special education teachers who have completed a special needs education course].

N = 26

(5 Strongly agree, 4 Agree, 3 Fair, 2 Not agree, 1 Never agree).

Source: Kawaguchi and Kuroda (2013).

Further, there were many teachers who were clearly opposed to inclusive education in their schools. The following teacher's opinion is representative of the reality in school settings:

> How can we care for children with disabilities when there are already too many children to fit into the classrooms? Without the support of parents and other children, it will have a negative impact not only on the children with disabilities but on all children, and it will place a heavy burden on the teachers. Won't this increase the teacher turnover rate? If there were special allowances for accepting children with disabilities, it might be different.
>
> (Ms. D.Y., primary school teacher, age unspecified)

These teacher voices reveal a frank recognition that, practically speaking, the introduction of inclusive education will not have the desired effect given the current situation in Malawi's primary schools. The typical opinion of teachers was that there is already a great shortage of teachers and it is not realistic to impose greater burdens on them. Indeed, Malawian education already suffers from overcrowding in classrooms, so there is little incentive for teachers to accept new 'time-consuming' children. Thus, given the current reality of teacher burdens and teacher scarcity in Malawian primary education, introducing inclusive education systemically from the top down will only lead to teachers' negative opinions about inclusive education. With the perception and likely the reality that teacher burdens will increase with the introduction of inclusive education, it will be difficult to obtain the desired educational effects.

While the Ministry of Education staff basically had a good impression of inclusive education, teachers tended to give either conditionally positive or negative opinions as shown above. The following response is representative of and pertinent to the question of how schools should realistically accept children and inclusive education:

> It is necessary for each school to recognise the type and degree of disability of the child in question, and then to make a comprehensive judgement based on the child's intentions, the wishes of the parents, the assignment of teachers and various other circumstances. In addition, the decision should ultimately be left to each school principal.
>
> (Mr. P.K., primary school principal, 50s)

Thus, given Malawi's limited resources, it is not a matter of choosing between special needs education and inclusive education, but of choosing the type of education that best suits each individual student. This is the reality of the reception of inclusive education in Malawian schools. Observation of inclusive education classes confirmed that some inclusive education classes in fact employed pedagogy reminiscent of early integrated education while others conducted general education in parallel with special needs education by enlisting the help of parents and fellow teachers.

In practice, therefore, we can see that the norm of inclusive education undergoes a process of localisation, as local norm-takers adapt the reception of the norm to the reality of the local context. Localisation 'involves changing the formal shape and content of foreign ideas on the basis of the recipient's own prior beliefs and practices' (Acharya, 2018, p. 45).

Parent reception of inclusive education policy: the meaning of 'inclusivity' at the local level

Further examination of the reception of inclusive education at the local level focuses on the perspectives of parents. As seen above, there is no special preparation or budget allocation for inclusive education in Malawi, and the policy is to simply welcome children into school. As a result, visually impaired children who can understand what the teacher is saying can benefit from classroom instruction, but children with intellectual disabilities or emotional disorders just sit in the classroom, an example of so-called 'Dumping Education'.

In light of this situation, some parents prefer to send their children to other schools in the hope of receiving a proper education rather than forcing their children to attend public schools offering 'inclusive education'. Currently, Malawi is experiencing a rapid increase in the number of private and non-formal schools, causing a state of confusion with the many different types and qualities of schools. According to education statistics for 2020, about 40% of school-aged children in primary school do not attend public schools (Ministry of Education, 2021).

Even from this limited data snapshot, it is apparent that the number of children attending non-public schools is increasing every year, and many children with disabilities attend non-formal schools run by foundations and NGOs. Many expect that the implementation of diverse forms of education will promote the creation of inclusive education in Malawi. Yet on the other hand, there is concern that the previously described lack of preparation for inclusive education will deepen educational inequality between disability types as it expands. In other words, it is causing polarisation in which only children who can easily be included are included in public schools and those who cannot continue to be marginalised. This is an interesting example of how attempts at educational Capacity-building by external donors in fact serve to exacerbate existing and emerging polarisation dynamics that run counter to the ethos and practice of inclusive education. Further, given the general dynamics of teacher transfers, there is a possibility that knowledgeable, experienced and motivated teachers will leave public schools and move to non-formal schools where they will be paid more. While the government will benefit from budget cuts if education becomes more informalised, there is also concern that the government would be less involved in the content and management of education.

Findings and discussion

As we have seen, although the Malawi government has adopted inclusive education policy at the national level, implementation has been inadequate. Schools and teachers are left to enact the policy while facing the realities of the current educational situation, leading to various issues. While Malawi's unique approach to disability and education suggest that a shared philosophy of inclusive education exists, the reality in the classroom is that inclusive education is not often practiced. Instead, educators faced with practical and structural barriers strive to provide the best education possible through a combination of special and integrative education.

This 'Malawian-style inclusive education' has been enabled in part by inadequate preparation of schools due to a lack of funding and support for teacher training at the national level. There have been no resolutions to issues of teacher training or the scale of inclusive education practice, such as who will be responsible for teaching inclusive education or whether a whole-school or classroom-based approach is appropriate. Further, a lack of continuous government funding for inclusive education initiatives means that public schools are unable to meet the needs of the community.

Therefore, the norm of 'inclusive education' as recognised at the global level is diluted at every layer of society until transformed into integrated education at the local level, where only the students who can keep up with general education classes are included. For the rest, they are left to search for a school that can meet their needs.

Conclusion

Inclusive education is a focal point of international frameworks including the United Nations SDGs. This study has shown how the concept of inclusive education has been disseminated from the regional to the national level and subsequently, how it has been received at the local level.

By analysing field data from Malawi, the study reveals that the development of inclusive education has been ad hoc rather than deliberate or planned. Further, the study has illuminated the plight of the local schools and communities endeavouring to realise inclusive education despite endless barriers and few options. Yet, this situation cannot simply be dismissed as a policy translation failure. Instead, it reflects the reality of Malawi's openness to global education policy and offers a glimpse into the ingenuity of Malawian schools and communities. Rather than insisting on an idealised form of inclusive education, schools worked within their limited resources, utilising special and integrated education to try to meet student needs.

Yet, from the perspective of policy makers and international organisations, greater efforts are needed to ensure the intended philosophy of inclusive education policy is effectively implemented. With needs such as support for teacher training and system-wide educational transformation, there is a renewed urgency for international cooperation engaging a strategic, long-term approach.

Funding and acknowledgements

The data used in this paper are based on field surveys conducted under JSPS KAKENHI Grant Numbers JP21653094, 'Research on "Regional" of education in developing countries – A challenge for theorisation of international policy framework' (PI: KURODA Kazuo), and JSPS KAKENHI Grant Numbers JP 22252006, 'Comparative study on the various roles of school education in the transforming communities of Southern and Eastern African countries' (PI: SAWAMURA Nobuhide). We would like to take this opportunity to express our sincere gratitude to those involved.

Note

1 The 'Convention on the Rights of Children with Disabilities' was ratified in Malawi in 2009 and the 'Disability Discrimination Act' was authorised in 2012. In comparison to other Southeast African countries, Malawi's signing and ratification of these conventions occurred at an early stage. The ratifications, however, were not tied to any new budget allocations, structural changes or staffing, resulting in so-called 'empty' ratification.

References

Abosi, O., & Koay, T. L. (2008). Attaining development goals of children with disabilities: Implications for inclusive education. *International Journal of Special Education*, *23*(3), 1–10.

Acharya, A. (2018). *Constructing global order: Agency and change in world politics.* Cambridge University Press.

JICA. (2011). *Malawii Shakai/Keizai Purofairu* [Malawi socio-economic profile]. JICA Malawi Office.

Kawaguchi, J., & Kuroda, K. (2013). Kokusaiteki kyouikuseisaku agenda no genchi tekigousei ni tsuite [The conformity of an international education policy agenda at the local level: A case study of inclusive education policy in Malawi]. *Nihon Hikaku Kyouiku Gakkai* [Comparative Education], *46*, 61–79.

Ministry of Education. (2001). *Policy Investment Framework 2001.* Lilongwe, Malawi.

Ministry of Education. (2004). *National Policy on People with Disabilities.* Lilongwe, Malawi.

Ministry of Education. (2007). *The National Policy on Special Needs Education.* Lilongwe, Malawi.

Ministry of Education. (2021). *EMIS, Malawi Education Statistics.* Malawi National Statistic Bureau, Zomba.

UNESCO International Bureau of Education. (2008). *Concept paper for the Preparatory Conference of the African region for the 48th session of the International Conference on Education (ICE) 'Inclusive education: Major issues and priorities in Africa'.* [Unpublished work].

World Bank. (2021). Trading economics. Retrieved August, 2022 from https://tradingeconomics.com/malawi/gdp

8 Challenges for diffusing Global Citizenship Education in Japan

Leyla Radjai

Introduction

Sustainable Development Goal (SDG) 4.7 calls on countries to 'ensure that all learners acquire the knowledge and skills needed to promote sustainable development through education, among other means, for sustainable development and sustainable lifestyles, human rights, gender equality, promotion of a culture of peace and non-violence, global citizenship and appreciation of cultural diversity and of cultural contributions to sustainable development' (United Nations, n.d.). This new target, which was not included in the previous Millennium Development Goals, places novel emphasis on the value of education, going beyond the former focus of access to education.

Since its establishment in 1945, the United Nations Educational, Scientific and Cultural Organization (UNESCO) has proposed a variety of values-related education projects that focus on the challenges of global society. Education for International Understanding (EIU), which was proposed in 1950, was the first initiative and has the longest history. The idea behind UNESCO's proposal for the EIU initiative was that achieving international understanding among people through education was essential to maintaining peace after the war, as mentioned in the UNESCO Constitution:

> Ignorance of each other's ways and lives has been a common cause, throughout the history of mankind, of that suspicion and mistrust between the peoples of the world through which their differences have all too often broken into war.
>
> (UNESCO, n.d.-a)

Since then, UNESCO has proposed several values-related education programmes such as Promoting Tolerance (1995), Education for All (2000), Culture of Peace (2000), Dialogue among Civilizations (2001) and Rapprochement of Cultures (2013). Among the various values-related education frameworks proposed by UNESCO, two programmes that UNESCO is focusing on as its top priority areas today are Education for Sustainable Development (ESD) and Global Citizenship Education (GCED) (Kobayashi, 2018).

DOI: 10.4324/9781003205951-11

GCED seems to receive more attention and adoption in policy, management, programmes, and teaching and learning activities, in the context of international higher education, especially in the field of social science. Many universities see their roles as responding to the need to produce global citizens capable of meeting the demands of the twenty-first century (Hammond & Keating, 2018). Although GCED is defined and referenced internationally as one of the targets of SDG 4.7, as with any other international concept or framework, its implementation reflects different local and regional realities. The adaptation of GCED in higher education policy in Japan is no exception, where concerns about GCED have interplayed with ongoing higher education policy conversations and reform efforts. In this research, I investigate how the diffusion of the concept of GCED has been hindered in higher education policies in Japan by using qualitative research methods such as document analysis and interviews with key informants.

Global Citizenship Education

UNESCO defines global citizenship and GCED as follows:

> A sense of belonging to a broader community, beyond national boundaries, that emphasises our common humanity and draws on the interconnectedness between the local and the global, the national and the international. GCED aims to equip learners of all ages with those values, knowledge and skills that are based on and instill respect for human rights, social justice, diversity, gender equality and environmental sustainability and that empower learners to be responsible global citizens. GCED gives learners the competencies and opportunity to realise their rights and obligations to promote a better world and future for all. GCED builds on many related fields such as human rights education, peace education, education for international understanding and is aligned with the objectives of education for sustainable development (ESD).
>
> (UNESCO, 2015a)

This concept of a global citizen is not new and has a long-rooted philosophical history, including the idea of 'world citizen' proposed by Socrates or 'cosmopolitan citizenship' by Immanuel Kant (Schattle, 2009). Furthermore, educational efforts to develop global citizens have already been taking place since around the 1990s through scholars and educators such as Pike and Selby (1988) and organisations like Oxfam, before it became an element of the SDGs (Oxfam, 2015; Pike & Selby, 1988)

GCED encompasses various concepts such as citizenship, globalisation and the role of education in globalisation, and therefore it is difficult to fully agree on and define GCED across all fields of research and practice (Harada, 2019). There are multiple interpretations of global citizenship (UNESCO, 2014) and various researchers have attempted to categorise the concept of global citizenship and GCED to date. These include the categorisation of soft and critical GCED presented by Andreotti (2014) and cosmopolitan-based

Table 8.1 Core conceptual dimensions of GCED

Cognitive	*Socio-emotional*	*Behavioural*
To acquire knowledge, understanding and critical thinking about global, regional, national and local issues and the interconnectedness and interdependency of different countries and populations	To have a sense of belonging to a common humanity, sharing values and responsibilities, empathy, solidarity and respect for differences and diversity	To act effectively and responsibly at local, national and global levels for a more peaceful and sustainable world

Source: (UNESCO, 2015b)

and advocacy-based global citizenship presented by Oxley and Morris (2013). Among these different models, Schattle (2009) points out that 'awareness', 'responsibility' and 'participation' are the three most shared concepts in the discourse of global citizenship.

With the official inclusion of GCED in the SDGs since 2015, UNESCO, as the central agency for promoting GCED, has published various guidelines and reports on GCED in order to bring coherence to the concept. The following are the three core conceptual dimensions of GCED as defined by UNESCO (Table 8.1).

As with Schattle's (2009) three concepts of GCED and UNESCO's three dimensions of GCED, it is evident that GCED consists of knowledge, skills and values for the learner to embody and practice. Although every element of GCED is important for learners of all ages, since it includes educating for competencies such as critical thinking and engaging with national or global issues, not all educators are prepared to teach such content, especially at the primary and secondary education levels (Chung & Park, 2016). Therefore, it seems that GCED is mainly discussed in the context of higher education since these skills are valued in the global market and knowledge-based society.

Internationalisation of higher education in Japan

GCED is often discussed in connection with the internationalisation of higher education. The ambition of many internationalisation efforts is to develop students' intercultural awareness and competencies (Leask, 2015) and to nurture graduates who are capable of communicating, engaging and working in a culturally diverse globalised environment (Killick, 2014). There are many phrases used by international organisations to describe the competencies and skills needed for students, such as twenty-first-century skills, used by the Organisation for Economic Co-operation and Development (OECD) and Asia-Pacific Economic Cooperation (APEC), global competence by the OECD, and global citizenship by UNESCO. To respond to these international norms and challenges of globalisation, many higher education institutions attempt to internationalise in different ways with a different focus.

As for Japan, Kayashima (2019) identifies three main higher education policy efforts: (1) inviting international students; (2) institutional reform to accommodate those international students; and, most recently, (3) nurturing domestic students as global jinzai (Global Human Resources). Historically, the focus of investment of the Japanese government for the internationalisation of higher education used to be mainly on receiving international students. Japan's first official international higher education policy effort started in 1983 with 'The International Students 100,000 Plan', which aimed to increase the number of international students on Japan's university campuses. The number increased as planned; however, in Japan, as a non-English speaking country, several challenges in accommodating international students emerged, and institutional services and educational programmes had to be reformed. Those reforms and efforts included establishing English medium instruction courses, departments and degrees, recruiting English speaking faculty and academics, expanding strategic partnerships with foreign universities and establishing international offices (MEXT, 2008). This type of initiative to internationalise institutions began in the early 2000s as Ministry of Education, Culture, Sports, Science and Technology (MEXT) introduced funded programmes such as the 21st Century Centre of Excellence Programme, the Global Centre of Excellence Programme and the Super Global University Programme.

Shifting from an international student-focused policy, recently, Japan has increased investments and programmes for Japanese students to gain global competencies by providing scholarships and funds to study abroad. As a result, 'global jinzai (Global Human Resources)', a phrase that refers to a person with global competencies, is now one of the most frequently used terms by the Japanese government when international higher education is discussed. The reason behind this shift is the shrinking domestic market due to a declining birth rate and decrease in the working-age population in Japan (Yonezawa, 2014) as well as concern about the 'inward tendency' of Japanese students (Ota, 2011). Given that, the increase in international competition in the global market made Japan prioritise the development of 'Global Human Resources', and internationalisation of higher education has become one of the measures to achieve this goal (MEXT, 2013).

Internationalisation of higher education in Japan is a national strategy (Ota, 2011), and has been driven by competitive funding projects such as the Global 30 project (2009–2013), Go Global Japan project (2012–2016) and the Top Global University project (since 2014) (Ota, 2018). As a result, the term 'global' has been used for naming newly established programmes at the universities selected for these projects. There are many 'global' courses and programmes intended to develop students' global competencies. However, although there are many 'global' initiatives at university and policy levels, global citizenship or GCED are not the terms they have been using. There appears to be hesitation to use and diffuse the term 'global citizenship' in Japan. In this chapter, I attempt to identify the factors that are preventing the 'global citizenship' from being diffused in Japan's higher education policy.

Methodology

In this study, qualitative research methods such as document analysis and interviews with key informants were used. International higher education policy documents published by MEXT, and documents related to human resources and youth published by other governmental organisations were analysed to understand whether and to what extent the concept of GCED is included in Japanese higher education policy. Meeting minutes of the Japanese National Commission of UNESCO, an institution within MEXT where the role is the promotion of UNESCO-related programmes and activities in Japan's education sector, were also analysed. Among all the meetings listed on the website, those where GCED was discussed were selected and analysed to understand the discussions and arguments behind the adoption of UNESCO principles into the Japanese education sector. In total, 11 meetings held from 2017 to 2019 were selected. Also, interviews with three key informants who are/were in the education sector (government, NGO and university) in Japan were conducted, and questions regarding educational programmes and activities of ESD and GCED promoted by their organisation were asked.

Findings

In analysing the data, it became evident that although there are many opinions and arguments that the Japanese government needs to enhance its efforts in the area of GCED, the topic has not been well represented or discussed in higher education policy in Japan. Instead, another SDG 4.7 target 'Education for Sustainable Development' and 'Global Human Resources' have frequently been discussed and promoted. By analysing the data, I identified four possible barriers to the diffusion of GCED. They are: (1) the politics of international norms; (2) the existence of competing terms; (3) challenges in translation and implementation in practice; and (4) the existence of dominant stakeholders.

The politics of international norms

SDG 4.7 lays out a variety of values-related education themes, which have been incorporated through a series of meetings and conferences involving various stakeholders (King, 2017). It is considered one of the most inclusive processes, and that is also why so many different concepts are included in one target, SDG 4.7. Among them, ESD was strongly supported by Japan, while GCED was a programme promoted by South Korea.

ESD was initiated by Japan's then Prime Minister Koizumi and adopted as an official programme of the United Nations at the Johannesburg Summit in 2002, and with Japan's effort, the 2005–2014 period was designated as the United Nations Decade of Education for Sustainable Development (UNDESD), which has become widely known and considered important by educators. Hence, Japan has been actively promoting ESD since the beginning of the UNDESD (Cabinet Office, 2021). Especially since MEXT and the Japanese National Commission for UNESCO designated UNESCO Schools as centres for promoting ESD in 2007, the principles of ESD have become widely known and diffused among Japanese educators. A variety of research and educational practices on ESD have been developed in schools, universities, research institutes and government agencies, including boards of education, as well as NGOs and private companies. In 2016, the ESD Activity Support Centre was established at the United Nations University in Tokyo as a joint institution of MEXT and the Ministry of the Environment, and also in 2017, the Japanese Society for ESD was established and, in that way, ESD activities became more and more popular in Japan (Kobayashi, 2018).

On the other hand, GCED is a programme adopted by the United Nations in response to the 'Global Education First Initiative' launched by former UN Secretary-General Ban Ki-moon, a South Korean diplomat, in 2012. The Asia-Pacific Centre of Education for International Understanding (APCEIU), an institute (Category II) of UNESCO in Seoul, has been playing a leading role in the subsequent development of GCED.

In the discussions and the meeting minutes of the Japanese National Commission of UNESCO of MEXT, most of the discussions regarding SDG 4.7 relate to ESD matters; however, when topics related to GCED are initiated, GCED is frequently introduced as a 'programme promoted by South Korea' (Minutes of Japanese National Commission of UNESCO Meeting, 14/7/2015, 21/1/2016, 28/1/2016, 1/2/2016, 23/8/2016, 29/1/2018 (MEXT, n.d.)). It indicates that among the policymakers, ESD is labelled as a Japanese initiative and GCED as a South Korean one, rather than both just being SGD 4.7 targets or goals that should be promoted internationally. The political conflicts between the main actors and stakeholders of SDG 4.7, ESD and GCED, may be hindering the promotion of GCED in Japan's education policy.

Having said that, there are also opinions that Japan and South Korea should cooperate and promote GCED and ESD together since they share similar values in education:

> I understand that our neighbour, South Korea, has put a lot of effort into the GCED, both in its budget, for its activities within South Korea, and UNESCO activities, which are also quite large in scale. However, ESD and GCED are not in any way rivals, and I believe that SDG 4.7 can only be achieved if they develop in a mutually complementary manner. In fact, when I attended several meetings on GCED, ESD was always mentioned, and since ESD has been active for a longer period of time, there seems to be a great deal of interest in learning from it.
>
> (Minutes of Japanese National Commission of UNESCO Meeting, 29 January 2018 (MEXT, n.d.))

There seems to be a dilemma for both Japan and South Korea in wanting to promote their own initiatives nationally and internationally rather than other countries' initiatives, while they also see potential for it to develop if they work together as a supplementary concept. In fact, it was mentioned by one of the key informants that Japan and South Korea cooperated with each other to make sure that values-related education was included in the SDGs since there was some opposition from other parties to including values-related education as an international norm and goal. However, after adopting both concepts in SDG 4.7, they have not been actively cooperating with each other.

Existence of competing terms

In higher education policy, the term 'Global Human Resources' (GHR) is used and discussed frequently in Japan. Although GHR and global citizenship sound similar and both terms indicate characteristics and elements of people needed in this globalised world, they are very different concepts, which emerged from a different set of problems and perspectives. Table 8.2 compares the elements of GHR and global citizenship.

Table 8.2 Comparison of the elements of GHR and global citizenship

	Global citizenship	*GHR*
Cognitive	To acquire knowledge, understanding and critical thinking about global, regional, national and local issues and their interconnectedness	To acquire deep understanding of Japanese culture, strong language skills, educational and professional skills cultivated from a broad perspective and media literacy
Socio-emotional	To have a sense of belonging to a common humanity, sharing values and responsibilities, empathy, solidarity and respect for differences and diversity	To have an identity as a Japanese and intercultural understanding
Behavioural	To act effectively and responsibly at local, national and global levels for a more peaceful and sustainable world	To have a sense of responsibility, leadership, communication skills and cooperativeness to build relationships across different languages, cultures and values; willingness to take on new challenges and initiatives, ability to find and solve problems and to create new value; and a sense of social contribution that extends to the next generation

Source: The Council for the Promotion of Global Human Resource Development through Industry-Academia Collaboration (2011); The Council on Promotion of Human Resource for Globalization Development (2011); UNESCO (2015b)

As can be seen from the comparison, while global citizens are described as people needed to achieve a symbiotic society and who have a sense of 'belonging to a common humanity', the concept of GHR as defined by the Japanese government emphasises 'a deep understanding of Japanese culture' and 'identity as a Japanese' aiming to nurture people who can work internationally in the global market as a Japanese. We can see a nationalistic portrait of people in what Japanese higher education policy is aiming for.

'Differences and conflicts of interest between national citizenship and global citizenship' (Wintersteiner et al., 2015), and 'how to simultaneously promote global solidarity and individual competitiveness' (UNESCO, 2014) are two frequently discussed issues of GCED. There have been debates about whether education, especially higher education, should cultivate a national identity or a cosmopolitan global identity. Higher education institutions were originally cosmopolitan institutions, spaces for the gathering of researchers, educators and students interested in specific topics regardless of where they came from. However, with the establishment of the modern nation-state, higher education institutions and universities became national institutions promoting national identity (Kuroda, 2013). Now what we have around the world as higher education institutions or universities are mostly national institutions that intend to internationalise themselves (Ebuchi, 1997), mainly preparing their students for international job markets (Yonezawa, 2014). Although the human resources required by each country have changed due to globalisation, it may still not be exactly the human resources needed to resolve global issues such as global citizens. We all agree that international and global issues are every nation-state's responsibility; however, different countries have different priorities. National interests are not always identical to the interests of the global community (Chung & Park, 2016), and that could be another reason why GCED cannot take the place of GHR.

Having mentioned the differences between GCED and GHR, these two concepts also have some common elements in terms of human resources that are needed to achieve peace and sustainability. These include the ability to consider issues from a broad perspective, understand different cultures and act independently with a sense of responsibility to contribute to the next generation. GHR programmes could also contribute to the development of global citizenship, and Japan can claim that it contributes to the goal of GCED by promoting GHR. However, it seems difficult to promote GCED as a policy and use the term GCED when a similar term with an overlapping but significantly different meaning that emerged from different needs is already rooted and prioritised in higher education policy.

Challenges in translation and implementation in practice

Incorporating any new programme into policy takes time, as it requires not only a clear understanding of the concept but also its significance as well as the development of measures and indicators to plan implementation and evaluation. The concept of GCED is very ambiguous. Even if everyone agrees that the concept is important, how to translate the concept and its three dimensions into educational practice is another question (Wintersteiner et al., 2015):

> In SDG 4.7, there are many vague targets, such as ESD, Culture of Peace, and GCED. I believe that indicator setting will become a very important step for the international community.
>
> (Minutes of Japanese National Commission of UNESCO Meeting, 14 January 2016 (MEXT, n.d.))

In the case of Japan, as mentioned, ESD programmes had already started before the inclusion of ESD in SDG 4.7. Even though the concept of ESD is arguably as ambiguous and vague as GCED, in practice, it has been discussed with a focus on environmental issues. Since it has been in practice in Japan for many years already, experience and established best practices of ESD among different stakeholders make it easier to further promote ESD in the education sector:

> Recently, society's understanding of ESD has been deepening, but if GCED is introduced again, there will be confusion. Therefore, I really feel that it is necessary to organise them in an understandable way.
>
> (Minutes of Japanese National Commission of UNESCO Meeting, 23 August 2016 (MEXT, n.d.))

> The GCED should be carefully considered in light of international trends in education, its consistency with domestic education policy, and its impact on UNESCO Schools that have been working hard to implement ESD.
>
> (Minutes of Japanese National Commission of UNESCO Meeting, 1 February 2016 (MEXT, n.d.))

Moreover, some aspects of GCED could be deemed controversial and political, as it requires critical thinking regarding global issues, including democracy and human rights. As such, some organisations might find it difficult to put into practice. Chung and Park (2016) point out that there are tensions among practitioners, as GCED requires them to re-examine existing perceptions, values, beliefs and worldviews. This also means that it might challenge the status quo:

> I think that the GCED contains elements that not all Asian countries can necessarily get on board with. But at least Japan, South Korea, and some Southeast Asian countries can get on board and work together if they look at it from a broad perspective.
>
> (Minutes of Japanese National Commission of UNESCO Meeting, 28 January 2016 (MEXT, n.d.))

Eventually, UNESCO (2015b) published guidelines and a way for localising GCED, but it is still a lot of work for practitioners to review and transform their current programmes.

Existence of dominant stakeholders

All of the above-mentioned reasons are linked to the fact that the main stakeholder in the education sector, including international higher education in Japan, is the government, or more specifically, MEXT:

> What can we do when private organisations, NGOs, and civil society are having conversations that are in line with the values that UNESCO is advocating, but the government does not agree? If the government disapproves of the proposed project, they cannot implement it. So, no matter how good UNESCO and civil society think the project is, there is a dilemma of not being able to proceed unless there is an acceptance system on the part of the government. GCED is one such example.
>
> (Minutes of Japanese National Commission of UNESCO Meeting, 29 January 2018 (MEXT, n.d.))

The Japanese National Commission for UNESCO provides funds to organisations, agencies and universities to promote UNESCO-related activities. These funding projects are the UNESCO Platform for Future Co-Creation project, Subsidy for UNESCO activities for Official Development Assistance, the ESD promotion project for GHR development and the project to promote the development of leaders for achieving the SDGs (ESD). Two of these projects clearly mention ESD in their titles and aim to promote ESD. Higher education institutions are also receiving these funds (mainly from the latter three); however, there are no accepted project titles that include GCED:

> The objective and goal of both ESD and GCED are the same, and it is just a matter of words. It is not really our goal to label what we do as ESD or GCED. If anyone asks, we might say yes, we work on those targets, but what we care the most is to solve the issue. You can call it ESD or GCED; we don't care.
>
> (Interview with a key informant, 5 August 2021)

The same applies to the funding projects provided by MEXT for the internationalisation of higher education. As mentioned, Japanese higher education internationalisation is initiated 'top-down' by the government, and the funding sources of most of the universities' international activities come from the MEXT projects that are aimed at nurturing GHR. It will be easier for the universities or any other organisations to use the phrases and terms favoured or promoted by the government in their proposals in order to receive funding.

Conclusion

In this chapter, four obstacles to the diffusion of GCED in Japan are identified and discussed. They are: (1) the politics of international norms; (2) the existence of competing terms; (3) challenges in practical implementation; and (4) the existence of dominant stakeholders. However, it is worth mentioning that even among government officials, practitioners and policymakers, there are different opinions on whether Japan should actively participate in and promote GCED. For instance, based on the minutes of the meetings of the Japanese National Commission of UNESCO, there were both groups of committee members who believed Japan should actively take part in GCED activities and those who disagreed. Those who were in favour of participating recognised the differences between ESD and GCED, and the importance of GCED. They suggested that GCED and ESD should be promoted together as complementary concepts. On the other hand, those who disagreed argued that GCED could be a part of ESD activities, and they emphasised the similarities between GCED and ESD rather than the differences. They argued that the use of the term GCED might confuse actors already engaging in ESD activities.

When a state resists incorporating a norm as a policy, local practitioners and other actors could put pressure on the state by having active partnerships with the international community on a specific issue, which is known as a 'boomerang effect' (Keck & Sikkink, 1999). Yet, the reason this does not happen in Japan, and GCED is not adequately diffused, is because there are few actors who are willing to actively advocate GCED or challenge the policymakers. This can be attributed to the fact that GCED is vague as a concept which makes it difficult to understand and implement. Moreover, there are other similar-sounding, frequently used terms, such as ESD and GHR, and practitioners may not particularly feel the need to use the term GCED which may not be widely known. Conversely, if actors had a good understanding of GCED and had been active in recognising its importance, the policymakers' response might have been different. Therefore, the first step necessary for the diffusion of GCED in Japan is to clarify what exactly it is and how it differs from other concepts such as ESD and GHR, and to recognise the significance and value of each concept.

References

Andreotti, V. O. de. (2014). Soft versus critical Global Citizenship Education. In S. McCloskey, (ed.), *Development education in policy and practice*, (pp. 21–31). Palgrave Macmillan.

Cabinet Office. (2021). *Kodomo to wakamono hakusho* [White paper on children and youth]. www8.cao.go.jp/youth/whitepaper/r03honpen/pdf_index.html

Chung, B. G., & Park, I. (2016). A review of the differences between ESD and GCED in SDGs: Focusing on the concepts of Global Citizenship Education. *Journal of International Cooperation in Education*, *18*(2), 17–35.

Ebuchi, K. (1997). *Daigaku kokusaka no kenkyu* [Study on the internationalization of universities]. Tamagawa Daigaku Shuppanbu.

Hammond, C. D., & Keating, A. (2018). Global citizens or global workers? Comparing university programmes for global citizenship education in Japan and the UK. *Compare: A Journal of Comparative and International Education*, *48*(6), 915–934.

Harada, A. (2019). Global citizenship kyoiku ni kansuru kenkyudoukou [A literature review of Global Citizenship Education]. *Bulletin of the Graduate School of Education, the University of Tokyo, 59*, 197–206.

Kayashima, N. (2019). *Dagaku no kukusaika to ODA sanka* [Internationalization of higher education and ODA participation of Japanese university]. Tamagawa University Press.

Keck, M. E., & Sikkink, K. (1999). Transnational advocacy networks in international and regional politics. *International Social Science Journal, 51*(159), 89–101.

Killick, D. (2014). *Developing the global student.* Routledge.

King, K. (2017). Lost in translation? The challenge of translating the global education goal and targets into global indicators. *A Journal of Comparative and International Education, 47*(6), 801–817.

Kobayashi, M. (2018). UNESCO no chikyushiminkyouiku ga tsuikyu suru nouryoku [Skill analysis for Global Citizenship Education (GCED) of UNESCO: Prospect of values education in the age of globalization]. *Bulletin of College of Education, Tamagawa University, 18*, 19–32.

Kuroda, K. (2013). Ajia ni okeru chiikiteki koutoukyouiku gabanansu no tenkai [Development of regional higher education governance in Asia]. In K. Kuroda (Ed.), *Ajia no koutoukyouiku gabanansu* [Asian regional governance of higher education] (pp. 3–25). Keisoshobo.

Leask, B. (2015). *Internationalizing the curriculum.* Routledge.

MEXT. (2008). *Monbukagaku hakusho* [White Paper on Education, Culture, Sports, Science and Technology]. www.mext.go.jp/b_menu/hakusho/html/hpaa200901/1283098_004_01.pdf

MEXT. (2013). *Kyouiku shinkou kihon keikaku* [Basic plan for the promotion of education]. www.mext.go.jp/a_menu/keikaku/detail/__icsFiles/afieldfile/2013/06/14/1336379_02_1.pdf

MEXT. (n.d.). *Nihon UNESCO kokunai iinkai gijiroku haifu shiryou* [Minutes of Japanese National Commission of UNESCO Meeting]. Retrieved August 20, 2021, from www.mext.go.jp/unesco/002/006/1308017.htm

Ota, H. (2011). Daigaku kokusaika no doukou oyobi nihon no genjou to kadai: higashi ajia to no hikaku kara [University internationalization trends and Japan's challenges and prospects: An East Asian comparative study]. *Journal of Multimedia Education Research, 8*(1), S1–S12.

Ota, H. (2018). Internationalization of higher education: Global trends and Japan's challenges. *Educational Studies in Japan: International Yearbook, 12*, 91–105.

Oxfam. (2015). *Education for global citizenship A guide for schools.* https://oxfamilibrary.openrepository.com/bitstream/handle/10546/620105/edu-global-citizenship-schools-guide-091115-en.pdf?sequence=11&isAllowed=y

Oxley, L., & Morris, P. (2013). Global citizenship: A typology for distinguishing its multiple conceptions. *British Journal of Educational Studies, 61*(3), 301–325.

Pike, G., & Selby, D. (1988). *Global teacher, global learner.* Hodder and Stoughton.

Schattle, H. (2009). Global citizenship in theory and practice. In R. Lewin (Ed.), *The handbook of practice and research in study abroad: Higher education and the quest for global citizenship* (pp. 3–20). Routledge.

The Council for the Promotion of Global Human Resource Development through Industry-Academia Collaboration. (2011). *Sangakukan ni yoru globarujinzai no ikusei no tameno senryaku* [Strategies for developing global human resources through industry-academia-government collaboration]. Tokyo.

The Council on Promotion of Human Resource for Globalization Development. (2011). *An interim report of the council on promotion of human resource.* Tokyo.
UNESCO. (2014). *Preparing learners for the challenges of the 21st century.* Retrieved August 20, 2021 from https://unesdoc.unesco.org/ark:/48223/pf0000227729
UNESCO. (2015a). *Global Citizenship Education (GCED) UNESCO's approach.* Retrieved August 20, 2021 from www.unesco.org/new/fileadmin/MULTIMEDIA/HQ/ED/pdf/questionsanswers-21jan-EN.pdf
UNESCO. (2015b). *Global citizenship education topics and learning objectives.* UNESCO. https://unesdoc.unesco.org/ark:/48223/pf0000232993
UNESCO. (n.d.-a). *UNESCO constitution.* Retrieved August 20, 2021, from http://portal.unesco.org/en/ev.php-URL_ID=15244&URL_DO=DO_TOPIC&URL_SECTION=201.html
UNESCO. (n.d.-b). *What is global citizenship education?* Retrieved August 20, 2021, from https://en.unesco.org/themes/gced/definition
United Nations. (n.d.). *SDG indicators.* Retrieved August 20, 2021, from https://unstats.un.org/sdgs/metadata?Text=&Goal=4&Target=4.7
Wintersteiner, W., Grobbauer, H., Diendorfer, G., & Reitmair-Juárez, S. (2015). *Global citizenship education: Citizenship education for globalizing societies.* Klagenfurt: Zentrum für Friedensforschung und Friedenspädagogik.
Yonezawa, A. (2014). Japan's challenge of fostering 'global human resources': Policy debates and practices. *Japan Labor Review*, *11*(2), 37–52.

Section 4

Full and productive employment and decent work (SDG 8)

9 Gender equality and decent work

Japan

Thais Favero Souza

After a long and difficult fight, the protection of women's rights as international human rights has finally reached a level in which gender equality and women's right to work, included within the general guarantee of decent work, are considered an integral part of the United Nations' (UN) human rights agenda, and are also incorporated respectively as the deeply interconnected Goals 5 and 8 of the Sustainable Development Goals (SDGs).

However, a huge gap between state commitment to and state compliance with both goals remains. This is clear in Japan, which faces hurdles in areas directly and indirectly related to gender equality and women's right to work. Although an 'elite' developed country, which has ratified some of the relevant international treaties, has created some domestic law following international norms and has been vocal about using women in the labour force, Japan's efforts have not been translated into reality.

In this chapter, I analyse the connection between gender equality and decent work, and use the hybrid 'spiral model' to look into how the adoption of these SDGs and other instruments have affected the processes of diffusing and implementing women's right to work in Japanese society. First, I introduce the historical development of Goals 5 and 8 and clarify both their negative and positive developments. Next, I relate the theoretical basis of the hybrid spiral model to its usefulness in identifying issues in norm diffusion and norm implementation processes, focusing on how complementing it with theories of norm localisation and norm contestation and applying the concept of norm diffusion through a feminist approach can improve the use of the model. Then, making use of the spiral model framework, I proceed to analyse the introduction of the SDGs and other fundamental international principles, treaties and guidelines into Japanese domestic laws and policies, focusing on the importance of mainstreaming gender, on how female empowerment must be taken further than simply being a tool for economic development, and on the culturally, economically and politically-backed unbalanced power relations existent between female actors and key institutional players. Through this analysis, I aim to suggest how this has affected Japan's persistently lacking levels of commitment and compliance concerning women's right to work.

DOI: 10.4324/9781003205951-13

Guarantees of gender equality and decent work in the MDGs and SDGs

Constantly evolving and following the changes in the world's needs, the Millennium Development Goals (MDGs), followed by the 2015 SDGs are the frameworks which have been guiding the international community's practices since the turn of the millennium. Considering their accolades and criticisms, I will focus on analysing how the MDGs and SDGs approached gender equality and decent work, two of the most basic and essential human rights needed to achieve the financial, economic and political transformation required by the 2030 Agenda for Sustainable Development.

Changing the mindset concerning decent work: from a lack of mention in the MDGs to an individual goal in the SDGs

Work is a fundamental part of life in society. It takes up a huge number of hours of people's lives and defines the way they see themselves as members of their workplace and as individuals in private. Conscious of these aspects, the International Labour Organization (ILO) has continuously hailed decent work as 'the best way to avoid a life of poverty' (International Labour Organization, 2001, para. 32), and the UN as an institution that respects the fundamental rights of the worker, based on international human rights instruments (UN Committee on Economic, Social and Cultural Rights, 2006, paras. 7–8). These organisations include decent work in their legal instruments and encourage member states to create policies that contemplate the realisation of full employment and decent work.

Regardless, the MDGs failed to include decent work in the original objectives, only mentioning it in indicator 11 of Goal 3 on gender equality, and in Goal 8 on developing a global partnership, with regard to work for youth (United Nations Development Group, 2003). Not even the 2007 addition of a new target on full and productive employment for all, including women and young people, could remedy the negative consequences for the goals' realisation. This weak and delayed attempt was only a symbolic response to criticism, distant from human rights treaties and ILO conventions, lacking basic aspects such as deadlines and a plan of action, and failing to bring about positive change (Frey & MacNaughton, 2016, p. 6).

Pushed by the constant rise in unemployment rates and the 2008 worldwide economic crisis, the ILO, non-governmental organisations (NGOs), workers and trade unions lobbied for a more effective goal. The result was Goal 8 of the SDGs, which aims to 'promote sustained, inclusive and sustainable economic growth, full and productive employment and decent work for all' (United Nations General Assembly, 2015, p. 19). According to Frey and MacNaughton, it was promising that the goal included women and all people as subjects deserving of full employment and decent work, and that it was connected to the ILO monitoring mechanisms. However, its promotional aspect, its distancing from relevant human rights obligations under international law, and the conditioning of full employment and decent work to economic growth worked to undermine the goal's potential and its intrinsic and instrumental value as an internationally protected human right (Frey & MacNaughton, 2016, p. 2, pp. 7–8). For Goal 8 to overcome such setbacks and serve its purpose of furthering human rights standards, including gender equality and women's right to work, there must be a change in the way it is interpreted and translated into international and domestic policies.

The continuous struggle towards gender equality: how MDG 3 evolved into SDG 5

Compared to the right to decent work and full employment, the protection of gender equality was contemplated relatively earlier in Goal 3 of the MDGs. However, the MDGs in general were criticised for being too simplified and narrow, not having effective targets and lacking focus on fundamental issues such as human rights (Odera & Mulusa, 2020, p. 96). Goal 3 also suffered from these issues, being limited to the field of education.

Aiming to revamp this lacklustre approach, the SDGs were established with a broader perspective, including economic, social and environmental dimensions of development, clear means of implementation and cutting deeper into the issues plaguing the world. SDG Goal 5 on gender equality encompasses this cross-cutting aspect, both as a stand-alone goal and by spreading the protection of gender equality all over the framework. For example, it is present in Goal 8 on decent work, via indicators that include disaggregated data by gender (MacNaughton & Frey, 2015, p. 653). Furthermore, to enhance this holistic framework, Goal 5 should be applied in tandem with other human rights instruments. Beate Rudolf is incisive with regard to using the Convention on the Elimination of All Forms of Discrimination Against Women (CEDAW) as a globally binding standard for women's rights protection and the guiding recommendations of its committee as a guide to achieve the successful implementation of the SDGs (Rudolf, 2020).

However, the goals are not free of criticism. According to Odera and Mulusa, too few indicators reference women and have internationally established standards, and some goals lack gender specific language or deal with issues in a gender-neutral way (Odera & Mulusa, 2020, pp. 99–101). The lack of pertinent qualitative and quantitative gender sensitive targets and indicators makes identifying the most pressing issues women face in both private and public spaces an even more daunting task. Goal 5 specifically suffers from the constant underinvestment in policies for gender equality and women's empowerment (Sen, 2019), and from the overconcentration of gender-related policies and funding in areas such as health and education, to the detriment of reaching equality in economic, political and productive sectors (Odera & Mulusa, 2020, pp. 107–108). The SDG-led efforts of governments and businesses towards signing trade agreements, creating public–private partnerships, calling for trade liberalisation and pushing for economic growth must consider how they directly affect women, thus including in their foundation gender equality and prioritising regulations which protect social, economic and civil rights. Powerful players need to be held accountable and include the spirit of international women's rights protection in their interpretation and implementation of international legal documents (Odera & Mulusa, 2020, p. 111).

To overcome some of this criticism, the aspirational Goal 5 should be connected to progress in other specific SDGs. Specifically concerning women's right to work, it must be analysed together with Goal 8, and the aforementioned issue concerning the connection between decent work and economic growth must be revisited through its gender equality aspect. When the goal prioritises economic growth in its industrial, neoliberal-based sense as the main solution for gender inequality and lack of female empowerment, it overlooks the effect global economic governance policies have on women's human rights (Ponte & Enríquez, 2016), focuses on the creation of employment opportunities, and tends to disregard basic labour standards, social protections and social dialogue (MacNaughton & Frey, 2015, p. 655). This directly affects the implementation of Goal 5, stopping women from enjoying and taking advantage of the economic growth that they are key participants in achieving. Putting aside the fact that ideally Goal 8 should only include the right to decent work and full employment, it is frustrating that 'economic growth' was selected over 'sustainable economic development' to feature within the decent work agenda (MacNaughton & Frey, 2015, p. 659), allowing for economic growth to be disconnected from the improvement of educational, social, environmental and technological aspects of society in the goal's implementation process. These human rights-based guarantees should not be paired with potentially prejudicial neoliberal ideas of economic growth (Lapinskaitė & Vidžiūnaitė, 2020, pp. 117–118).

Regardless of improvements in the framework, much work remains. Goal 5's range of women's rights protections, which include ending discriminatory practices within the realm of work, should be coupled with interpreting Goal 8's mention of 'economic growth' as being 'sustainable economic development', and with understanding the realisation of gender equality and women's rights as a goal in itself, regardless of economically-driven aspects. Only this human rights-based, comprehensive and uniform approach can allow gender equality and women's empowerment to become an established concept to which all actors will thoroughly commit and comply.

Understanding the gap between commitment and compliance: the relevance of the spiral model of norm diffusion for domestic implementation

The persistence of problems in the SDGs is aggravated by the fact that their implementation in both developed and developing countries has been largely lagging behind (Gennari & Navarro, 2020). To better understand this situation, it is important to look at it through an appropriate theoretical lens, which in this book is the hybrid version of Risse, Ropp and Sikkink's spiral model of norm diffusion.

Building on Chapter Two, I will focus on how Checkel's theory of different types of socialisation, theories of norm localisation and a feminist approach to the topic can help identify issues surrounding domestic commitment and compliance with guarantees of gender equality and decent work.

The spiral model as a useful tool to understand norm diffusion

The spiral model is a state of the art ideal-typical framework with a good explanatory power of individual cases and a conceptual structure for analysing the commitment/compliance gap (Souza, 2020, p. 10), which allows for the identification of 'messy' points within implementation processes. The hybrid version of the model draws together elements from other approaches to norm diffusion and expands the understanding of socialisation processes, including ideas of instrumental rationality (logic of consequences), normative rationality (logic of appropriateness) and communicative rationality (logic of arguing) (Börzel & Risse, 2012, p. 5). This change in perspective regarding socialisation processes is relevant when looking at and setting subdivisions for the model's five phases of implementation: (repression (phase 1); denial (phase 2); tactical concessions (phase 3); prescriptive status (phase 4); rule-consistent behaviour (phase 5)), aiming to clarify why so many countries remain stuck between phases 3, 4 and 5.

In short, the spiral model is a useful tool to analyse issues and successes in diffusing international norms of various kinds, including those at the softer end of the soft law continuum such as the SDGs. Using this model, it is possible to identify the level of respect states have towards human rights, and to consider which modes of action and mechanisms of diffusion might be the most effective for the implementation of such imprecise aspirational objectives.

Checkel's different types of socialisation: pushing for the internalisation of the concepts of gender equality and decent work

The connection of Checkel's theory on processes of socialisation and the spiral model allows for the suggestion that socialisation, divided into Type I/socialisation or Type II/persuasion, can differently affect the movement of actors between phases of commitment and compliance. Although reaching Type I socialisation is considered sufficient for compliance in some cases (Risse & Sikkink, 2013, pp. 284–285), the lack of compliance found among states shows that more is needed when it comes to women's rights. Thus, in this hybrid version of the spiral model, the concept of and the need for persuasion are used as a magnifying glass on commitment/compliance processes. In phase 3 of the model, instrumental concessions made by actors could be divided into concessions based on calculations of benefit and/or to avoid criticism from others, and concessions that are legitimacy-based, containing somewhat valid reasoning. Depending on the kind of concession, in phase 4 we could find a situation in which states act either because they were truly persuaded ('sincere' ratification), or because they are just following a social script without internalisation ('tactical' ratification). This difference could help explain situations where countries are unable to proceed to phase 5 and reach satisfactory levels of implementation.

This approach would allow the dissection of the ongoing processes and the issues concerning the commitment/compliance gap in the guarantee of gender equality and decent work. These rights have been constantly mitigated for economic, cultural and political reasons, showing that states have not been fully persuaded of their importance, and that internalisation of the principles behind the SDGs is needed for their implementation.

The importance of localising international women's rights norms

Localisation, in the context of the SDGs, can be understood as 'the process of defining, implementing and monitoring strategies at the local level for achieving global, national and subnational' targets (Odera & Mulusa, 2020, p. 110). In the same sense, Acharya's theory of norm localisation digs deeper into the processes of using soft law to establish consensus between external actors and internal actors, and among internal actors themselves through dialogue and adaptability. He argues that localisation goes further than finding 'differences' or 'matches' between principles (Acharya, 2004, pp. 242–244), instead being 'the active construction (through discourse, framing, grafting and cultural selection) of foreign ideas by local actors, which results in the former developing significant congruence with local beliefs and practices' (Acharya, 2004, p. 245). The key is to find balanced adaptive processes that respect the role of local actors and take into consideration the intersectional cultural and customary background and context that shape a state and its citizens, all without disregarding the importance of foreign actors in this dialogue (Souza, 2020, pp. 44–45).

Efforts towards achieving the SDGs in the context of countries with diverse cultural, economic and political backgrounds depend exactly on this kind of strong but flexible approach, based on a high level of dialogue. This is especially the case for rights such as gender equality and decent work, which face many hurdles in their implementation as they deal directly with changing longstanding patriarchal social standards, culturally based customs, established work culture and professional status-quo, neoliberal economic policymaking. Processes of norm diffusion must aim to become a bridge between universally accepted human rights paradigms and local traditional positions concerning such rights.

A feminism-based approach to multiculturalism and norm contestation: breaking the illusion of gender neutrality

Researching women's rights and looking at the topic through a feminist lens go hand in hand. Neither domestic cultural practices and internationally sanctioned norms are gender neutral, which must be considered to analyse the conflict between guaranteeing universal women's rights and protecting multicultural expressions, as well as the engagements feminist scholars have had with constructivism and norm contestation.

Although different cultures must be respected and protected, blindly and neutrally prioritising cultural rights of minority groups over the protection of women's rights goes directly against the internationally agreed principles that guarantee that women should not be disadvantaged in any way by their sex. Regardless, violation of women's rights continuously happens publicly and privately, behind the veil of sovereignty. The application of norm localisation could be useful to overcome societal customs that endorse disparities in power between the sexes and facilitate the control of men over women.

Similarly, looking at constructivist approaches to international law through the lens of feminist norm contestation shows that power relations and their impact on international norms are not gender neutral. True illustrates this when she criticises how constructivists tend to oversimplify norms and how feminist analysis aims to overcome these ideas of neutrality and bring normative change, using critical methods to problematise old norms and establish new ones (True, 2013, p. 73–77). Thus, international legal documents and frameworks such as the SDGs should be interpreted and implemented considering the gendered and dynamic processes at work in their adoption.

Incorporating this view into the spiral model clarifies that the diffused norms usually include normalised, static, male-centred and discriminatory ideas concerning gender equality. This could affect why norms emerge and appear to diffuse quickly only up to a certain phase, rarely achieving their intended effectiveness. To overcome this, norm diffusion must consider ideas of norm localisation and feminist critique, aiming for a more discursive approach that uses conscious acts of persuasion towards true norm internalisation. True protection of gender equality and decent work is based on both protecting and empowering women according to their needs, and it requires change in the whole internalised construction of gender roles and in patriarchal, male-dominated legal, social and economic institutions.

The Japanese approach to the SDGs' implementation

Japan's positive initiatives

Japan, as an advanced economy and a democratic developed country, has long been at the leading edge of the development of international legal documents, and it has willingly signed up to most of the relevant international documents on human rights, including those concerning women's rights and the right to work, actively introducing many of these international norms into its domestic legislation.

As for the SDGs, Japan has accepted them and even contributed to various dialogues even before the international community's discussion became fully in progress, succeeding in incorporating the concept of relevant development agendas. The government established the SDGs' Promotion Headquarters in May 2016, aiming to guarantee a comprehensive and effective governmental approach to implementing the 2030 Agenda. In the same year, it held the SDGs' Promotion Roundtable Meeting, since then consistently setting up SDGs' Action Plans and the promotion of guiding principles, demonstrating leadership in many areas (Ministry of Foreign Affairs of Japan, 2020).

In the field of gender equality and decent work, Japan has put much effort into creating policies that support women's empowerment and active participation in the workforce, through the Council for Gender Equality and other organs which form the Framework for Promotion of Gender Equality (Gender Equality Bureau Cabinet Office, 2020). Starting with the adoption of CEDAW and the creation of the Equal Employment Opportunity Law back in 1985, the government has consistently updated its legal provisions for the protection of women's rights to decent work. Other laws dealing with the eradication of gender discrimination include the 1999 Basic Act for a Gender-Equal Society, the Basic Plan for Gender Equality (now on its fifth formulation), the 2016 Act on Promotion of Women's Participation and Advancement in the Workplace and the 2018 Act on Promotion of Gender Equality in the Political Field. They attempted to prioritise the guarantee of women's rights in the workplace, female empowerment and the expansion of their participation in all fields of society, and originated a variety of policies aiming to 'build a society where women can shine' and to reach a '30% by 2020' goal of increasing the share of women in leadership positions in all fields of society.

Following the spirit of both Goals 5 and 8 of the SDGs, Japan has attempted to create a system that emphasises the importance of women pursuing a work life of their own volition, full of opportunities and that considers the impact that traditional practices and gender roles have on women's lives, at the same time that it provides evaluation tools to publicity analyse and quantify the efforts of companies towards a less discriminatory working environment for women (Gender Equality Bureau Cabinet Office, 2020, pp. 28–29).

Japan's lack of successful implementation

While in theory there has been commitment to guaranteeing female empowerment and active participation in society, a deeper look into Japan's case shows that these efforts do not translate to the daily lives of women. Patriarchal attitudes and deep-rooted stereotypes regarding gender roles persist in the media and in education and consequently, also in the workplace.

Japan has not managed to eliminate or even satisfactorily improve issues such as indirect discrimination in the workplace, the considerable and stagnant gender-pay gap, the persistent M-shaped curve in the ratio of women's labour participation, the fact that employment rates in all age groups remain lower for women than for men, that most working women are in lower positions, that they are more prone to take low paying part-time jobs (Gender Equality Bureau Cabinet Office, 2020, pp. 8–10), that a dual track career system persists, that sexual harassment and detrimental treatment due to marriage, pregnancy and childbirth, etc. persist (Government of Japan, 2014, para. 299). The lack of intention towards creating an independent national human rights institution, ratifying the CEDAW Optional Protocol or ILO Convention No. 111, and the refusal of male-dominated Japanese courts to even apply these or other international women's rights norms in their judicial decisions also deserves criticism.

Ranked 121 out of 153 countries in the Gender Gap Index of the World Economic Forum (2019), Japan's gender gap is by far the largest among all advanced economies and the country keeps losing position, especially in the economic and political arenas. There are some damning statistics: only 15% of senior and leadership positions are held by women; 56% of female workers hold irregular positions, against only 22% of men; the share of time that women spend in unpaid care and domestic work is over five times that of men; the number of men taking childcare leave is as low as 6.16% (Gender Equality Bureau Cabinet Office, 2020). Japan had to push back fundamental and widely publicised targets such as the '30% by 2020' goal (Hori, 2020). These figures show that Japan's low ranking is not unwarranted.

Also, Japanese civil society is aware of this gap in treatment between men and women (Gender Equality Bureau Cabinet Office, 2020, p. 18), and considering that the work culture is centred on men, the fight to guarantee gender equality, empowerment and decent work for women becomes ever harder. It is clear that Japan needs to own up to its labour-related shortcomings and deeply rethink how to make the basis of decision-making, political and economic institutions more female friendly, addressing masculine approaches to power and discriminatory and threatening practices, and introducing more accessible childcare options for both parents, if it desires to achieve better results within the next ten years.

Using the spiral model to understand Japan's commitment and compliance to gender equality and decent work

After understanding the historical development of the SDGs, the usefulness of the spiral model of norm diffusion, and how Japan has been dealing with the need to abide by international legal instruments and put them into practice, we can draw conclusions and identify pressing issues.

It is clear thar Japan has been lacking in commitment and compliance with international women's rights norms and thus remains stuck far below *rule-consistent behaviour*. Even though Japan has tried to bring the topic of gender equality in labour and society to the forefront with policies and laws, these have not achieved the expected success. In fact, Japan could be positioned in the phase of *prescriptive status* when it comes to the right to work, perhaps even close to the phase of *tactical concessions* when complying with related international recommendations. Moreover, concerning the country's refusal to sign relevant international instruments such as the CEDAW Optional Protocol, the country could even be placed within the phase of *denial*, albeit close to *tactical concessions*.

This situation is complex. The influence of cultural and social conditions plays a huge role when looking at women's work-related situation in Japan. Conservative ideas concerning how women and men should behave are still internalised and externalised, and they culminate in persistent labour-related problems. Japan also tends to downplay the importance of international law in shaping the domestic legal framework. By refusing to implement the CEDAW committee's recommendations and to ratify the CEDAW Optional Protocol, for example, Japan limits both the access of its citizens to the international legal arena and their knowledge of basic gender equality-related principles. Similarly, the Japanese domestic legal, administrative and juridical landscape has not caught up to international standards. Laws and policies are often inadequate and made of suggested guidelines; male-dominated courts, legislatures and decision-making organs reinforce a picture of gender inequality and hinder any significant societal change (Souza, 2020, pp. 7–8).

The hybrid spiral model, read together with theories on different types of socialisation, norm localisation and through a feminist lens, allows a deeper look into these issues and the identification of the main ones. These theories are relevant in the process of understanding that compliance can only be effectively and continuously reached if it is seen as a dynamic social process that depends on actors being truly persuaded of the importance of such norms, which then makes it possible to redefine such actors' values and priorities.

Japanese female activists connected to the issue of women's right to work in Japan have shed light on the usefulness of the model (Souza, 2020) and on which issues should also be tackled immediately in SDG-based policies. With regard to the application of Acharya's norm localisation theory, attempts to forcefully change behaviours were pointed out as ineffective and counterproductive. Educational measures, bottom-up initiatives, transnational influence and mimicry are useful ways to help gradually adapt international norms and achieve true change in the understanding and implementation of women's rights, without falling into the trap of neocolonialistic approaches.

The relationship between Japanese feminist movements and the fight for women's right to work also turned out to be singular. Although it is intuitive to think that the 1970s women's liberation movement or even modern feminist theories would be deeply connected to the creation of work-related organisations, this was not the case. Feminist theory or feminist movements were seen instead as more of a sociological movement, and this separation might have even contributed to the persistent and negative gender-neutral approach in labour-related laws and policies. Thus, urging Japanese female leaders to go deeper into feminist waters could offer a wider variety of insights, creating necessary intersections between women's right to work and other issues, such as the treatment given to different kinds of marginalised workers (Souza, 2020, p. 221).

Interestingly, Japan's placement within the phases of the spiral model was confirmed by interviewed activists. In an illustration of the theory of organised hypocrisy, Japan has been masking its logic of consequences under a logic of appropriateness, tactically adapting and enacting legislation in order to avoid stronger direct criticism. It 'talks the talk' but does not 'walk the walk', showing a lack of persuasion related to guaranteeing women's right to work because it is the right thing to do. Governmental and economic players, moved by strategic calculation, recognise that it is beneficial to act under the script agreed internationally, but continue to make decisions under a logic of consequences, creating quick and palliative solutions simply to improve the economy.

This misguided focus reinforces the criticism towards SDGs 5 and 8 and the harmful gender-neutral work-related policies that they have given rise to. In fact, the discourse that 'economic growth will bring gender equality' has been disproven by the persistence of gender disparities regardless of the success of economic policies. In a world supported by patriarchy and neoliberalism, women bear the brunt of the economic financial crisis, which culminates in privatisations, fewer opportunities for regular employment and in cuts in public expenditure, welfare policies and social protection (Odera & Mulusa, 2020, p. 100, 104). The COVID-19 crisis exacerbated this issue, as reports show that Japanese female workers were disproportionately affected by the crisis (Shuto, 2021; Urasaki, 2021; Zhou, 2021). The pandemic shone a spotlight on the flawed, economy-driven governmental efforts on gender equality, and made it crystal clear that women's right to work needs to be perceived as a universal right and a pure sustainable development goal, not as a response to economic or demographic pressures.

Lastly, the model's presumption that there will be constant interaction between domestic and international actors served to pinpoint another possible setback to women's rights diffusion. While there seemed to be some level of transnational engagement in the 1970s and 1980s, more recent activities of Japanese organisations appear to lack this exchange. International movements like #metoo did not make sufficient domestic impact, and national grassroots movements like the #kutoo lacked strong dissemination abroad. Aspects contributing to this unsatisfactory transnational mobilisation and to the early demobilisation of domestic actors may include the lack of language skills and technological proficiency, the older age of the leading activists, the low number of people actively taking part in the movements, the persistent hierarchical cultural aspects of Japan and the need to still focus on commitment issues as Japan fails to ratify relevant international treaties (Souza, 2020, p. 222). By identifying such issues and this deviation from the model, it is possible to understand the situation better and suggest ways of tackling it.

Conclusion

In conclusion, Japanese women deserve more effective policies that guarantee equality, and not to be treated as a cheap and disposable workforce, as scapegoats in times of economic crisis. They should not be bearing alone most of the responsibilities at home and in childrearing at the same time that they are also expected to heavily contribute to family earnings. As the SDGs themselves have made clear, unpaid care and domestic work must be recognised and valued. In the same sense, Japanese men, who control the positions of power in the majority of political, legal and economic institutions responsible for creating and implementing top-down policies on gender equality, must do better. A male-led Japan, together with other powers, adopted the SDGs and thus, needs to take charge and responsibility not only in the creation of intersectional policies that tackle women's rights, but also by strengthening accountability mechanisms with the participation of civil society and clear indicators and benchmarks.

The effective design and implementation of laws and plans based on SDGs 5 and 8 and on other international women's rights principles, set apart from economic motivations, is bound to improve the lives of all working and non-working persons. It will bring about change in the toxic aspects of workplace culture; it will help contain harmful gender stereotypes; it will balance housework and childrearing responsibilities, and create a healthier and fairer idea of family. And above all, women's rights must still be protected because it is the right thing to do. Only with persuasion this deep and clear, with a true 'transformative approach' towards gender-unequal power dynamics and structures (Odera & Mulusa, 2020, p. 108) that deals with the issues defined by the application of the hybrid approach to the spiral model, will it be possible to achieve longstanding and strong foundations for Japanese commitment to and compliance with women's rights, specifically the right to work and consequently, to see Japan move to a position of rule-consistent behaviour.

References

Acharya, A. (2004). How ideas spread: Whose norms matter? Norm localization and institutional change in Asian regionalism. *International Organization*, *58*(2), 239–275.

Börzel, T. A., & Risse, T. (2012). From Europeanization to diffusion: Introduction. *West European Politics*, *35*(1), 1–19.

Frey, D. F., & MacNaughton, G. (2016). A human rights lens on full employment and decent work in the 2030 Sustainable Development Agenda. *SAGE Open*. https://doi.org/10.1177/2158244016649580

Gender Equality Bureau Cabinet Office. (2020). *Women and men in Japan 2020*. Government of Japan. www.gender.go.jp/english_contents/pr_act/pub/pamphlet/women-and-men20/index.html

Gennari, P., & Navarro, D. K. (2020, January 14). Are we serious about achieving the SDGs? A statistician's perspective. *IISD SDG Knowledge Hub*. https://sdg.iisd.org/commentary/guest-articles/are-we-serious-about-achieving-the-sdgs-a-statisticians-perspective/

Government of Japan. (2014). *Seventh and eighth periodic reports on the implementation of the Convention on the Elimination of All Forms of Discrimination against Women* (CEDAW/C/JPN/7-8). www.mofa.go.jp/files/000051250.pdf

Hori, K. (2020, June 26). Japan gov't to push back 30% target for women in leadership positions by up to 10 years. *The Mainichi*. https://mainichi.jp/english/articles/20200626/p2a/00m/0fp/014000c

International Labour Organization. (2001). *Poverty reduction and decent work in a globalizing world* (GB.280/WP/SDG/1). International Labour Office, Working Party on the Social Dimension of Globalization. www.ilo.org/wcmsp5/groups/public/---ed_norm/---relconf/---reloff/documents/meetingdocument/wcms_078848.pdf

Lapinskaitė, I., & Vidžiūnaitė, S. (2020). Assessment of the sustainable economic development goal 8: Decent work and economic growth in G20 countries. *Economics and Culture, 17*(1), 116–125.

MacNaughton, G., & Frey, D. F. (2015). Decent work, human rights and the sustainable development goals. *Georgetown Journal of International Law, 47*. http://dx.doi.org/10.2139/ssrn.2613999

Ministry of Foreign Affairs of Japan. (2020) *Japan's efforts for achieving the SDGs*. Government of Japan. www.mofa.go.jp/policy/oda/sdgs/pdf/Japans_Effort_for_Achieving_the_SDGs.pdf

Odera, J. A., & Mulusa, J. (2020). SDGs, gender equality and women's empowerment: What prospects for delivery? In M. Kaltenborn, M. Krajewski, & H. Kuhn (Eds.), *Sustainable Development Goals and human rights. Interdisciplinary studies in human rights, vol 5*. Springer, Cham. https://doi.org/10.1007/978-3-030-30469-0_6

Ponte, N. B., & Enríquez, C. R. (2016) Agenda 2030: A bold enough framework towards sustainable, gender-just development? *Gender & Development, 24*(1), 83–98. https://doi.org/10.1080/13552074.2016.1142227

Risse, T., & Sikkink, K. (2013). Chapter 15 – Conclusions. In T. Risse, S. C. Ropp, & K. Sikkink (Eds.), *The persistent power of human rights: From commitment to compliance* (pp. 275–295). Cambridge University Press.

Rudolf, B. (2020). Freedom from violence, full access to resources, equal participation, and empowerment: The relevance of CEDAW for the implementation of the SDGs. In M. Kaltenborn, M. Krajewski, & H. Kuhn (Eds.), *Sustainable Development Goals and human rights. Interdisciplinary studies in human rights, vol 5*. Springer, Cham. https://doi.org/10.1007/978 3 030 30469-0_6

Sen, G. (2019). Gender equality and women's empowerment: Feminist mobilization for the SDGs. *Global Policy, 10*, 28–38.

Shuto, W. (2021, January 14). *The failed promise of workplace equality in Japan: A view from the trenches*. Nippon. www.nippon.com/en/in-depth/d00653/

Souza, T. F. (2020). *Women's rights implementation stuck in time and hindered by tradition: Analyzing Japan's persistent commitment/compliance gap regarding women's right to work through the lens of a "spiral model" of feminist norm diffusion* (Unpublished PhD thesis). Waseda University.

True, J. (2013). Chapter 4 – Feminist problems with international norms. In J. A. Tickner, & L. Sjoberg (Eds.), *Feminism and international relations: Conversations about the past, present and future* (pp. 73–88). Routledge.

United Nations Committee on Economic, Social and Cultural Rights. (2006). *ICESCR General Comment* No. 18. United Nations.

United Nations Development Group. (2003). *Indicators for monitoring the Millennium Development Goals*. United Nations. http://unstats.un.org/unsd/publication/seriesf/seriesf_95e.pdf

United Nations General Assembly. (2015). *Transforming our world: The 2030 Agenda for sustainable development*. (U.N. Doc. A/RES/70/1). United Nations. www.un.org/ga/search/view_doc.asp?symbol=A/RES/70/1&Lang=E

Urasaki, Y. (2021, May 1). *Women and temps hit hardest by Japan's job market upheaval.* Nikkei Asia. https://asia.nikkei.com/Economy/Women-and-temps-hit-hardest-by-Japan-s-job-market-upheaval

World Economic Forum. (2019). *The Global Gender Gap Report 2020.* Retrieved from http://www3.weforum.org/docs/WEF_GGGR_2020.pdf

Zhou, Y. (2021). How women bear the brunt of COVID-19's damages on work. *Japan Labor Issues*, *5*(28), 2–8.

10 Tackling forced labour in Thailand

The role of the EU and ILO

Paul Bacon and Nishkhan Usayapant

Introduction: joint recognition of improved fisheries standards in Thailand

The Thai fisheries case is a successful example of the diffusion of Sustainable Development Goal (SDG) 8 by the European Union (EU). The EU used the economic conditionality of the fisheries 'yellow card' as the driver for this. This economic threat produced significant behavioural change from the Thai government, in two ways. Firstly, the Thai government significantly improved its fisheries management, respecting SDG Goal 14. Secondly, the EU also simultaneously funded a major International Labour Organization (ILO) Capacity-building project, the Ship-to-Shore project, which aimed to improve human rights and prevent/mitigate forced labour in the Thai fisheries industry, respecting SDG Goal 8.

The two relevant SDG goals are defined as follows:

> **Goal 8: Decent work and economic growth**
>
> **Target 8.7:** Take immediate and effective measures to eradicate forced labour, end modern slavery and human trafficking and secure the prohibition and elimination of the worst forms of child labour…
>
> **Goal 14: Conserve and sustainably use the oceans, seas and marine resources for sustainable development**
>
> **Target 14.4:** By 2020, effectively regulate harvesting and end overfishing, illegal, unreported and unregulated fishing and destructive fishing practices and implement science-based management plans, in order to restore fish stocks in the shortest time feasible…

There were two main sources of complementary pressure from the EU. The first of these was the fisheries yellow card issued by the Directorate-General for Maritime Affairs and Fisheries of the European Commission (DG Mare), and the subsequent confidential dialogue between the EU and the Thai government as part of this process. The EU is working to close the loopholes that allow operators to profit from illegal, unreported and unregulated (IUU) fishing activities. The

DOI: 10.4324/9781003205951-14

EU regulation to prevent, deter and eliminate IUU fishing entered into force on 1 January 2010. The Commission is working actively with all stakeholders to ensure coherent application of the IUU regulation. Only marine fishery products accompanied by catch certificates validated by the competent flag state can be imported into the EU. The EU regularly updates the IUU vessel list. It includes IUU vessels identified by regional fisheries management organisations (European Commission, 2022). The IUU regulation can take steps against states ignoring illegal fishing activities: the Commission first issues a warning (yellow card), then if the country is still not complying, it will identify the country as non-cooperating (the so-called red card) and place it on the list of non-cooperating countries. Fisheries products from the country in question will then be banned from the EU market (European Commission, 2022)

The second source of pressure was the 'Ship-to-Shore' project, which was administered by the ILO and funded by the EU. The EU provided 3.7 million euros of support for this Capacity-building project, which had a new stand-alone forced labour law as one of its main objectives. We can see that the two sources of pressure were complementary from the jointly-managed way in which the yellow card was lifted. On 8 January 2019, the EU formally announced the lifting of the yellow card for Thailand in recognition of the substantive progress Thailand had made in tackling IUU fishing since 2015. Representing the Thai government, General Chatchai Sarikulaya, Deputy Prime Minister, travelled to Brussels to take part in the joint press conference with H.E. Mr. Karmenu Vella, European Commissioner for Maritime Affairs and Fisheries. He emphasised the successful cooperation between Thailand and the EU in combatting IUU fishing. To quote the Thai Ministry of Foreign Affairs:

> The yellow card issued by the EU prompted Thailand to overhaul its entire fishing industry to meet international standards. … Thailand has pledged to ensure that the working conditions in its domestic fishing industry meet the International Labour Organization (ILO) standards. … Thailand will also take the lead by becoming the first country in Asia to ratify the ILO Work in Fishing Convention, 2007 (C188) by the end of January 2019. On the same occasion, the EU Commissioner … commended the success of Thailand in tackling IUU fishing in all dimensions and the accomplishment of the Thai government to address the labour issue in the fisheries sector.
>
> (MOFA, Thailand, 2019)

The two dimensions of the EU's pressure, the yellow card and the ILO Ship-to-Shore project were not officially directly connected, as human rights protection is not strictly part of the remit of DG Mare. This separation is made clear in official statements, such as that cited directly below. However, the Thai government clearly understood that it needed to improve its human rights record in the fisheries industry, as well as improving its record on IUU fishing before the EU yellow card could be lifted. On the European side:

> the Commission also recognises the efforts demonstrated by Thailand to tackle human trafficking and to improve labour conditions in the fishing sector. While not part of the bilateral dialogue on illegal, unreported and unregulated fishing, the Commission and the European External Action Service have addressed with Thai authorities the serious human rights abuses and forced labour in the fishing industry. Thailand has recently announced the ratification of the International Labour Organisation's Convention No. 188 on Work in Fishing (C188), the first country in Asia to do so.
>
> (European Commission, 2019)

Therefore, we can see official recognition from both the Thai government and the European Commission that EU norm diffusion was successful in this case with regard to both fisheries governance and human rights. In the discussion below, we attempt to explain how this success occurred, and which mechanisms of norm diffusion were in play. Next, before outlining the nature of the argument being made, it is necessary to offer some background about how to conceptualise EU norm diffusion, and the importance of case study work in third countries.

Case study work on SDG norm diffusion in third countries[1]

Somewhat curiously, there has been very little work on EU SDG norm diffusion in third countries beyond the European neighbourhood.[2] To understand why this is so, it is necessary to consider Ian Manners' seminal Normative Power Europe (NPE) article. For Manners, famously, not only is the EU constructed on a normative basis, but this 'predisposes it to act in a normative way in world politics … the most important factor shaping the role of the EU is not what it does or what it says, but what it is' (p. 252). The EU possesses the 'ability to define what passes for "normal" in world politics', which is 'ultimately, the greatest power of all' (p. 236, 253). There are four stages in Manners' analysis. He first explains the EU's normative difference (historical context, hybrid polity and political-legal constitution), and the EU's normative basis (five core norms of peace, liberty, democracy, the rule of law and human rights). He then offers an explanation of how norms can be diffused, identifying six methods of norm diffusion (contagion, informational, procedural, overt, transference diffusion and cultural filter). Finally, Manners uses his norm diffusion framework to analyse four clusters of death penalty situations in accession candidate countries and neighbours, and offers four sketches identifying which methods of diffusion were deployed in each of these situations (2002, pp. 244–252).

Identifying the EU's normative difference and normative basis in this way was ground-breaking. However, in this chapter we focus on developing the third and fourth elements in Manners' analysis, by using a norm diffusion framework to analyse a concrete country case study in which the EU has attempted to diffuse anti-forced labour norms. Following the publication of Manners' article, most subsequent analyses of NPE that have framed the mainstream debate have focused on developing the first element of Manners' analysis, looking at normative difference, and the issue of what type of power the EU is or should be. In this article, however, we park the issue of EU actor identity. This is partly because the specific analysis of norm diffusion is often marginalised in this highly politicised meta-debate, and partly because the concepts of normative, civilian, postmodern and ethical power are not very clearly defined; Pace (2007), for example, has suggested that the concept of NPE is a 'semantically empty notion'. Lastly, there is considerable overlap between these various concepts and each approach asserts that the EU does or should seek to diffuse human rights norms. If our focus is on EU norm diffusion, it is therefore not strictly necessary to first take a position on what type of actor the EU is.

According to Forsberg (2011, p. 1191), in the debate over NPE, at least five kinds of criteria for identifying a normative power have been used: having a normative identity; having normative interests; behaving in a normative way; using normative means of power; and being able to achieve normative ends. We focus on the fourth and fifth of these criteria, with an emphasis on whether the EU is able to achieve normative ends, assessing the extent to which the EU contributes concretely to the diffusion of human rights norms. We suggest that whether the EU has the capacity to define what passes for normal is not the main question. The main question is whether, how and to what extent the EU is able to diffuse the human rights norms which constitute the normative basis of NPE. Only then can we build a meaningful picture of whether the EU actually makes a normative difference, rather than simply being normatively different. We should do as Manners does in his 2002 article, where he actually discusses case studies of norm diffusion, but not as he says, when he argues that we should focus on what type of actor the EU is.

Manners' own norm diffusion criteria, and his demonstration of how such criteria can be applied to case studies, have not been picked up on and developed in mainstream EU studies. This is partly because subsequent scholars have followed Manners' headline advice to focus on what the EU is, as a result of which meta-arguments about the nature of EU identity have dominated mainstream scholarship on NPE. However, it is also partly because Manners' own criteria were 'briefly outlined', 'unclear' and 'unspecified', and not convincingly developed and systematically applied throughout the course of his article (Forsberg, 2011, p. 1196). We seek to address these shortcomings in Manners' criteria by adapting and applying a different set of criteria developed by Börzel and Risse (2012), which have been widely used in the Europeanisation literature. Some of the criteria Börzel and Risse use overlap with and build on those used in the 'spiral model' approach (Risse & Ropp, 2013), which itself builds on pioneering work on the 'boomerang effect' by Keck and Sikkink (1998). Börzel and Risse have historically confined the scope of application of their diffusion framework to EU member states, acceding states, states in the EU neighbourhood and other regional organisations (Börzel & Risse, 2012, p. 6). However, we seek to demonstrate how their approach can be expanded to analyse EU relations with third countries beyond the European neighbourhood. And, in particular, to an analysis of the EU's efforts at SDG norm diffusion in Thailand.

At present there is also very little systematic case study research in English on EU SDG norm diffusion with regard to third countries beyond the neighbourhood, and almost no work of this kind on the Asia-Pacific region. There is potentially a major and profoundly under-investigated research programme here. It is time to recognise and address these various oversights, and pursue this particular untaken normative turn.

Overview of the argument

Below, we describe how the EU was successful in four ways that can be concretely benchmarked: there was behavioural change on the part of the Thai government; the Thai government ratified important international agreements related to forced labour; the Thai government meaningfully transposed the content of at least one of these agreements into domestic law; and finally, there has been sustained compliance with ILO standards and SDG norms on the ground. We discuss the introduction of an amendment to the Thai Anti-Human Trafficking Act (AHTA), which establishes forced labour as a stand-alone crime separate from human trafficking. We also analyse the ILO Ship-to-Shore Endline survey, which identifies real improvements in the working conditions on the ground in Thailand. Of the four most important reports connected to this case study, three are produced by the ILO, as a result of major project funding by the EU. These include an ILO Baseline report (ILO, 2017), an ILO Endline report (ILO, 2020) and an ILO legal Gap Analysis (ILO, 2018). The fourth is a major Human Rights Watch report on the Thai fisheries industry (Human Rights Watch, 2018).

Börzel and Risse define norms as 'expectations of appropriate behaviour based on a given collective identity', and diffusion as 'a process through which ideas, normative standards, or … policies and institutions travel across time and space' (2012, p. 4, 5). Following their example, the dependent variable we analyse here is 'domestic or regional institutional change which can be traced to the EU's direct or indirect influence' (p. 14). In its attempt to diffuse human rights norms, the EU often relies on external incentives (*conditionality*), on the one hand, and technical and financial assistance (*Capacity-building*), on the other. Conditionality 'tries to manipulate the cost–benefit calculations of target actors through creating positive and negative incentives', while Capacity-building 'by contrast, provides target actors with additional resources enabling them to make choices to begin with' (Börzel & Risse, 2012, p. 7). While Börzel and Risse identify conditionality and Capacity-building as one mechanism, we follow Risse and Ropp, (2013, pp. 14–16), in dividing them into two separate mechanisms.

In their discussions of EU norm diffusion capacity, Börzel and Risse make two tentative distance-related claims: firstly, that the further one goes from Europe, the weaker the EU's diffusion power becomes (p. 2); and secondly, mostly indirect mechanisms are in play when the EU is able to engage in norm diffusion beyond the European neighbourhood (p. 15). And yet, one can make a reasonable case that the EU has had a positive impact, actively contributing to the process of SDG norm diffusion in Thailand. If true, this finding challenges the two claims made by Börzel and Risse above. We argue that there is strong evidence that *conditionality* has worked in the fisheries case. There are also examples of significant *Capacity-building*. Conditionality and Capacity-building are both 'direct' mechanisms of diffusion, according to Börzel and Risse. Happily, we believe, Börzel and Risse's pessimism about the EU's capacity for direct norm diffusion far from Europe is misplaced in this Thai case. In the next section, we explain why Thailand is vulnerable to EU economic conditionality.

Thailand's asymmetric interdependence vulnerability: the basis for EU conditionality

Thailand has long been recognised as having a substantial problem with IUU fishing. Thailand is the thirtieth largest economy in the world with a GDP of US$404 billion, and the Thai seafood industry employs more than 800,000 people, while seafood exports are valued at $5.5 billion (Human Rights Watch, 2018). A growing number of independent reports over the past decade have documented abuses of workers trafficked onto Thai fishing vessels, including forced labour and the use of extreme violence. One report by UNIAP found that 59% of trafficked migrants interviewed aboard Thai fishing vessels reported witnessing the murder of a fellow worker. A Human Rights Watch report claimed that 90 out of 138 fishers interviewed in 2016 had been victims of forced labour, and 95 of 248 interviewees across the fishing industry as a whole had been victims of human trafficking (Human Rights Watch, 2018).

In June 2014, the Guardian newspaper reported that fish caught by victims of trafficking working aboard Thai fishing boats were being used to feed shrimp grown and exported for sale. Ten days later, the US Department of State downgraded Thailand in its annual Trafficking in Persons report to Tier 3. Numerous media reports raised serious concerns about killings, beatings and trafficking of fishers, many from Burma and Cambodia. The European Commission in April 2015 issued a 'yellow card' warning to Thailand, identifying it as a possible non-cooperating country in fighting IUU fishing. A subsequent 'red card' would lead to EU sanctions (Human Rights Watch, 2018). The fisheries yellow card was lifted in January 2019, after 3.5 years.

In 2017, the total trade between the EU and Thailand was 37.352 billion euros, with 22.309 billion of this made up of Thai exports to the EU, and 15.043 billion made up of EU exports to Thailand. Thailand is ranked as the seventeenth biggest exporter into the EU market by volume, and the EU is the twenty-sixth biggest importer into the Thai market by volume. Overall, Thailand is the twenty-fourth most significant trade partner of the EU. From a Thai perspective, the EU is ranked by volume as the third most significant importer of goods from Thailand. There was a trade deficit of 7.266 billion in 2017 'in favour' of Thailand, which is good for business but creates vulnerability on the Thai side to sanctions or the threat of sanctions. EU trade with Thailand is 1% of total EU trade, but Thailand's trade with the EU makes up 9.5% of Thailand's total trade (all figures above from European Commission, 2018). There is thus also a considerable interdependence asymmetry between the two polities. The Thai fish product sector is worth $5.5 billion per year, and in 2016 the EU imported 426 million euros ($496.5 million) of seafood products from Thailand, which was a significant drop from 476 million euros the year before. The EU nevertheless remains Thailand's third largest market for seafood exports after the US and Japan, and consumes 12% of the 1.8 million tons of seafood Thailand exports annually (Macan-Markar, 2017). EU trade in general, and EU fisheries trade in particular, are both highly significant for Thailand.

Successful EU conditionality in action in both the fisheries and forced labour sectors

The Thai Department of Fisheries responded extremely promptly to EU, US and ILO pressure. It established a new fisheries law, the Royal Ordinance on Fisheries (2015), enacted and entered into force in November 2015. The law empowers relevant authorities to combat IUU fishing and unlawful labour practices in the fishing and seafood industries. A brief summary of the main measures adopted by the government is offered below. A fuller list could easily run to several pages. The extent of the reforms, and the speed of the response indicates the success of EU conditionality in this case. The measures taken address fisheries management, but also human rights abuses. The measures have been highly successful with regard to fisheries governance. Legislation has been and will be passed, and this legislation has been comprehensively implemented.

Under the provisions of the new law, measures of *Monitoring, Control and Surveillance* are applied to Thai-flagged overseas fishing vessels. This aims to prevent, deter and eliminate IUU fishing by Thai-flagged fishing vessels operating outside Thai waters (United Nations Ocean Conference, 2021). *Fisheries Monitoring Control*, including a *Vessel Monitoring System* is the key tool for monitoring of these vessels' fishing operations at sea. According to the new fisheries law: a port-in and port-out control scheme has been implemented by *32 Port-in, Port-out Centres* along the coastline; all fishing vessels must be inspected regarding physical conditions, fishing gear and other required documents (e.g. vessel registration, fishing licence, fishing log-book, etc.) before permission for porting out and porting in (United Nations Ocean Conference, 2021). Regarding inspection and control, the *Fishing Information System*, an integrated database system of fishing vessels, gear and crew, has been put in place and upgraded. Inspections of fishery products during landing at port and offloading have been strengthened. As specified by fisheries law, observers on board are required for fishing vessels and carriers operating outside Thai waters. For ensuring catch traceability, the Thai government has upgraded the catch certification scheme and strengthened traceability document requirements. One hundred per cent of Thai-flagged fishing vessels operating inside and outside Thai waters are controlled, monitored and inspected (United Nations Ocean Conference, 2021). Overall, the Thai authorities have responded comprehensively with regard to the EU yellow card in the realm of fisheries governance.

In addition to making technical changes, the Thai government recognised the important role of migrant workers in supporting the Thai fishing and seafood processing industries. Regulatory changes were made to facilitate the regularisation of illegal migrant workers in the sector and provide registered workers with greater flexibility in obtaining and extending their work permits (MOFA Thailand, 2020). Firstly, the government started a new round of registration of illegal migrant workers on fishing vessels and in seafood processing factories (for nationals of Cambodia, Lao PDR and Myanmar). By February 2016, over 130,000 undocumented migrant workers in the fisheries sector registered. Second, the government confirmed its commitment to a non-deportation policy. Third, the Thai Ministry of Labour revised rules to provide migrant workers with greater flexibility to change employers. Fourth, the governmental Policy Committee on Migrant Workers compiled policy recommendations for future reform of the labour migration system. These included revision of laws and regulations and anti-trafficking plans. One of the key reform objectives is to eliminate illegal labour brokers (MOFA Thailand, 2020).

Further, a number of important conventions relating to forced labour were ratified (see Kadfak & Linke, 2021, pp. 4–6; MOFA, Thailand, 2020; Tavornmas & Cheeppensook, 2020, pp. 678–682 for more detailed information). First, the Thai Ministry of Labour revised the Ministerial Regulation on Labour Protection in Sea Fishery Work, which had taken effect in December 2014. The Ministerial Regulation re-asserts existing provisions to meet international standards, including those in the ILO Work in Fishing Convention (No. 188). Key provisions of the Ministerial Regulation include prohibition of recruiting workers under 18 years of age on fishing boats, compulsory rest hours and holidays, mandatory signed work contracts, crew lists, and requirements on training and welfare of workers. Second, the Cabinet approved the ratification of the ILO's Occupational Safety and Health Convention No. 187 in September 2015. Third, concerned agencies reconsidered existing laws and the necessary revisions of the law in order to ratify the ILO's Work in Fishing Convention No. 188. This happened in early 2019. Fourth, the AHTA was amended to include a new stand-alone section on forced labour (ILO, 2020, p. I).

Benchmarking successful norm diffusion

The most important effort to prevent and reduce unacceptable forms of work in the Thai fishing industry came in the form of the EU-funded ILO Ship-to-Shore project, launched in 2016. The project worked alongside the Thai seafood supply chain with the Royal Thai government, workers' and employers' organisations, and civil society organisations to advance four objectives: (i) strengthen the legal, policy and regulatory framework; (ii) improve the labour inspectorate's ability to move against forced labour and other rights abuses; (iii) improve compliance with ILO core labour standards and establish a complaints mechanism across the supply chain; and (iv) increase access to support services for workers, especially victims of labour abuses. Of these four objectives, strengthening the legal framework has progressed furthest.

How do we know when attempts at human rights norm diffusion have been successful? Risse and Ropp identify several benchmarks. These include, but are not confined to, the following:

1. Behavioural change of state actors.
2. State ratification of relevant international human rights conventions and protocols.
3. Transposition of these international commitments into domestic law.
4. Sustained compliance with international human rights in the case specified (Risse & Ropp, 2013, pp. 6–10).

With regard to the first two benchmarks, in this chapter we have already explained how the Thai government has changed its behaviour, and also ratified several relevant international instruments. In what follows, we next want to note an example of successful transposition of international standards on forced labour into domestic legislation, meeting the third benchmark, through the Thai AHTA. We will also refer to improvements that are quantifiable as a result of the ILO Endline report produced by the Ship-to-Shore project. This report identifies evidence of improved human rights standards, and therefore a substantial degree of compliance on the ground with international standards on forced labour, thereby meeting the fourth benchmark.

Examples of successful diffusion of the SDG 'decent work' goal on the ground

Amendment of the Thai AHTA

Thailand's AHTA was introduced in 2008. The original AHTA listed instances of exploitation to include prostitution and other forms of sexual exploitation, forced organ removal for trade, and extortion as well as forced labour and services. It also provided a broad definition of forced labour to be a situation in which 'a person is forced to work or provide services by putting that person in fear for life, freedom and property, by means of intimidation, or use of force, causing that person to involuntarily comply'. This definition is more or less in line with the definition of forced labour adopted in the ILO's Convention on Forced Labour (C29), which Thailand ratified long ago. However, forced labour was not originally recognised as a stand-alone offence in earlier versions of the AHTA. The law was previously set up in such a way that if you wanted to prosecute a forced labour offence, you also had to prove the victim of forced labour had also been trafficked.

Over the past few years there has been growing scrutiny of Thailand's human trafficking record and numerous reports on forced labour issues. The Thai government has faced pressure from other actors, mainly the EU and the US, to revamp its existing legislation, measures and enforcement capacity, and improve the situation. A key objective of the ILO Ship-to-Shore project was to provide support for the Thai government in preparing for the ratification of the ILO's *Protocol on Forced Labour* (P29) as well as a call for additional ratification of the *Work in Fishing Convention* (C188). Along with the preparation for P29 ratification, the ILO also led a legal Gap Analysis study.

The Gap Analysis study suggested that a new stand-alone provision in the AHTA was needed, to ensure that forced labour can be established as a separate offence independent of human trafficking. This is important so that people who are victims of forced labour, but not of human trafficking, can be protected. Following the successful identification of this legal gap, a drafting committee was established to formulate legislation that would fill it. After a series of drafts and consultations, it was concluded that the existing AHTA would be amended. Rather than creating an entirely new act, a stand-alone forced labour offence would be incorporated into the existing AHTA. This means that the AHTA would be amended to include clauses specifically identifying forced labour as a separate offence from human trafficking. Forced labour as a separate offence is now recognised, alongside but distinct from, the existing offence of human trafficking. This includes trafficking of individuals for the purpose of exploiting them in forced labour scenarios. This indicates that within the most updated AHTA there are two channels through which forced labour could be prosecuted–either as part of human trafficking or as a stand-alone offence in itself. The EU heavily funded the ILO project through which the AHTA was managed, monitored and ultimately amended. The EU also consistently stated that its objective was the creation of a stand-alone offence in Thai law. Ultimately, the EU was able to achieve its objective.

In this example, the EU engaged in Capacity-building by funding the ILO and several domestic non-governmental organisations (NGOs) with expertise in human rights law. And the ILO and the NGO experts in turn worked on the ground in the local target state, in this case Thailand, to engage in the socialisation of the Thai government. For Börzel and Risse, processes of socialisation 'often result in complex learning by which actors redefine their interests and identities' (2012, p. 7). In some cases, this can mean that domestic actors are socialised directly by the EU. Sometimes, however, domestic dynamics replace international dynamics. For Börzel and Risse:

> Socialisation also relies on domestic actors, but the ways in which domestic actors facilitate reforms are different. Norm entrepreneurs ... socialise domestic actors into new norms and rules of appropriateness through persuasion and social learning, and they redefine their interests and identities accordingly.
>
> (2012, pp. 7–8)

The EU-funded efforts of the ILO and the NGO experts was an important Capacity-building effort that increased their socialisation capabilities. What this also suggests is that we need to specify an additional category of diffusion: *where an external norm sender such as the EU successfully builds the capacity of local non-state actors (through financial assistance, knowledge transfer, etc.) enabling them to act as direct diffusers of the human rights norm in question, in the local domestic context of the target state.* The local norm entrepreneurs were the ILO and the local Thai human rights experts. In this particular case, from an EU perspective, the diffusion has become indirect, because this is now being carried out by local intermediaries. These local non-state actors are themselves engaging in direct diffusion, but the EU is now working through intermediaries and proxies, local norm entrepreneurs or norm carriers in the target state. Following Bacon and Nakamura, (2021), we tentatively refer to this process as '*mediated local diffusion*'.

Improvement in the labour conditions of workers in the Thai fisheries sector

The Ship-to-Shore project was also responsible for the creation of an ILO Endline survey. This report was produced and published in March 2020. The Endline report made direct reference to the findings of the earlier ILO Baseline project report, to see how much progress, if any, had been made. It is clear from the Endline report that significant progress has been made across a number of human rights labour standards. We identify some of the headline positive findings below. Nevertheless, although progress has been meaningful and extensive, there is still room for improvement.

Among surveyed fishers, 51% remembered signing a contract. Of these, the proportion who reported being given a copy of their contract increased significantly from 14% in 2017 to 79% in 2019. Nearly all seafood workers (97%) who recalled signing contracts reported being given a copy (ILO, 2020). Large proportions of workers surveyed in 2019 said their contract stated their salary (around 70%) and their ability to quit their job (around 80%). But of the roughly half of surveyed fishers who recalled signing a contract, the proportion of workers whose contract was written in their native language decreased from 66% in 2017 to 51% in 2019. For seafood, this figure declined from 77% to 55% (ILO, 2020). This is due in part to use of a revised Government-provided work contract in 2018 that was only available in the Thai language, and the lack of a legal requirement that contracts be provided for workers in their native languages. In 2017, the earlier forms were available in Thai, Burmese, Khmer and English.

The average monthly pay, which included overtime, bonuses and piece-rate pay or 'share of the catch' was higher for respondents working in fishing than in seafood processing. Workers surveyed in 2019 in both sectors reported higher average monthly pay than those surveyed in 2017: average monthly earnings among fishers surveyed increased by 28%, from THB 9,980 to THB 12,730. Monthly pay increased by 15% for seafood workers, from THB 9,270 to THB 10,640 (ILO, 2020). There are two important factors that help to explain this significant improvement in wages between the two surveys. Firstly, there was a tight labour market for fishers, and this forced employers to bid up wages to attract and keep fishers. Secondly, a 2018 Ministry of Labour requirement that fishers be paid electronically via bank accounts introduced a verifiable pay record and greater attention to wage violations in an industry with obscure pay practices (ILO, 2020). The 2019 survey sample was geared towards larger fishing vessels and seafood factories where pay is generally higher. And the growth in monthly pay in both sectors has outpaced growth in the legal minimum wage across Thailand as a whole. As a result, compliance with wage laws has improved. Compliance with the minimum wage requirements among workers surveyed increased from 74% (2017) to 96% (2019) in fishing. And in the seafood sector, compliance with the minimum wage requirements rose from 67% (2017) to 94% (2019) (ILO, 2020). Again, this is an improvement.

In 2017, a significant proportion of fishers surveyed (22%) were paid only with a share of catch, not with a fixed wage. Some 15% of fishers reported receiving a fixed wage combined with a share of catch, and only 39% were paid only a fixed monthly wage. By 2019, all fishers reported that they were paid either a fixed monthly wage (85%) or by a combination of a salary plus a share of the catch (ILO, 2020). This is a further highly significant demonstration of the fact that the working conditions of workers on the ground were substantially improving. The proportion of seafood workers who received a fixed salary showed a smaller increase, from 10% in 2017 to 26% in 2019. The vast majority of seafood workers in 2019 (74%) reported that they received a fixed salary combined with piece-rate pay (ILO, 2020).

Fishing workers reported working 6.4 days per week and seafood workers, 6.0 days. These figures are very close to the legal limit for a single working week. These figures are also largely unchanged since the 2017 survey. Workers in both the fishing and seafood processing sectors reported working an average of nine hours each day (ILO, 2020). For seafood workers, this is unchanged since the 2017 survey, but among fishers it represents a decline from an average 11 hours. There are no effective limits on overtime in Thailand: a 14-hour working day, six days a week, is permissible in both seafood processing and fishing. Some buyers of Thai seafood now require lower limits of their suppliers and nine- and ten-hour workdays (54- and 60-hour workweeks) are routine for 73% of the seafood workers surveyed (ILO, 2020).

Project researchers also asked additional questions of workers who have worked for five or more years, since 2015 when reform of the Thai fisheries industry began in earnest. These 165 workers—of whom one-third were Thai and two-thirds were Cambodian or Myanmar—rated a dozen work issues of the kind addressed above as generally ‘better’, ‘about the same’ or ‘worse’ than five years earlier. For seafood workers, the top three improvements were work benefits received (70%), work safety (68%) and housing conditions (65%). For fishers, the top reported improvements were found in salaries (58%), housing conditions (51%) and work location (50%) (ILO, 2020). This five-year period spans the duration of the Ship-to-Shore project and allows us to see that significant improvements were made during this time.

Conclusion

In the Thai case study we looked at in this chapter, the EU has successfully diffused environmental norms relating to fisheries governance. Moreover, in the field of human rights, the EU has also successfully diffused SDG norms relating to decent work and forced labour. This resulted in behavioural change by the Thai government, the ratification of several important international treaties and conventions, the transposition of the content of these treaties into Thai domestic law, and substantial compliance with SDG standards on forced labour inside Thailand. Concretely, the working conditions and living standards of those working in the Thai fisheries industry have improved considerably, and it is possible to trace this improvement through an analysis of the Baseline and Endline reports of the ILO. Furthermore, the ILO Ship-to-Shore project was at the core of these positive developments, and this project was heavily and exclusively funded by the EU. A combination of EU *conditionality* and *Capacity-building* has therefore proved to be highly successful. We can also say that various actors within Thailand have been *socialised* into respecting labour rights. Finally, we can see that the work of the ILO and the various Thai human rights NGOs on the ground is an example of '*mediated local diffusion*', where actors funded by the EU engage in direct SDG norm diffusion on the territory of the target state. Although Börzel and Risse claimed that Capacity-building is not particularly important the further away we move from Europe, we found several examples of Capacity-building being useful, the most obvious of which is the Ship-to-Shore project. And although Börzel and Risse suspect that direct methods of norm diffusion are unlikely to be successful the further one travels away from Europe, conditionality, Capacity-building and socialisation are all direct forms of norm diffusion. Ultimately, the EU *was* able to exercise a significant degree of normative power and successfully diffuse SDG norms related to decent work in this case study.

Notes

1 This section draws extensively on Bacon and Nakamura (2021).

2 In this chapter and in the book as a whole we consider the SDGs through the lens of norm diffusion. However, the SDGs and the broader project of sustainable development can and have been conceptualized in a number of other ways; for example as part of the liberal project (Inoguchi & Bacon, 2001); as a human security approach (Bacon, 2014); and as a strategic narrative (Bacon & Burton, 2018).

References

Bacon, P. (2014). The politics of human security in Japan. In *Human security and Japan's triple disaster* (pp. 34–50). Routledge.

Bacon, P., & Burton, J. (2018). NATO-Japan relations: Projecting strategic narratives of 'natural partnership' and cooperative security. *Asian Security*, *14*(1), 38–50.

Bacon, P., & Nakamura, H. (2021). Diffusing the abolitionist norm in Japan: EU 'Death Penalty Diplomacy' and the gap between rhetoric and reality in EU–Japan relations. *Journal of Common Market Studies*, *59*(5), 1230–1246.

Börzel, T. A., & Risse, T. (2012). From Europeanisation to diffusion: Introduction. *West European Politics*, *35*(1), 1–19.

European Commission. (2018). *DG trade, EU-Thailand trade figures, 2017*. https://ec.europa.eu/trade/policy/countries-and-regions/countries/thailand/

European Commission. (2019, January 8). *Commission lifts 'yellow card' from Thailand for its actions against illegal fishing*. https://ec.europa.eu/commission/presscorner/detail/en/IP_19_61

European Commission. (2022). *Oceans and fisheries, 'Illegal Fishing'*. Retrieved January 2022, from https://ec.europa.eu/oceans-and-fisheries/fisheries/rules/illegal-fishing_en

Forsberg, T. (2011). Normative power Europe, once again: A conceptual analysis of an ideal type. *Journal of Common Market Studies*, *49*(6), 1183–1204.

Human Rights Watch. (2018). *Hidden chains: Rights abuses and forced labour in Thailand's fishing industry*. www.hrw.org/report/2018/01/23/hidden-chains/rights-abuses-and-forced-labor-thailands-fishing-industry

ILO. (2017). *Ship-to-shore: Gap analysis of the Work in Fishing Convention, 2007 (No. 188), and Thai national laws, regulations and other measures concerning conditions of work on board fishing vessels*. www.ilo.org/wcmsp5/groups/public/---asia/---ro-bangkok/documents/publication/wcms_557738.pdf

ILO. (2018). *Ship-to-shore: Baseline research findings on fishers and seafood workers in Thailand*. www.ilo.org/wcmsp5/groups/public/---asia/---ro-bangkok/---sro-bangkok/documents/publication/wcms_619727.pdf

ILO. (2020). *Ship-to-Shore: Endline research findings on fishers and seafood workers in Thailand*. www.ilo.org/wcmsp5/groups/public/---asia/---ro-bangkok/documents/publication/wcms_738042.pdf

Inoguchi, T., & Bacon, P. (2001). Sovereignties: Westphalian, liberal and anti-utopian. *International Relations of the Asia-Pacific*, *1*(2), 285–304.

Kadfak, A., & Linke, S. (2021). Labour implications of the EU's illegal, unreported and unregulated (IUU) policy in Thailand. *Marine Policy*, *127*, 104445.

Keck, M. E., & Sikkink, K. (1998). *Activists beyond borders: Advocacy networks in international politics*. Cornell University Press.

Macan-Markar, M. (2017, July 26). *Thai seafood industry grapples with international scrutiny*. Nikkei Asian Review. https://asia.nikkei.com/Economy/Thai-seafood-industry-grapples-with-international-scrutiny2

Manners, I. (2002). Normative power Europe: A contradiction in terms? *Journal of Common Market Studies*, *40*(2), 235–258.

MOFA, Thailand. (2019, January 8). *EU announced the lifting of a yellow card for Thailand*. www.mfa.go.th/en/content/5d5bd20115e39c3060027699?page=5d5bd3cb15e39c306002a9ac&menu=5d5bd3cb15e39c306002a9ae

MOFA, Thailand. (2020). *Thailand's fisheries reform: Progress and way forward in the fight against IUU fishing and forced labor*. Royal Thai Embassy Washington DC. https://thaiembdc.org/2016/03/07/thailands-fisheries-reform/

Pace, M. (2007). The construction of EU normative power. *Journal of Common Market Studies*, *45*(5), 1041–64.

Risse, T., & Ropp, S. (2013). Introduction and overview. In T. Risse, S. C. Ropp, & K. Sikkink (Eds.), *The persistent power of human rights: From commitment to compliance* (Vol. 126). Cambridge University Press.

Tavornmas, A., & Cheeppensook, K. (2020). Shaping ocean governance: A study of EU normative power on Thailand's sustainable fisheries. *International Economics and Economic Policy*, *17*(3), 671–685.

United Nations Ocean Conference (UNOC). (2021). *Thailand's actions on combating IUU fishing*. Retrieved January 7, 2022, from https://oceanconference.un.org/commitments/?id=18205

11 Diffusion of labour rights

Georgia 2003–2019

Shukuko Koyama

Introduction

This chapter looks at the labour rights components of Sustainable Development Goal (SDG) 8, in particular, Target 8.8 'Protect labour rights and promote safe and secure working environments for all workers, including migrant workers, in particular women migrants, and those in precarious employment'. It explores dynamics in the process of adopting the labour rights norms that are embedded in SDG 8 and analyses factors affecting the norm diffusion process by taking an example from Georgia.

Since its independence in 1991, Georgia has undergone a massive socio-economic and political transition. In the late 1990s and early 2000s, the country experienced two violent territorial conflicts in Abkhazia and South Ossetia, while corruption penetrated throughout society. In 2003, a mass demonstration which came to be known as the Rose Revolution ushered in Mikheil Sasakasvhili as president. Under the Saakashvili administration, a number of radical deregulation reforms took place. The war with Russia in August 2008 and the subsequent global economic crisis had a serious impact on its economy, which led to a change of government in 2013. Despite the crises, Georgia had mostly experienced solid GDP growth during the period between 2003 and 2019.[1] During this timeframe, Georgia also saw a swing in the treatment of international labour rights norms. The Saakashvili government's neoliberal reforms touched upon all policy areas, including the labour field. For instance, the 2006 Labour Code dismantled the Labour Inspectorate and the Employment Agency, and dissolved the Georgian Labour Administration. Following the change of government in 2013, however, the new government took positive steps to protect labour rights in an effort to develop a labour regime in compliance with international labour standards.

This chapter investigates what factors drove the process of labour rights norm diffusion in Georgia by using the spiral model. Between 2003 and 2019, Georgia's labour rights norm diffusion process progressed from repression (phase 1), denial (phase 2), to tactical concession (phase3), but it has stagnated in the transition from phase 3 to prescriptive status (phase 4) (Risse, Ropp & Sikkink, 1999). Being informed by Acharya's work on local actors (Acharya,

DOI: 10.4324/9781003205951-15

2004) and True's critique regarding the need for greater focus on domestic and international subjects (True, 2011), this chapter focuses on local actors, their dynamics, and the interaction between local and international actors in the different phases of labour rights norm diffusion in Georgia.

The next section examines the labour rights norm diffusion process under the Saakashvili government between 2003 and 2012, considered as being in phase 1 (repression). It analyses how the political and economic orientation among local political elites resisted labour rights protection norms. The third section explores the period between 2013 and 2019 in which Georgia witnessed a shift from phase 2 (denial) to phase 3 (tactical concession). The fourth section examines an emerging social activism in Georgia and its role in advancing labour rights norm diffusion. The chapter concludes by examining the applicability of the spiral model to the Georgia case, and the implications of findings from the Georgia case study for norm diffusion research.

Repression and denial: 2003–2012

Between 2003 and 2012, Georgia was under the Saakashvili administration which implemented a wide range of societal reforms. Unlike his predecessor, the former Soviet foreign minister Eduard Shevardnadze, western educated Saakashvili explicitly expressed an intention to join the North Atlantic Treaty Organization (NATO) and the European Union (EU). However, this political aspiration for integration with the west did not mean the standardisation of labour rights practice with international labour standards. The economic development model adopted by the Saakashvili government aimed at making Georgia the 'Switzerland of the region with elements of Singapore' and turning the country into a business hub (De Waal, 2011, p. 3). This economic aspiration was followed by a series of deregulations. During the time when Saakashvili was in power, Georgia went through drastic neoliberal reform efforts and became one of the world's most business-friendly countries, according to the World Bank (2016).

Using spiral model terminology, labour rights norm diffusion in the early period of the Saakashvili regime can be considered to be in the 'denial' phase. An illustrative example of the Saakashvili government's denial of labour rights norms' is the introduction of the 2006 Labour Code. The 2006 Labour Code dismantled the Labour Inspectorate and the Employment Agency, and dissolved the Georgian Labour Administration, which brought an end to labour rights inspections in the country. These changes in the Labour Code violated international labour standards.[2] The political stance of the domestic political elites is the main factor that explains persistent resistance to labour rights norms. Having garnered popular support by claiming the need for reform in the 2003 Rose Revolution, implementing reform was a political *raison d'etre* for Saakashvili and the small circle of young political elites associated with him. Giga Bokeria, a former activist who led the Rose Revolution, and who was a politician under the Saakashvili administration, explained that the reforms needed to be carried out rapidly because 'We have lost so much time and we need to catch up' (De

Wall, 2011, p. 3). After they arrived in power, they implemented reform of government institutions to demonstrate their difference from the old generation associated with *nomenklatura*, socialism and the Soviet times represented by Eduard Shevardnadze, the predecessor of Saakashvili. The Saakashvili administration hastened to implement deregulation reforms and anti-corruption campaigns to replace the influence of the Shevardnadze regime, especially during the first few years of their administration. The leading figure in the neoliberal school in Georgia under Saakashvili was Kakha Bendukidze. Having established himself as a successful businessperson in Russia, Bendukidze returned to Georgia in 2004, joined the Saakashvili administration as the Minister of Economy, and then Minister for the Coordination of Economic Reforms until 2008. Being a radical liberal, Bendukidze was almost hostile to regulation and considered the EU as 'a bureaucratic trap for Georgia' and even labelled his compatriots who called for more regulations to align with the EU as 'betrayers' (De Wall, 2011).

The inadequate labour inspection system and other changes in labour governance following the 2006 Labour Code drove the norm diffusion process to advance from repression to the denial phase, by inducing a 'boomerang effect' from the international community. International actors such as the EU, the International Labour Organization (ILO) and the US Department of Labour criticised the Saakashvili government for the changes to the Labour Code, and other actions in 2006. For instance, the EU tried to impose conditionality. In 2008, a Deep and Comprehensive Free Trade Areas (DCFTA) with the EU was offered to Georgia, provided that Georgia met some conditions to make labour legislation conform to EU standards. The conditions included an amendment to the Labour Code to protect workers' rights (Commission of the European Communities, 2008). Despite pressure from the international community, however, the Georgian government refused to accept the introduction of the labour rights norms, and regarded most of these criticisms as 'an unnecessary burden' (Diakonidze, 2016, p. 157). The EU, usually an international actor with the leverage to advance the promotion of human rights norms in its eastern neighbourhood countries, could not exert much influence on the labour rights diffusion process during the Saakashvili period. A few days after the EU offered the DCFTA, the government signed a Memorandum of Understanding with the International Monetary Fund (International Monetary Fund, 2008) to take 'responsibility not to undertake these institutional reforms in the near future (Papava, 2013, p. 94). Labour rights' norm diffusion did not progress any further until Saakashvili was replaced by a new leader in 2013.

From denial to tactical concessions: 2013–2019

The labour rights norm diffusion process enjoyed some progress in the early days of the newly elected government led by Bidzina Ivanishvili and his party, Georgian Dream (GD). GD had appealed to the general public by pledging more spending on welfare. Ivanishvili, a billionaire businessman and the founder of GD, also pledged to implement several social policies and continue to aim at

Euro-Atlantic integration (Civil Georgia, 2012). Once elected, the GD-led government amended the 2006 Labour Code to reintroduce some rules. The government also established a Labour Conditions Inspection Department in 2015. Having signed an Association Agreement with the EU in 2016, Georgia took a number of positive steps towards raising the conformity of Georgian labour laws and practices with international labour standards. Additionally, Georgia ratified the Revised European Social Charter 22/08/2005, accepting the Revised Charter's 98 paragraphs. Compared to its neoliberal predecessor, the GD-led government encompassed a wider range of actors from across the political spectrum: between 2016 and 2019, the GD formed a coalition with the Social Democrats for the Development of Georgia, who advocated for an amendment of the constitution to include social rights.[3]

Throughout this period, the international community continued to pressure the Georgian government. The International Trade Union Confederation (ITUC), for instance, pressured the GD on workers' rights as soon as they had defeated the Saakashvili government in the 2012 election (International Trade Union Confederation, 2012). The EU continued its advocacy through the negotiation process that took place prior to and after the signing of the Association Agreement with Georgia in 2016.[4] Despite pressure from human rights norms-promoting international actors, the gap between the Georgian labour rights situation and international labour standards remained.[5] There were few efforts to change the labour standards situation through the existing state and private sector institutions. A lack of will to change labour conditions was particularly prominent among employers, as one observer noted that the Labour Code situation in Georgia is 'a paradise for employers and hell for employees' (Pertaia, 2017).

When the SDGs' framework was introduced to Georgia in 2016, the United Nations (UN) could have been well-placed to encourage the Georgian government and relevant stakeholders including businesses to promote labour rights issues in the country. However, compared with the EU imposing conditionality, the UN has a more peripheral role. When the SDGs' framework was introduced to Georgia in 2016, the 'UN Partnership for Sustainable Development 2016–2020' was developed with jobs, livelihood and social protection as focus areas,[6] but no outcomes were explicitly dedicated to the promotion of labour rights issues. The UN agencies' assistance is provided in the area of rural employment, vocational education and training, capacity development of labour market actors and women's economic empowerment (Government of Georgia, 2016). An informal working group consisting of line ministries and UN agencies was established in 2016. In 2017, the SDGs' council (the Council of Public Administrative Reform and Sustainable Development Goals) was established (State Audit Office of Georgia, 2019, p. 14). The SDGs' council later established four working groups: Social Inclusion, Economic Development, Democratic Governance, and Sustainable Energy and Environmental Protection. Goal 8 is covered by the working groups on Social Inclusion and Economic Development, co-chaired by the Ministry of Labour, Health and Social Affairs, United Nations Children's Fund (UNICEF), Education for all (Social Inclusion), the Ministry of Economy and Sustainable

Development, United Nations Development Programme (UNDP) and a non-governmental organisation, the Caucasus Environmental NGO Network (CENN) (Economic Development) (Bobghiashvili, 2019, p. 12). These working groups are to provide 'professional assistance to realisation of SDGs through strategic planning, integrated implementation and effective monitoring of the 2030 Agenda' (State Audit Office of Georgia, 2019, p. 19). However, the structure of the working groups, the roles of the member bodies, and the goals and functions of the working group members are not clearly defined (State Audit Office of Georgia, 2019, p. 20). When it comes to actual implementation, the framework and institutional arrangements lack substantial action plans. Georgia's State Audit Office complains that 'Georgia does not have a clear and comprehensive long-term and medium-term view about the means of implementation required for realisation of SDGs and the corresponding targets' (State Audit Office of Georgia, 2019, p. 24). The State Audit Office reports a set of challenges facing SDG promotion efforts such as the lack of sufficient involvement of relevant stakeholders in the SDG council and working groups. The office also reports that no concrete roles nor action plans are defined for the members of the council and working groups, and that responsible bodies are not assigned for SDG targets and specific roles and responsibilities for goals are absent (State Audit Office of Georgia, 2019, p. 6). As of 2019, no official national 2030 agenda document has been approved (State Audit Office of Georgia, 2019, p. 17). In this manner, the SDGs' framework itself remains rhetorical and has not been associated with domestic practices.

As this section has examined, between 2003 and 2019, the labour rights norm diffusion process in Georgia moved from denial to tactical concessions, following the government change in 2013 and by responding to the international community's continued pressure. Having made partial concessions such as the reintroduction of some labour regulations, however, Georgia has been stumbling regarding the further advancement of the norm diffusion process. Direct norm diffusion mechanisms such as EU conditionality, as well as UN assistance through the SDGs' framework have had limited influence in advancing norm diffusion beyond the tactical concessions' phase.

Beyond tactical concessions? The emergence of bottom-up mobilisation

When Georgia became a member state of the Council of Europe in 1999, then Prime Minister, Zurab Zhvania famously declared at the Parliamentary Assembly: 'I am Georgian and therefore I am European' (Council of Europe, n.d.). The same phrase was repeated by another Georgian Prime Minister, Mamuka Bakhtadze, in 2019 when Georgia took the chair of the Council Europe (Council of Europe, 2019). The labour rights norm diffusion process in Georgia discussed in this chapter points out that Europeanisation has not accompanied normative identity transformation, as far as labour rights practices are concerned.

However, if we turn our eyes to civil society and other local actors outside the state institutions, a different conclusion can be drawn about the norm diffusion process in Georgia. Risse, Ropp and Sikkink claim that rule-consistent behaviour requires continuous mobilisation and pressure from domestic organisations in a bottom-up fashion (1999, p. 33). What has been taking place in Georgia's civil society can be considered as just such an active bottom-up mobilisation for labour rights norm diffusion, in parallel to the stagnated top-down approach.

A call for more just labour practices has increasingly grown among workers and in civil society in Georgia. Since two consecutive fatal incidents in a coal mine in 2018, demands for improving workers' safety increased both domestically and internationally. A series of strikes by workers including mine workers of the Tkibuli coal mine in Imereti and glass factory workers in Ksani shed light on hazardous working conditions and poor labour rights practices (Solidarity Center, 2016). Responding to the demand for the introduction of regulations for better labour rights practices, the head of the Georgian Employers' Association's legal committee noted that 'we don't flatly oppose them, but we want to go slower' (Human Rights Watch, 2019, p. 12). Georgia may still remain in the tactical concessions' phase. However, the growing bottom-up movement puts pressure on Georgian employers to make more concessions.

While these strikes themselves follow quite traditional labour union practices and tactics, what is notable about this movement is that it is part of a wider spectrum of social movements that is calling for the alignment of a wide range of other human rights with European and international standards.[7] Efforts to bring in social rights in Georgia are not something new. For instance, Social Democrats for the Development of Georgia (Social Democrats) and its leader, Gia Zhorzholiani have been long-term political actors since the liberal national movement in the 1980s. The Social Democrats tried to incorporate social rights into the constitution when they were forming a coalition with the GD party, though without success. The older generation has not been able to garner popular support especially among the younger generation who had been born after Soviet dissolution and grown up in a Georgia aspiring to be a European country. A new rhetorical approach that can reflect social, central-left values was required to mobilise wider support for social values to be implemented in practice. The movement in the late 2010s had an additional layer of local actors that emerged from outside the existing socialist movements.

It was these new emerging local actors that added a strong voice for social justice in Georgia. One example is Auditorium #115, established in early 2016. It was initially a student group occupying Tbilisi State University's auditorium calling for education reforms (Pertaia, 2017). They called for improvements in labour practices as 'a member of Auditorium #115 associates the lack of labour rights to an economic agenda of deregulation, blaming political elites for maintaining the status-quo' (Pertaia, 2017). What is notable about the new actors is that they are loosely associated with other individuals and do not adopt a consolidated form of organisation, as in the case of the previous generation.

Instead, most of the individual actors/participants take part in demonstrations in their available time, and do not engage in social activism as full-time non-governmental organisation (NGO) workers. They do not necessarily identify themselves as socialists, either. For instance, not all members of Auditorium #115 considered themselves to be 'leftist' (Pertaia, 2017). What has taken place since in the bottom-up movement in the late 2010s in Georgia is to overwrite the old image of socialism with a Soviet connotation, with central-left values and social rights norms under a new identity narrative as being European.

While the local actors engaged in these social movements do not necessarily belong in a conventional way to organised groups, this does not mean that the new social movement elements do not associate with international actors. On the contrary, there is an active collaboration between international and local actors to promote norms on labour rights and other human rights. The collaboration efforts use a wide range of formats including organising workshops, running advocacy campaigns and conducting investigative and/or policy-oriented research. These collaboration efforts go beyond direct mechanisms such as Capacity-building and involve activities that aim at bringing normative changes. In these endeavours, the boundary between local and international actors blurs as both engage in activities largely on an equal footing.[8]

One concrete example is a transnational workshop jointly organised by Georgian, German and French organisations in September 2018.[9] Entitled 'Between a Rock and a Hard Place? Georgian, German and French Perspectives on European Values and Euro-Atlantic Integration', the workshop gathered young individuals from the three countries and reflected on European values (Georgian Institute of Politics, 2018). The biggest drivers in the collaboration are the EU and its member states, namely, France and Germany. Their strategy to engage with this type of local actor is not mere capacity development, which has an aim of enhancing administrative abilities of local actors. Rather it is more encouraging activities aimed at sharing European values and promoting and constituting European identity, targeting the local actors in Georgia, particularly the youth. This phenomenon could be understood as an example of 'mediated local diffusion' (Bacon & Nakamura, 2021, p. 1243). In mediated local diffusion, local non-state actors act as direct diffusers of the norm in question in the local domestic context (Bacon & Nakamura, 2021). To take Georgia's labour rights norm diffusion to a later phase of the spiral model, the direct mechanisms of conditionality and Capacity-building may have limited impact. Instead, efforts to raise the profile of European values and identity among the local actors in Georgia seem to be contributing to the consolidation of the bottom-up movement for empowering labour rights.

Conclusion

This chapter examined dynamics, processes and actors in labour rights norm diffusion in Georgia between 2003 and 2019. As seen in the chapter, in terms of stages of the spiral model, norm diffusion in Georgia shifted from the repression phase to the tactical concessions' phase over this period in response to the international community's pressure. This chapter has shown that, instead of the conventional international actors, it is the local actors such as social movement activists, supported by their transnational networks that are advancing the norm diffusion process in a bottom-up manner. As illustrated in this chapter, direct mechanisms of diffusion such as EU conditionality matters in the earlier norm diffusion phases. However, we are yet to see whether such mechanisms drive the labour rights norms in Georgia to the deeper diffusion phases.

This chapter demonstrated the usefulness of the spiral model in understanding dynamics, processes and actors in the early phases of labour rights norm diffusion in Georgia, i.e. the repression, denial and tactical concessions' phases. Additionally, this chapter has also shown the importance of examining the roles and dynamics of local actors other than the state and other formal actors for better understanding factors in the norm diffusion phases beyond tactical concessions. The Georgia example in this chapter suggests that more nuanced understanding of local actors is required in order to better analyse factors which could drive the norm diffusion process from the tactical concessions' phase, to prescriptive status and rule-consistent behaviour.

What the bottom-up rights-based movement suggests is that the traditional strategy of labour strikes still has a certain leverage in forging improvements in labour rights practices. What the case of Georgia has also shown is that traditional labour activism has now been joined by a new generation of social activists who carry European identity. For the young generation, labour rights and other human rights are not something external to be adopted, but rather an integral part of their 'own' identities. This way, instead of 'localising' the international labour rights norms, these local actors take the rights as an integral part of their own European identity. For local actors in Georgia, the rights-based norms are not foreign norms but something that they are equipped with naturally due to their European identity.

The case of Georgia has also demonstrated the close interaction and collaboration between local civil society actors and international actors, especially through transnational networks. Further research would benefit from a closer examination of the intersection between the local and international actors, to better understand which mechanisms are being deployed to help the diffusion process progress. In doing so, we may benefit from considering another level of actors in addition to local and international actors, i.e. meso-level actors, and which mechanisms contribute to empowering them. As illustrated in the recent social movements in Georgia, there are organisations consisting of internationally-educated Georgian staffers at international organisations, activists in social movements, and Georgian and transnational civil society organisations. They play an active role as interlocutors to promote labour rights norms. We would also benefit from further investigation of the role these actors' identities play in labour rights and other norm diffusion processes in Georgia, as well as which diffusion mechanisms are in play when higher education programmes such as Erasmus+ are contributing to the development of their identities.

Notes

1 Georgia's average economic growth rate was 5% per annum between 2005 and 2019 (World Bank, n.d.).

2 In the same year, the unemployment benefits system was also abolished.

3 Social Democrats for the Development of Georgia (Social Democrats) is a centre-left party established in 2010. Although it has advocated for social rights to be included in the constitution it has not been a strong driver for social rights norms to become socialised in Georgia. It came into parliament from 2016 and formed a coalition with Georgian Dream. The Social Democrats split with Georgian Dream over pension and justice reform issues in 2019.

4 Other international actors that expressed their criticism over labour rights practices in Georgia include the High Representative of the EU for Foreign Affairs and Security Practice, the EU at the 2019 EU–Georgia Annual Human Rights Dialogue, the European Committee of Social Rights and the UN Working Group on Business and Human Rights.

5 For instance, Georgia has not yet ratified the Council of Europe's Additional Protocol providing for a system of Collective Complaints.

6 The SDGs' framework states two outcomes, i.e. 1) by 2020 poor and excluded populations have better employment and livelihood opportunities; and 2) by 2020 vulnerable groups have access to a proactive and inclusive gender and child sensitive social protection system that addresses major vulnerabilities. (Government of Georgia, 2016).

7 Leading figures in these social movements include Giorgi Tabagari (Director of Tbilisi Pride) and Shota Digmelashvili and Salome Barkeri of Sirtskhvilia (Shame) movement.

8 For instance, Human Rights Watch conducted research on labour rights violations in the mining sector in Georgia and ran a series of advocacy campaigns in 2019 in tandem with its Georgian counterparts, Human Rights Education and Monitoring Center, and Solidarity Network. The Georgian Institute of Politics hosts an international team of researchers consisting of Georgian and non-Georgian analysts, carrying out policy-oriented research and monitoring. The Georgian Institute of Politics is also a member of the Organization for Security and Co-operation in Europe (OSCE) network of think tanks and academic institutions.

9 The three-day workshop was co-organised by the Georgian Institute of Politics based in Tbilisi, Polis180 based in Berlin and Argo based in Paris, with financial assistance from France and Germany.

References

Acharya, A. (2004). How ideas spread: Whose norms matter? Norm localization and institutional change in Asian regionalism. *International Organization*, *58*(2), 239–275.

Bacon, P., & Nakamura, H. (2021). Diffusing the abolitionist norm in Japan: EU 'Death Penalty Diplomacy' and the gap between rhetoric and reality in EU–Japan relations.

Journal of Common Market Studies, *59*(5), 1230–1246. https://doi.org/10.1111/jcms.13177

Bobghiashvili, G. (2019) *Nationalization of SDGs in Georgia: 3-year summary* [PowerPoint presentation]. Retrieved 1 March 2022, from http://dezvoltaredurabila.gov.ro/web/wp-content/uploads/2019/04/1.5.-Giorgi-Bobghiashvil-Nationalization-of-SDGs-in-Georgia-1.pdf

Civil Georgia. (2012, April 21). *Ivanishvili's political party launched*. Civil Georgia. https://civil.ge/archives/186312

Commission of the European Communities. (2008). *Communication from the Commission to the European Parliament and the Council, Eastern Partnership* (SEC [2008] 2974/3). Commission of the European Communities.

Council of Europe. (n.d.). *Welcome to the council of Europe in Georgia*. Retrieved August 15, 2021, from www.coe.int/en/web/tbilisi/field-office/overview

Council of Europe. (2019). *Manuka Bakhtadze, Prime Minister of Georgia* (Speech made to the Assembly), 10 April 2019. Retrieved August 15, 2021, from www.assembly.coe.int/nw/xml/Speeches/Speech-XML2HTML-EN.asp?SpeechID=289&a1=0&p2=0

De Waal, T. (2011). *Georgia's choice: Charting a future in uncertain times*. Carnegie Endowment for International Peace. https://carnegieendowment.org/files/georgias_choices.pdf

Diakonidze, A. (2016). Superficial institutions and challenges of re-regulation in the Republic of Georgia. *Caucasus Survey*, *4*(2), pp.149–164. https://doi.org/10.1080/23761199.2016.1188489

Georgian Institute of Politics. (2018, September 27). *Between a rock and a hard place? Georgian, German and French perspectives on European values and Euro-Atlantic integration #GEOEUvalues*. Retrieved August 15, 2021, from http://gip.ge/between-a-rock-and-a-hard-place-georgian-german-and-french-perspectives-on-european-values-and-euro-atlantic-integration-geoeuvalues/

Government of Georgia. (2016). *United Nations partnership for sustainable development (Framework Document) Georgia 2016–2020*. Retrieved August 15, 2021, from https://georgia.un.org/sites/default/files/2020-05/UNPSD.pdf

Human Rights Watch. (2019). *No year without deaths: A decade of deregulation puts Georgian miners at risk*. Human Rights Watch.

International Monetary Fund. (2008). *Georgia: Letter of intent, memorandum of economic and financial policies, and technical memorandum of understanding* (9 September 2008). International Monetary Fund.

International Trade Union Confederation. (2012). *Workers rights in Georgia* (a letter by Michael Sommer, the President of ITUC, and Sharan Bourrow, General Secretary of ITUC, addressed to Bidzina Ivanishvili, Prime Minister of Georgia [14 November 2012]). ITUC.

Papava, V. (2013). *Economic reforms in post-communist Georgia: Twenty years after*. Navinka.

Pertaia, L. (2017). Are Georgian's disparate left-wing protesters consolidating into a coherent political force? (16 February 2017). *OG Media*.

Risse T., Ropp, S. C., & Sikkink, K. (1999). *The power of human rights: International norms and domestic change*. Cambridge University Press.

Solidarity Center. (2016). *Georgia coal miners, factory workers win two key strikes* (17 May 2016). Retrieved August 15, 2021, from www.solidaritycenter.org/georgia-coal-miners-factory-workers-win-two-key-strikes/

State Audit Office of Georgia. (2019). *Performance audit of preparedness for implementation of Sustainable Development Goals.* State Audit Office of Georgia.

True, J. (2011). Chapter 4 – Feminist problems with international norms: Gender mainstreaming and global governance. In J. A. Tickner, & L. Sjoberg (Eds.), *Feminism and international relations: Conversations about the past, present and future* (pp.73–88). Routledge.

World Bank. (n.d.). *The World Bank in Georgia: Overview.* Retrieved August 15, 2021, from www.worldbank.org/en/country/georgia/overview

World Bank. (2016) *Doing Business 2016.* Retrieved August 15, 2021, from www.doingbusiness.org/en/reports/global-reports/doing-business-2016

12 Mainstreaming animal welfare

The role of EU trade policy

Stephanie Ghislain

Introduction

In the context of the recent COVID-19 pandemic, the question of how we treat animals has become even more central than before. About 75% of emerging infectious diseases that have affected people over the past three decades originated in animals and one of the major drivers behind the spread of zoonoses is the pressure on biodiversity created by the loss of habitat, which is, in turn, caused by the vast changes in land and sea use operated for agricultural purposes, especially for the intensification of animal farming. Yet, despite the interactions existing between animal welfare and many aspects of sustainability, the concept is not explicitly mentioned in the United Nations (UN) Sustainable Development Goals (SDGs).

This chapter will start by questioning the reasons behind this absence. Then, adopting the position that the SDGs can be seen as dynamic and constantly reformulated in practice, it will illustrate how animal welfare could be mainstreamed in the implementation of the SDGs by describing the interactions between animal welfare and SDG 8, which focuses on decent work and economic growth. This first part will end with a state of play of the global debate on animal welfare and the SDGs and with an assessment of the possibilities to see a spiral model of norm diffusion being developed on this norm at a global level.

The second section of the chapter will switch to the regional level and focus on the EU, where there has been a growing crystallisation around the normative inclusion of animal welfare in the implementation of the SDGs. Arguing that trade policy is considered a strong channel of norm diffusion for the European Union (EU), the section will describe the extent to which this normative approach on animal welfare and the SDGs has been adopted in the field of EU Trade Policy, both from a legal perspective—in Free Trade Agreements (FTAs) or in strategy documents—and from a practical one—in the implementation of FTAs. It will then look at how the EU chooses to use its trade policy to start a spiral model of norm diffusion around animal welfare by presenting three case studies, Chile, Ukraine and Canada, which will allow us to draw conclusions and open further reflections on the tools the EU has at its disposal to promote norms through trade policy.

DOI: 10.4324/9781003205951-16

Animal welfare—a missing dimension of the UN Sustainable Development Agenda?

Some of the 17 SDGs are connected to animals. In the cases of SDG 15 (Life on land) and SDG 14 (Life below water), they target animals as species, rather than as individuals. Yet, the Sustainable Development Agenda's vision states that it envisages 'a world [...] in which humanity lives in harmony with nature and in which wildlife and other living species are protected'. Protecting animal welfare is thus essential to sustainable development in its own right, even though neither the SDGs nor the more specific targets listed for each include an explicit mention of animal welfare.

The struggle to define animal welfare—from five freedoms to five domains

The World Organisation for Animal Health (WOAH, formerly known as OIE), which has also covered animal welfare since 2004, simply defines the concept as 'the physical and mental state of an animal in relation to the conditions in which it lives and dies' (OIE, 2019). The organisation also incorporated into its guiding principles the 'five freedoms'. This notion, which was established in the early 1990s and is now widely recognised (RSPCA, 2021), establishes that animals should be provided with at least five freedoms, namely the freedom from hunger, thirst and malnutrition; from physical and thermal discomfort; from pain, injury and disease; from fear and distress; and finally to express normal patterns of behaviour.

More recently, other notions have entered the debate such as the principle that animals should live 'a good life' or a 'life worth living'. The proponents of such concepts argue that the five freedoms are often misunderstood as an objective to be fully achieved, while an animal cannot be entirely free from certain of the negative experiences referred to in the list. The decades of progress in animal welfare science, as well as the changes in societal acceptance of certain animal treatments, led to an updated version of the theoretical framework around animal welfare, which now defines animal welfare as 'a state subjectively experienced by an animal; (..) a state within the animal' (Mellor, 2016). Subsequently, the focus shifted to the idea that animals should be provided with opportunities to have positive experiences, while negative experiences should be minimised. This approach is called the 'five domains'. The first four—nutrition, environment, health and behaviour, which are more physical or functional domains—shape the fifth one: the animal's mental state. Many animal protection organisations have now adopted such concepts.

The struggle to include animal welfare on the global agenda

While the animal movement succeeded in including a commitment to building a 'humane' society in the Johannesburg Declaration on Sustainable Development (United Nations, 2002) and a reference to the protection of living species in the

2015 Sustainable Development Agenda, it did not manage to obtain an explicit mention of the welfare of animals within the UN SDGs. The apparent reasons behind this absence could be categorised as normative and institutional.

From a normative perspective, the UN SDGs were developed around the needs of human beings, following an anthropocentric approach. In addition, as the process that led to the adoption of the UN Sustainable Agenda was open to multi-dimensional stakeholders, many issues were in competition to be addressed in the future SDGs.

The institutional structure of the animal movement may also have played a role. With the dismantling of the World Society for the Protection of Animals in 2014, there was no unified voice for the animal movement, and back then, only a few animal protection organisations advocated at UN level. It was only in 2017 that these organisations decided to form the Animal Issues Thematic Cluster (AITC) in order to formalise their involvement at UN level. The AITC operates under the 'Non-Governmental Organisation (NGO) Major Group', one of the nine groups within the system created by the UN to ensure the participation of civil society in UN decision-making.

Another institutional aspect that can be raised to explain the absence of commitments on animal welfare in the SDGs is the absence of binding global commitments in the field. Indeed, the standards produced by WOAH are only recommendations.

Mainstreaming animal welfare in the implementation of the UN SDGs

In addition to being intrinsically connected to sustainable development, animal welfare is also positively correlated with most SDGs (Keeling et al., 2019), which means that the achievement of these SDGs partly depends on improving animal welfare. Considering the SDGs as a dynamic concept, animal welfare could represent a new frontier, as proven by developments that occurred in the implementation of the SDGs.

Firstly, recent years have seen the appearance of the concept of 'One Welfare', which emerged both from the vision that animal welfare is linked to sustainable development and from concerns about contentious trade-offs between animal welfare, human well-being and environmental sustainability. This principle was first suggested by Colonius and Earley in 2013 and can be seen as complementing 'One Health', a concept already adopted by most international organisations, and in line with the 2017 OIE Global Animal Welfare Strategy.[1]

Secondly, animal welfare is one of the concepts identified by the 2019 UN Global Sustainable Development Report as missing from the initial Sustainable Development Agenda. This report, published by an independent group of experts to inform the work of the UN High Level Political Forum (HLPF) on sustainable development, underlines that

> the clear links between human health and well-being and animal welfare is increasingly being recognised in ethics- and rights-based frameworks. Strong

governance should safeguard the well-being of both wildlife and domesticated animals with rules on animal welfare embedded in transnational trade.

Thirdly, 2019 also saw the publication of the first academic research on the interlinkages between the SDGs and animal welfare. This study assessed the interactions between the SDGs and animal welfare, in both directions. The conclusion of the exercise was that, even if animal welfare is not explicitly mentioned in the SDGs, it is positively linked with all of them, to various degrees. Greater animal welfare does not impede the achievement of any SDG, quite the contrary (Keeling et al., 2019) (Figure 12.1).

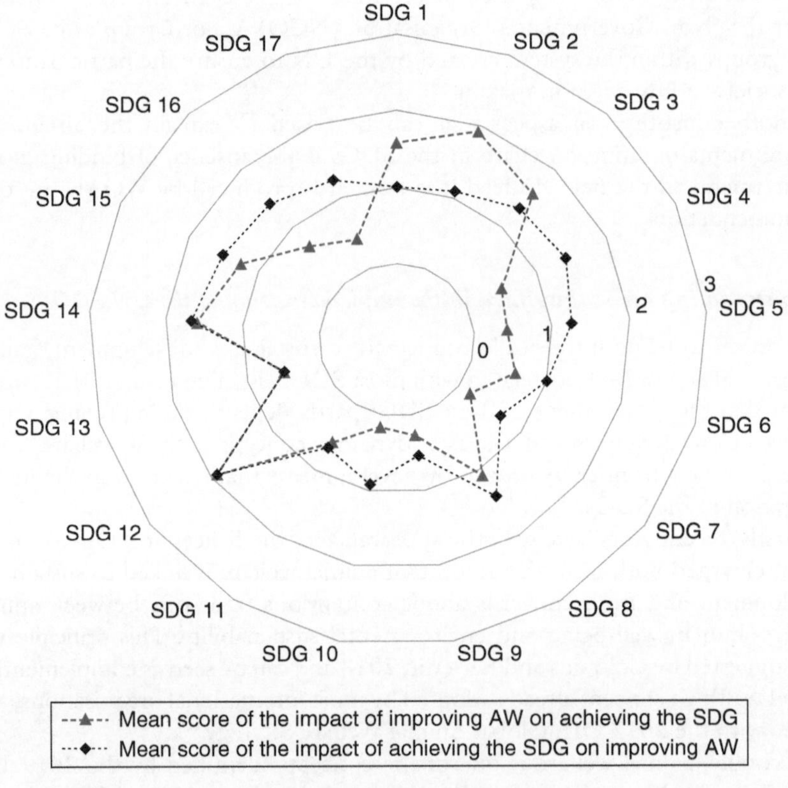

Figure 12.1 Overview of the average score for each Sustainable Development Goal (SDG)–animal welfare (AW) link.

Note: The green line (dashed line with triangles) refers to the impact of AW on achieving the SDG and the blue line (dotted line with squares) to the impact of the SDG on achieving improved AW (Keeling et al., 2019).

Animal welfare and the SDGs—the case of SDG 8

Animal welfare therefore interacts with the SDGs in many ways. An obvious exemplification of these interconnections is the spread of intensive farming. Scientific research reveals the 'inherent major disadvantages for animal welfare' of intensive animal confinement systems, such as the limitations on space in individual stalls restricting the movement of animals, or high stocking densities in groups increasing the potential for disease transmission and injurious contact with others. The International Finance Corporation noted that these systems lack 'the potential to provide satisfactory outcomes' for animals (International Finance Corporation, 2014). These systems also negatively impact the environment, as they lead to water, air and ground pollution, deforestation, and usually to an increase in greenhouse gas (GHG) emissions, especially due to deforestation potentially linked to animal feed production (IPBES, 2019). Farming systems with the potential to provide better animal welfare conditions are more likely to have a lesser impact on the environment, the climate and livelihoods. This section focuses on the latter: the impact of animal welfare standards on livelihoods.

SDG 8 promotes 'sustained, inclusive and sustainable economic growth, full and productive employment and decent work for all'. The contribution of higher animal welfare standards to three targets under SDG 8 will be assessed: full and productive employment and decent work (8.5), where success will be measured by looking at average hourly earnings and unemployment rates; quality of work (8.8), considering the frequency of injuries; and sustainable tourism (8.9), with as indicators the proportion of GDP and jobs generated by the tourism sector.

Animal welfare and full and productive employment and decent work (8.5)

The spread of intensive animal agriculture all over the world has had an impact on hourly earning rates and unemployment. José Graziano da Silva, the former Director General of the Food and Agriculture Organisation (FAO) confirmed with no ambiguity that: 'Smallholders must not be pushed aside by large capital-intensive operations' (Graziano da Silva, 2018). Industrialised systems typically employ fewer people than traditional ones, as many integral tasks become automated. Wages are low and the seasonal nature of the work creates prolonged job insecurity. The sector also employs many migrant workers who are especially vulnerable due to their precarious legal status. These workers are also particularly likely to experience poor working conditions, unfair wages and limited access to public services (HLPE, 2016). As the livestock sector is one that experiences growth, especially in developing countries (FAO, 2018), it is crucial to ensure such growth is fully inclusive and sustainable. Smallholders and smaller scale operations, where animal welfare can be respected, should be favoured to enhance animal productivity through improved health care, welfare and nutrition.

Another link exists between animal welfare and decent growth. For poorer populations, owning a strong working equid can also help build resilience. The extra income generated by working animals allows the owner to save money and reinvest to promote further growth and access to education. Around 200 million working animals are essential to the livelihoods of some of the poorest communities. In rural areas, working animals facilitate farming and transportation; they pull ploughs and carts, deliver goods to market, herd livestock and collect water from wells. Urban uses include construction, the transport of people and goods, and refuse collection. By enabling their owners to participate in work, they boost their economic capacity and revenues. Simple interventions to improve the welfare of working equids, such as improved access to good, affordable harnessing, hoof care and veterinary services, can empower owners to keep their animals healthy, therefore ensuring they remain productive (World Horse Welfare & The Donkey Sanctuary, 2017).

Animal welfare and quality of work (8.8)

People employed by larger industrial operations usually face poor working conditions, with a high level of occupational health hazards, such as diseases and injuries. One of the determining factors for worker safety in slaughterhouses is the speed of the line on which animals are processed. When the pace is very fast, workers face more risks of chronic physical ailments called musculoskeletal disorders (Lowe, 2016). A report by the US National Institute for Occupational Safety and Health published in 2015 noted that 76% of the workers in a plant located in Maryland had abnormal nerve conditions in at least one hand (Lowe, 2016). In 2014, US data showed that repetitive motion injuries among beef and pork processing workers were nearly seven times that of other private industries (Lowe, 2016), and US workers in all meat sectors were three times more likely to suffer serious harm than the average American worker (Levit, 2019). Line speed and general pace of the activities also impacts animal welfare. Scott David, who worked in a US slaughterhouse during a pilot programme to increase speed and lower inspections, denounced workers under pressure, 'beating, dragging, and electrically prodding pigs to make them move faster'(David, 2018; Scott-Reid, 2019).

Workers who face more animal suffering, in an environment operating at lower welfare standards, will also be more at risk of suffering psychological problems. A study commissioned by the French Ministry of Labour in 2011 lists contact with animal suffering as a negative factor (Gollac & Bodier, 2011). A study led in Turkey, where animals are not stunned before slaughter, also showed that butchers, especially those operating in slaughterhouses, demonstrated more psychological pain than office workers. The butchers operating in slaughterhouses had even higher levels of unpleasant body sensations, anxiety, hostility and psychoticism than butchers operating in other environments (Emhan et al., 2012).

Animal welfare and sustainable tourism (8.9)

Improving the welfare of wild animals by protecting them from being poached contributes to another target linked to SDG 8, that related to sustainable tourism.

Within the poorest populations, 600 million people rely on animals for their livelihood. Animals are not only fundamental in the agricultural sector, but also in tourism, especially in wildlife viewing activities. Eighty per cent of all trips to Africa aim at wildlife viewing. In 2018, the majority of the 350,000 jobs created in the tourism sector in Rwanda were related to gorilla trekking. In its 2018 report, the World Travel & Tourism Council noted that wildlife tourism accounted for five times more in the global GDP than wildlife trade (120 billion USD vs 23 billion USD). In 2017, this industry directly employed more than 9.1 million people, and generated another 21.8 million jobs indirectly (Dickinson, 2019). Keeping animals in the wild is thus an improvement to their welfare, but it also constitutes a boost for the economies of the countries from which these animals originate.

While there has been a growing understanding of the interactions between animal welfare and the SDGs in recent years, there is still no consensus at the global level on mainstreaming animal welfare in the implementation of the UN Sustainable Development Agenda. As the crystallisation of the animal welfare agenda remains difficult at the global level, it is not yet possible to observe the initial stages of a spiral model of norm diffusion at that level. However, it is worth questioning the state of play of such a spiral model at regional level and assess whether any regional consensus could be strong enough to foster international norm diffusion. The selected case study will be the EU, where the consensus around animal welfare and the SDGs is getting stronger. After looking into how such a regional consensus came to be, this chapter will investigate how the EU chooses to use its normative power through trade policy to foster a spiral model of norm diffusion on animal welfare and the SDGs.

Norm diffusion around animal welfare through EU trade policy

The European consensus on the importance of animal welfare is not recent, as confirmed by the recognition of animals as sentient beings included in the Treaty on the Functioning of the EU and by the legislation already existing in the field, at EU and member state levels. In parallel, the EU has also used its trade policy to promote animal welfare in third countries since 2002, well before the UN adopted its Sustainable Development Agenda. This section looks at how a consensus has recently crystallised around linking animal welfare and the SDGs, and at how such a consensus has been or can be reflected in the norm diffusion efforts the EU carries out through trade policy.

From the EU's agenda on the SDGs to EU trade policy

Animal welfare is increasingly recognised as an important element of sustainable production systems in the EU. In the recent consultation on the Future of Europe, one in seven European citizens designated animal welfare as a priority for the EU, in an open question (European Commission, 2019). Pushed by citizens and civil society, this norm was more easily adopted at the institutional level by the EU's Directorates-General working on environment and agriculture. Already back in 2012, before the adoption of the UN SDGs, then EU Commissioner for Agriculture, Dacian Cioloş stated, in a speech at a G20 meeting, that sustainable agriculture should aim at ensuring animal welfare (Cioloş, 2012). More recently, the new EU Food Policy, entitled 'Farm to Fork', has clearly put animal welfare at the heart of sustainable food systems (European Commission, 2020). In the field of trade policy, this norm has faced more contestation.

In the EU, this normative vision that animal welfare is linked to sustainable development has been promoted by animal welfare organisations, including more recently in the field of trade policy. Several factors contributed to make the sustainable development dimension of trade policy more relevant to animal welfare organisations. These factors are linked, on the one hand, to the political developments around EU trade policy and, on the other hand, to the rise of important global challenges.

Over the past decade, the EU's trade policy has moved towards a value-based model. The negotiations for the EU–US Transatlantic Trade and Investment Partnership (TTIP), which started in July 2013, generated a strong backlash among citizens and civil society. Debates around the potential impact of trade policy on non-trade issues, such as labour rights, the environment and animal welfare, grew louder. This is in part due to the introduction by the EU of a new generation of FTAs covering not only tariffs, but also aiming at lowering non-tariff barriers by harmonising standards. This objective brought fears of a race to the bottom, especially in fields like food safety or animal welfare. The politicisation of EU trade policy was also fuelled by the decision made in the Lisbon Treaties to grant to the European Parliament the power to veto these agreements. The European Parliament, being an elected institution, provided grounds for more intense lobbying by civil society on trade policy. In 2015, after the adoption of the UN SDGs, the EU responded to the criticisms expressed by civil society with the publication of a new trade strategy entitled *Trade for All* (European Commission, 2015). The strategy, which focused more on sustainable development, committed the EU to 'continuing its longstanding commitment to sustainable development in its trade policies [and] contributing to the newly agreed global SDGs under the 2030 Agenda for Sustainable Development'. Following this, the political environment became more open to discussing non-trade issues such as not only environmental and labour rights, but also animal welfare.

The EU's tool to address sustainability in trade agreements is the inclusion of Trade and Sustainable Development (TSD) chapters. These chapters have been heavily criticised in the past for lacking enforceability. This issue was one of the reasons behind the opposition that emerged against the ratification of the EU–Canada Comprehensive Economic and Trade Agreement (CETA).[2] Since then, the debate around the effectiveness of TSD chapters has not yet been settled, as demonstrated by the joint paper published in 2020 by the French and Dutch governments, which calls for tariffs to be linked to sustainability criteria (France & the Netherlands, 2020), and by the heated debates surrounding the ratification of the EU–Mercosur Agreement. In reaction, the European Commission launched a consultation on the matter in July 2021.

These discussions have fuelled hope that these chapters could eventually be strengthened and if so, that they could deliver better results, especially with the appointment in the EU of a new Chief Trade Enforcement Officer tasked with improving the implementation of FTAs, including TSD chapters. These developments created a renewed interest in TSD chapters among animal protection NGOs. EU FTAs have included provisions on animal welfare cooperation since 2002, with the adoption of the EU–Chile Association Agreement. Animal welfare provisions were initially part of the chapters on sanitary and phytosanitary (SPS) issues, but more recent EU trade agreements tend to include them in either a standalone chapter[3] or in chapters on regulatory cooperation.[4] There has never been a mention of animal welfare in the TSD chapters but, initially, animal protection NGOs did not push for this, as they considered these chapters as too weak.

Another factor that forced animal welfare organisations to develop a better narrative on TSD is the surge of global challenges, such as the climate and biodiversity crises, antimicrobial resistance and the spread of zoonoses. In fighting these battles, it is key to cooperate with partners, including through trade agreements, in order to find compromise solutions. It thus became crucial for animal protection NGOs to ensure animal welfare was understood as a dimension of sustainable development, and that it would not be traded off when collaborating on these issues with its partners.

The EU has not yet explicitly made animal welfare part of the TSD chapters, probably out of a fear that embracing a more comprehensive approach to sustainable development might lead to overloading the TSD chapters. However, the bottom-up effort of norm diffusion by animal protection NGOs has still seen results in the trade policy field. In 2018, the EU recognised, for the first time in the context of trade policy, the connection between improved animal welfare and sustainability of food production systems.[5] Such a wording can now be found in the EU–UK Trade and Cooperation Agreement. The EU 'Farm to Fork' strategy, which is described as 'central to the Commission's agenda to achieve the United Nations' Sustainable Development Goals (SDGs)' (European Commission, 2020), clearly states that trade policy must be coherent with the objectives of the strategy, which contains commitments to improving animal welfare. The strategy also calls for trade policy to be used to obtain ambitious commitments from third parties on animal welfare. Finally, the Trade Policy Review published in February 2021 confirmed that the EU will aim to include chapters on sustainable food systems, which will include provisions on animal welfare cooperation in all future EU FTAs. These chapters have been described as linked to both SPS and TSD chapters (European Commission 2021).

Mainstreaming the link between animal welfare and the SDGs in the implementation of FTAs

EU TSD chapters mostly focus on labour rights and environmental protection. They also refer to the UN Sustainable Development Agenda and the SDGs.

Even if current EU TSD chapters do not contain provisions on sustainable agriculture—although the sustainability of food systems is at the heart of the SDGs—the implementation of EU trade agreements, which is a more fluid political process, has provided increasing opportunities for norm diffusion around the link between animal welfare and the SDGs. These efforts have taken place at a horizontal level—between the parties in the implementing committees,[6] within the EU Domestic Advisory Groups[7] (DAGs) and between the different DAGs under the same agreement—but also at a vertical level, from the DAGs to the parties.

TSD committee meetings are the place where the parties meet to discuss their commitments to sustainable development and the SDGs. While in negotiations the EU's norm diffusion efforts might have faced denial, the conclusion of the agreement represents the results of tactical concessions on both sides. As agreements can be kept vague on purpose, the committee meetings also constitute a place where new tactical concessions will be made on how to interpret the norms that have been adopted. The DAGs have two normative functions. The first is to be the place where rule-consistent behaviour is monitored by civil society organisations. While only the parties can formally trigger the dispute settlement mechanism included in the FTA, DAGs can jointly denounce situations in which the norms are not respected, drawing the attention of the parties to a specific violation of commitments.

DAGs are also places where the norms can be diffused and, to a certain extent, localised. DAGs' meetings provide stakeholders with more access to officials, which increases accountability but also multiplies the channels for bottom-up norm diffusion. Acting in the EU DAGs, European civil society can strive to drive the EU's TSD agenda. Animal protection organisations have participated in most existing DAGs in the past five years and have managed to ensure that animal welfare is on the agenda of these meetings, promoting the normative approach that animal welfare connects to the achievement of the SDGs. This normative effort led by European organisations is also directed at the partner's civil society through institutional mechanisms such as joint meetings of the DAGs and the Civil Society Forum.[8] These yearly interactions allow organisations to establish contact and potentially find synergies in their agendas. It can also allow European animal protection NGOs to share their normative approach with their counterparts, possibly triggering a localisation of the norms. According to Acharya, localisation of the norms, which he defines as 'the active construction (through discourse, framing, grafting, and cultural selection) of foreign ideas by local actors, which results in the former developing significant congruence with local beliefs and practices' (Acharya, 2004, p. 245), is key to ensuring that a spiral model of norm diffusion reaches the final phase of rule-consistent behaviour. In turn, this adoption of the norms by local organisations can lead to a mirroring bottom-up normative effort in the partner country, which can have a much stronger effect than efforts carried out by foreign civil society organisations.

The efforts to raise animal welfare in the context of TSD chapters can be deemed successful insofar that, in their rules of procedure, current DAGs have often officially expanded their scope of work to all issues related to sustainable development, even if located outside TSD chapters. Overall, EU civil society organisations have pushed the EU to grant more consideration to animal welfare topics by leveraging their role within monitoring mechanisms under TSD chapters to encourage the EU to adopt more proactive stances with its trade partners.

Between adoption and contestation—norm diffusion around animal welfare in trade policy

The previous section explained that, while there is no agreement yet at the global level on the link between animal welfare and the SDGs, a consensus is emerging on this normative approach in the EU. In the context of trade policy, the EU's normative efforts have initially focused on animal welfare as a concept on its own. This is due to the fact that the EU's normative consensus around the need to ensure animal welfare dates further back. Therefore, we can observe a more clearly crystalised norm diffusion through trade policy around animal welfare as a standalone norm, rather than in conjunction with the SDGs. Yet, this normative connection with the SDGs is increasingly pushed by civil society through the more fluid implementation of existing EU FTAs. This section will thus look at how successful the EU's norm diffusion around animal welfare has been through existing FTAs (with Chile, Canada and Ukraine), and at the tools the EU could put in place to further develop these normative efforts.

Norm diffusion through the EU–Chile association agreement can be seen as a success. After the conclusion of this agreement—the first ever to include provisions on animal welfare cooperation—the country started a collaboration process with its European partners that led to the enactment of the first Chilean animal welfare law in 2008. In this case, the EU relied on socialisation tools—in the form of cooperation mechanisms—to generate a spiral model of diffusion that reached its final stage with the adoption by Chile of legislation reflecting norms promoted by the EU. This success, without using stronger tools, can be explained by the willingness of the partner, and thus, to a certain degree, by the localisation process followed by these norms. Before concluding the agreement, Chile was already discussing some of these norms internally, pushed by local and international animal protection groups. Soon after, it became, with Mexico and Uruguay, one of the leading forces behind the OIE Collaborating Centres on Animal Welfare for the Americas. Incidentally, Mexico is another country with which the EU could see a successful spiral model of norm diffusion around animal welfare. The modernised EU–Mexico Global Agreement—which has not yet been ratified—is the first EU trade agreement to contain a standalone chapter on animal welfare and antimicrobial resistance (Ghislain, 2018). Ahead of the ratification process, Mexico has continued to progress on animal welfare and took the first step towards banning animal testing for cosmetics (HSI/Mexico, 2020).

The case of the trade agreement between the EU and Canada reveals more contestation of EU norms. During negotiations, the EU had to make tactical concessions but still managed to get animal welfare listed as a potential topic for CETA's Regulatory Cooperation Forum (RCF). In the implementation phase, the EU formally suggested the welfare of animals on long distance transport as a topic to be addressed within the RCF. As Canada was in the process of reviewing its 30-year-old rules, which were still allowing for very long journey times in difficult conditions, the cooperation had the potential to produce concrete policy impact. However, after a few months, Canada adopted its new legislation without awaiting any outcome of this cooperation process. The EU's norm diffusion effort on animal welfare has thus faced much more resistance in Canada. In this case, the EU lacks the lever to foster a spiral model of norm diffusion, notably because of the weak outcome of the negotiations. The concessions the EU made on animal welfare to conclude the agreement, as well as the weakness of the objectives set for animal welfare cooperation, among which were information exchange (European Commission, 2020), also underline a lack of willingness to use more political capital to promote this norm. Yet, the EU–Canada RCF has recently adopted a joint statement on animal welfare recognising the concept as part of sustainable food systems (CETA Regulatory Cooperation Forum, 2021). This is progress and shows that framing animal welfare in a wider context, such as the SDGs, can help foster acceptance from partners.

With Ukraine being a neighbouring country, the dimension of norm diffusion is even stronger in EU–Ukraine relations. The EU–Ukraine Deep and Comprehensive Free Trade Agreement (DCFTA) granted Ukraine subsequent trade preferences but, in return, Ukraine committed to approximate the EU acquis in several fields, including animal welfare. In this case, the EU had both leverage and incentives to push for a strong outcome in negotiations, as Ukraine is an important player in the agri-food sector and thus, a potential competitor. Yet, Ukraine only adopted the needed animal welfare legislation five years later, in February 2021, with an implementation date set for 2026. This situation reflects the difficulty reaching the final stage of a spiral model of norm diffusion. In this case, the EU used the strongest of the soft tools, in the shape of a commitment to align standards. This is technically a persuasion tool that can help shape the partner's normative approach, but in practice there is a lack of leverage to push for the commitment to materialise. In 2021, the EU and Ukraine announced a review of the DCFTA's market access provisions. In that context, the EU could condition the granting of further trade preferences to Ukrainian animal products on the implementation of EU-equivalent animal welfare standards, which would mean escalating to harder policy tools.

The EU–Japan Economic Partnership Agreement is too recent to provide sufficient grounds for analysis but also contains provisions on animal welfare cooperation. It remains to be seen how the partners will make use of them and how Japan will react to the EU's attempts to diffuse this norm in the implementation phase.

Recent years have seen some successes for the EU's norm diffusion efforts around animal welfare, but also strong contestation from partners. Looking at the above cases, it seems the extent to which a norm is clearly defined and shared internally is crucial in the success of norm diffusion efforts. Subsequently, the decade-old consensus around animal welfare in the EU supports a better norm diffusion spiral model than what could be achieved, at this moment, around linking animal welfare to the SDGs. The efficacy of EU tools, such as provisions in trade agreements, and the willingness of the EU to use these tools externally, also shapes its ability to socialise, or even persuade, its partners, as well as other factors such as the capacity of partners to resist or the extent to which the norm has been localised. Nevertheless, the successes obtained by the EU in diffusing norms related to animal welfare have ultimately contributed to the achievement of the SDGs, given that, as demonstrated in the first part of the chapter, animal welfare is strongly connected to many of the SDGs.

Conclusions

In the EU, animal welfare is well recognised as an important dimension of sustainability. This normative connection has also been underlined in EU trade policy, but the first explicit reference to it can only be found in the recently signed EU–UK TCA. It is thus too early to assess the EU's norm diffusion effort around animal welfare and the SDGs. Nevertheless, the EU's normative outreach around animal welfare in the context of trade policy provides us with several useful case studies. The experience of the EU in using FTAs to diffuse its norms in the field has met mixed results. This is mostly due to the weakness of the tools the EU has relied upon—in most cases, cooperation mechanisms. The EU spiral model of norm diffusion only reached the final stage of rule-consistent behaviour with one partner, mainly because of the partner's willingness to adopt the projected norm, which had been fostered by a localisation process around this norm. When the EU has met resistance, it has been unable or unwilling to use the required levers to lift entrenched opposition. The EU has thus a capacity and does engage in norm diffusion using soft policy tools, but there is no willingness to level up this effort and engage more political capital. So far, EU trade policy has been able to put animal welfare on the agenda of its partners—achieving socialisation around this norm—but not always to shape how its partners consider animal welfare and how they behave—through persuasion. Nevertheless, the successes it has met in diffusing norms related to animal welfare clearly contributed to the achievements of the SDGs, as animal welfare is strongly connected to most of the objectives.

The case of the EU–Ukraine DCFTA has shown that even the strongest of the soft tools, which is a commitment to adopt the EU acquis, does not deliver easily. The difficulties faced by the EU in diffusing its normative approach on animal welfare raise the question of the need to develop more repressive tools—or sticks—or to widen the EU's negotiation toolbox with additional incentives—carrots—it can grant for tactical concessions. Several civil society actors have been calling on the EU to make more use of market access related tools in trade policy. With the release of ambitious strategies under the Green Deal, the years to come bring opportunities for the EU to rethink its trade policy and how it can better use trade agreements as part of its norm diffusion effort.

In addition to working on policy tools, better framing the narrative could also help generate more impact through norm diffusion on animal welfare in trade policy. With the growing importance of sustainable development and the adoption of the UN SDGs, civil society is already increasingly pressuring the EU to better consider the link between animal welfare and the SDGs in its normative efforts through trade policy. Clearly articulating an EU position on this normative connection between animal welfare and the SDGs—for instance through the concept of sustainable food systems—could give more ammunition to the EU in its effort to promote animal welfare through trade policy. Linking animal welfare to a concept that is better shared by all partner countries could also help crystallise a global consensus. This, in turn, might facilitate norm diffusion on animal welfare based on a spiral model at the global level.

Notes

1 The strategy is based on a vision of 'a world where the welfare of animals is respected, promoted and advanced, in ways that complement the pursuit of animal health, human well-being, socio-economic development and environmental sustainability'.
2 This opposition forced the adoption of an interpretative joint instrument calling for a review of CETA's TSD chapters 'with a view to the effective enforceability of CETA provisions on trade and labour and trade and the environment'.
3 As in the EU–Mexico Global Agreement.
4 As in CETA, the EU–Japan Economic Partnership Agreement and the EU–Vietnam Free Trade Agreement.
5 See for instance the EU's proposal to New Zealand for a chapter on sanitary and phytosanitary measures.
6 Once an agreement enters into force, the parties set up implementation committees based on the various chapters of the agreement.
7 In the case of most recent EU trade agreements, the TSD chapter imposes the appointment by each party of a domestic advisory group (DAG) composed of civil society organisations representing a wide range of interests. These DAGs are tasked with the monitoring of the implementation of TSD chapters.
8 According to most recent EU FTAs, the parties must organise a yearly Civil Society Forum open to all stakeholders.

References

Acharya, Amitav. (2004). How ideas spread: Whose norms matter? Norm localization and institutional change in Asian Regionalism. *International Organization*, *58*(2), 239–75. www.jstor.org/stable/3877858. Accessed 28 Aug. 2022

CETA Regulatory Cooperation Forum. (2021, July). *Joint statement by regulators on animal welfare*. Retrieved December 18, 2021, from https://trade.ec.europa.eu/doclib/docs/2021/august/tradoc_159774.pdf

Cioloş, D. (2012, June 21). *Europe's path towards sustainable agriculture* (speech at DG AGRI/DG DEVCO side event: Agriculture the way towards sustainability and inclusiveness G20/Rio de Janeiro). Retrieved December 18, 2021, from http://europa.eu/rapid/press-release_SPEECH-12-480_en.htm?locale=en

David, S. (2018, March 6). America's horrifying new plan for animals: Highspeed slaughterhouses. *The Guardian*, Retrieved December 18, 2021, from www.theguardian.com/commentisfree/2018/mar/06/ive-seen-the-hidden-horrors-of-high-speed-slaughterhouses#maincontent

Dickinson, G. (2019, August). Worth far more alive than dead: New research shows wildlife tourism is five times bigger than poaching. *The Telegraph*, Retrieved December 18, 2021, from www.telegraph.co.uk/travel/news/wildlife-tourism-wttc-poaching/

Emhan, A., Yildiz, A. Ş., Bez, Y., & Kingir, S. (2012). Psychological symptom profile of butchers working in slaughterhouse and retail meat packing business: A comparative study. *Kafkas Universitesi Veteriner Fakultesi Dergisi*, *18*(2). https://doi.org/10.9775/kvfd.2011.5494

European Commission. (2015). *Trade for all: Towards a more responsible trade and investment policy*, Retrieved December 18, 2021, from https://trade.ec.europa.eu/doclib/docs/2015/october/tradoc_153846.pdf

European Commission. (2019, April). *Online consultation on the future of Europe: Second interim report*, Retrieved December 18, 2021, from https://ec.europa.eu/commission/sites/beta-political/files/online-consultation-report-april-2019_en.pdf

European Commission. (2020, May). *A farm to fork strategy for a fair, healthy and environmentally-friendly food system* (COM/2020/381 final). Retrieved December 18, 2021, from https://ec.europa.eu/food/horizontal-topics/farm-fork-strategy_en

European Commission. (2020, October). *Comprehensive economic and trade agreement regulatory cooperation forum work plan*. Retrieved December 18, 2021, from https://trade.ec.europa.eu/doclib/docs/2020/october/tradoc_159008.pdf

European Commission. (2021, May 20). *Note for the attention of the Trade Policy Committee – Free Trade Agreements: Chapters on sustainable food systems* (WK 6723/202).

FAO. (2018). *World livestock: Transforming the livestock sector through the Sustainable Development Goals*. CC BY-NC-SA 3.0 IGO. Retrieved December 18, 2021, from www.fao.org/3/CA1201EN/ca1201en.pdf

France & the Netherlands. (2020). *Non-paper from the Netherlands and France on trade, social economic effects and sustainable development*. Retrieved December 18, 2021, from https://nl.ambafrance.org/Non-paper-from-the-Netherlands-and-France-on-trade-social-economic-effects-and

Ghislain, S. (2018). The EU-Mexico global agreement: A groundbreaking precedent for animal welfare in trade policy. *Global Trade and Customs Journal*, *13*(10), 472–474.

Gollac, M., & Bodier, M. (2011). *Mesurer les facteurs psychosociaux de risque au travail pour les maîtriser* [Measure psychosocial risk factors at work to control them] (Report commissioned by the French Labour Ministry to the Collège d'expertise sur le suivi des risques psychosociaux au travail). Retrieved December 18, 2021, from https://travail-emploi.gouv.fr/IMG/pdf/rapport_SRPST_definitif_rectifie_11_05_10.pdf

Graziano da Silva, J.(2018). *10th global forum for food and agriculture: Shaping the future of livestock – sustainably, responsibly, efficiently*. Retrieved December 18, 2021, from www.fao.org/director-general/my-statements/detail/en/c/1098613/

HLPE. (2016). *Sustainable agricultural development for food security and nutrition: What roles for livestock? A report by the High Level Panel of Experts on Food Security and Nutrition of the Committee on World Food Security*. Rome.

HSI/Mexico. (2020, March). *Mexican Senate passes bill to outlaw cosmetic animal testing*. Retrieved December 18, 2021, from www.hsi.org/news-media/mexican-senate-passes-bill-outlaw-cosmetic-animal-testing/

International Finance Corporation. (2014). *Good practice note on 'improving animal welfare in livestock operations'*. Retrieved December 18, 2021, from www.ifc.org/wps/wcm/connect/topics_ext_content/ifc_external_corporate_site/sustainability-at-ifc/publications/publications_gpn_animalwelfare_2014

IPBES. (2019). *Summary for policymakers of the global assessment report on biodiversity and ecosystem services of the Intergovernmental Science-Policy Platform on Biodiversity and Ecosystem Services*. IPBES Secretariat.

Keeling, L., Tunón, H., Olmos Antillón, G., Berg, C., Jones, M., Stuardo, L., Swanson, J., Wallenbeck, A., Winckler, C., & Blokhuis, H. (2019). Animal welfare and the United Nations Sustainable Development Goals. *Frontiers in Veterinary Science*, *6*. https://doi.org/10.3389/fvets.2019.00336

Levitt, T. (2019, September 18). US moves to scrap speed limits on pig slaughter lines. *The Guardian*. Retrieved December 18, 2021, from www.theguardian.com/environment/2019/sep/18/us-moves-to-scrap-speed-limits-on-pig-slaughter-lines

Lowe, P. (2016, August 11). *Working 'The Chain,' slaughterhouse workers face lifelong injuries*. NPR. Retrieved December 18, 2021, from www.npr.org/sections/thesalt/2016/08/11/489468205/working-the-chain-slaughterhouse-workers-face-lifelong-injuries?t=1590756619280

Mellor, D. J. (2016). Updating animal welfare thinking: Moving beyond the 'Five Freedoms' towards 'A Life Worth Living'. *Animals*, *6*(3), 21. https://doi.org/10.3390/ani6030021

OIE. (2019). *Terrestrial animal health code* [Volume 1]. Retrieved December 18, 2021, from https://rr-europe.oie.int/wp-content/uploads/2020/08/oie-terrestrial-code-1_2019_en.pdf

RSPCA. (2021, May). *What are the Five Freedoms of animal welfare?* Retrieved December 18, 2021, from https://kb.rspca.org.au/knowledge-base/what-are-the-five-freedoms-of-animal-welfare/

Scott-Reid, J. (2019, October 7). Advocates agree: Increasing kill line speeds puts animals and workers at risk. *Sentient Media*. Retrieved December 18, 2021, from https://sentientmedia.org/advocates-agree-increasing-kill-line-speeds-puts-animals-and-workers-at-risk/

United Nations. (2002, September 4). *Johannesburg Declaration on Sustainable Development*. Retrieved December 18, 2021, from http://un-documents.net/jburgdec.htm

World Horse Welfare & The Donkey Sanctuary. (2017). *Sustainable Development Goals: How the welfare of working equids deliver for development*. Retrieved December 18, 2021, from www.thedonkeysanctuary.org.uk/sites/uk/files/2018-03/sustainable-development-goals.pdf

Section 5

Conclusion

13 Norm diffusion, norm contestation and the SDGs

Paul Bacon, Mina Chiba, and Frederik Ponjaert

In this book we have sought to analyse how the Sustainable Development Goals (SDGs) are diffused, contested and implemented in practice through a series of original case studies. The United Nations (UN) adopted the 2030 Agenda for Sustainable Development in September 2015, comprising 17 SDGs and 169 targets, to be achieved by both developed and developing countries. This agenda is clearly the most significant global development agenda for the next decade and is taken extremely seriously within both Japan and the wider world. For example, Japan established the SDG Promotion Headquarters as a cabinet body headed by the Prime Minister in May 2016. The European Commission also issued a Communication on Implementing the SDGs in 2016. Japan and the European Union (EU) are two of the most significant development funders, and the SDGs are a priority for both.

Analysing the SDGs with appropriate rigour in turn creates two necessities: 1) Firstly, the necessity of conceptualising the SDGs as norms of global governance, in order to understand the ways in which they are contested at many levels. Fukuda-Parr and Muchhala (2020, pp. 1–3) argue that the SDGs offer a truly ambitious and 'transformative agenda' and mark a 'significant normative evolution in international development', as opposed to the MDGs, which were 'essentially an aid agenda'. Furthermore, 'the SDGs are a framework including a large number of norms' and themselves reflect the agency of 'norm entrepreneurs from the Global South'. However, some of the goals contradict and compete with each other, and there is also 'a growing recognition of the need to localise the SDGs' (Asian Development Bank, 2018, p. 2); 2) Once we recognise the necessity of studying the SDGs as norms, it is necessary to engage with cutting edge theories of norm diffusion. And these theories increasingly emphasise that if we want to understand processes of norm diffusion and norm contestation, we need to look far more extensively at activities that take place within the local politics of target states. This in turn necessitates detailed case study work, which entails extensive and deeply engaged fieldwork. We have tried to showcase exactly this type of engaged case study research in this edited volume.

We have sought to use the norm diffusion literature to offer practical insights and social learning on which types of policy diffusion approaches are successful and which are not. The book focused on three key SDGs: (1) SDG 3: healthy

DOI: 10.4324/9781003205951-18

lives and well-being; (2) SDG 4: promoting inclusive and equitable quality education; and (3) SDG 8: decent work and human trafficking. It should be noted that these particular SDGs also all fall within the official priority areas identified by the Japanese government (MOFA, 2016, p. 2). The book's objectives were threefold:

- To explore whether, how and why the selected SDG norms have been diffused, contested, transformed and implemented, across a series of original case studies.
- To explore the roles of different actors such as norm senders and norm receivers in the diffusion and possible localisation or rejection of the SDG norms.
- To explain which policy diffusion mechanisms successfully result in SDG norms being incorporated in national policies and implemented in accordance with international expectations.

One major shortfall of the academic literature is that many studies of the SDGs are policy-oriented. The SDGs are often treated as universally relevant prescriptions for the implementation of development goals. However, this policy approach fails to recognise the political dimension of the SDGs; that some norms might be opposed, contested and in need of localisation if they are to be successfully diffused to particular local contexts. Our project therefore adopted a more politically nuanced and theoretically sophisticated approach to studying the diffusion of the SDGs. Since the SDG literature is policy-oriented, SDGs are generally assumed to be static and their content is considered fixed. Their delivery and implementation are thus assumed to be a process of straightforward diffusion from norm senders to norm receivers. However, norm diffusion theories highlight that norms themselves are dynamic and that reconstitution of norm content can occur when there is norm contestation. We particularly suggest that it is more accurate to consider SDG implementation through the lenses of diffusion, contestation, subsidiarity, localisation and locally-mediated diffusion, rather than through a policy-oriented lens that misses the political conflict inherent in the contestation and possible implementation of the SDGs. Given the necessity of studying the implementation of the SDGs through the lens of norm diffusion, it is imperative to briefly return to definitions of these terms below.

First generation norm diffusion theory was somewhat West-centric, and made a series of unidirectional and 'linear' assumptions about the likely success of top-down Western pressure on target states (Jetschke & Liese, 2013). See also Keck and Sikkink's (1998) assumption that a 'boomerang' effect would occur when domestic opposition groups reached out to global civil society, which would then successfully target human rights abusing governments on their behalf. However, if the original focus in the norm diffusion literature was somewhat top-down and West-centric, later authors (Börzel & Risse, 2012) focused on both direct and indirect diffusion, and recognised that domestic mobilisation within target states was a key factor affecting norm diffusion. It was necessary, they argued, to look at the agency of target actors, potential norm-taking states, to see if they engaged in normative or functional emulation of norm-sending actors. Acharya (2018) further argued that target states can exercise agency by engaging in norm localisation or norm subsidiarity. Bacon and Nakamura (2021) suggested that we also need to look in more detail at the activities of norm-sending actors and their local proxies in target states. In other words, we need to look at 'locally-mediated diffusion', and also examine and explain in far more detail the interactions of norm senders and target actors on the local domestic 'battleground' of target states. While the original norm diffusion literature talked about the boomerang effect, in fact the actual interactions between global and local norm entrepreneurs, and the activities of actors within the target state were systematically and curiously under-researched. We aimed to address this gap in the literature by focusing in detail on what happens within target states.

Börzel and Risse define norms as 'expectations of appropriate behaviour based on a given collective identity', and diffusion as 'a process through which ideas, normative standards, or … policies and institutions travel across time and space' (2012, p. 4, 5). Following their example, the dependent variable we analysed here was 'domestic or regional institutional change which can be traced to the norm senders direct or indirect influence' (p. 14). In their attempts to diffuse human rights norms, norm senders often rely on external incentives (*conditionality*), on the one hand, and technical and financial assistance (*Capacity-building*), on the other. Conditionality 'tries to manipulate the cost–benefit calculations of target actors through creating positive and negative incentives', while Capacity-building, 'by contrast, provides target actors with additional resources enabling them to make choices to begin with' (Börzel & Risse, 2012, p. 7). Several of the chapters investigated Capacity-building within target states in detail.

Target actors are *socialised* into following rules when they recognise that the dominant script is regarded as the 'right thing to do'. *Persuasion* occurs at a thicker or deeper level, when actors internalise a particular norm as the right thing to do, not simply because they are capable of identifying with a dominant script which recognises this to be the case, but because they now themselves believe that the norm itself is substantively true or correct (Börzel & Risse, 2012, pp. 6–8). *Locally-mediated diffusion* takes place:

> when the norm sender successfully builds the capacity of local non-state actors (through financial assistance or knowledge transfer, among others) enabling them to act as direct diffusers of the human rights norm in question, in the local domestic context of the target state.
>
> (Bacon & Nakamura, 2021)

Localisation involves:

> changing the formal shape and content of foreign ideas on the basis of the recipient's own prior beliefs and practices … borrowing only those ideas which are, or can be made, congruent with local beliefs which may enhance

> the prestige of the borrower … pruning outside ideas to get rid of their undesirable elements, while finding a fit between the desirable elements and existing local beliefs and practices.
>
> (Acharya, 2018, p. 45)

Norm *subsidiarity* is a process whereby local actors create rules with a view to preserving their autonomy from neglect, violation or abuse by more central actors (Acharya, 2018, p. 47). The contributors to this volume focused more on the agency of norm receivers, and on the sociological analysis of interaction within the domestic arena of targeted states, which has historically been underspecified in the norm diffusion literature.

Crucially, what all of this means is that in order to study norm diffusion properly, there was a further imperative; to engage in detailed and extensive interviewing and fieldwork in states which are targets for the diffusion of particular SDG norms. This case study work involves talking to actors who exercise agency within the local target state in question. These could be a range of domestic, international and transnational actors. It was further necessary in each case to identify the key norm senders: international organisations such as the UN and its many agencies, such as the International Labour Organization (ILO); regional organisations, such as the EU and Association of Southeast Asian Nations (ASEAN); sovereign states, thinktanks, global human rights non-governmental organisations (NGOs), local NGOs, etc. For case study work it is ideally also necessary to profile and map the relevant domestic networks, stakeholders and influence multipliers within target states. Representatives of these actors then need to be interviewed, systematically and with care, and the results triangulated and corroborated. Understanding how and by which processes the SDGs are successfully implemented is highly significant.

Referring to Figure 13.1 below, first generation norm diffusion approaches focus on the mechanisms of diffusion used by norm senders, which can be found in the northwest quadrant. However, next generation norm diffusion theory recognises that we need to analyse what happens within the target state, represented here in the other three quadrants of Figure 13.1.

This could be additional norm-sending activity by actors located within the target state. For example, this could take the form of Capacity-building by a norm sender inside the target state or promotion of norms by local actors from within the target state. Examples of this would include the EU's funding of ILO legal Capacity-building projects in Thailand, as discussed in the chapter by Bacon and Usayapant. Or it could be positive, norm receptive activity on the part of the target state. This is indirect diffusion as outlined by Börzel and Risse, and can take the form of normative or functional emulation. Another example of positive agency on the part of actors in the target state is localisation. Finally, there could be non-receptive activity on the part of the target state or actors within the target state to particular attempts at norm diffusion. These could take the form of subsidiarity, as defined above, or outright spoiling.

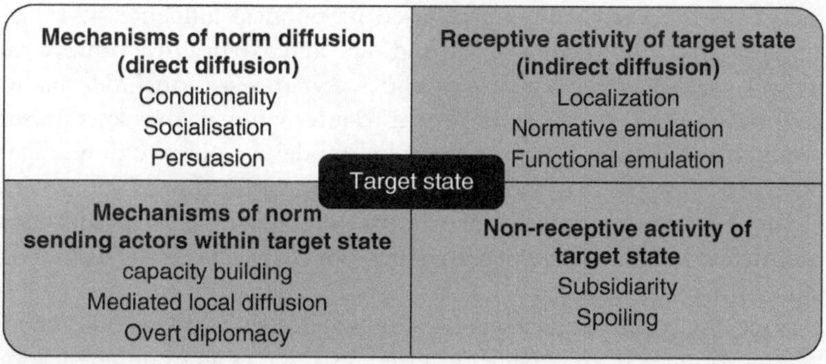

Figure 13.1 Norm diffusion activity within the target state.

Chapter One of the book sought to provide an overview of the SDGs as international norms and trace the emergence of international goals and targets in the context of development policy. Chapter Two introduced the 'spiral model', a state-of-the-art constructivist theory of norm diffusion and used it to explain the processes that could allow internationally sanctioned SDGs to be diffused to and implemented in a variety of states, and to clarify who has the normative power to put such diffusion into practice. Souza and Bacon focused on presenting the basic and most relevant points of the model, comprised of the model's logics of action and socialisation processes, its scope conditions, its direct and indirect mechanisms of diffusion and modes of action, and its five phases of implementation. In Chapter Three, Katsuma explains how there has been interdisciplinary norm diffusion in global health, from 'the right to health' to 'health for all' and then to 'universal health coverage.' The human rights norm associated with a 'right to health' was translated into a development norm encapsulating 'health for all'. Then, the development norm of 'health for all' became integrated with the health norm of 'universal health coverage', representing a strategic health policy to achieve SDG 3. Norm diffusion also took place within the concept of 'universal health coverage', from health to finance and then to politics, through global health diplomacy. Katsuma's research is fascinating because it shows that the content of norms can itself be fluid and contested.

In Chapter Four, Avramovska uses the concept of 'limited statehood' to explain how the Catholic Church in the Philippines became a powerful player in the domain of sexual and reproductive health. By adopting a historical perspective, she demonstrates how, in many ways, Philippine state consolidation was hindered, especially in its formative years. The difficulty for the Philippine state to consolidate has to be partly understood through the vast pre-existing institutional network of the Catholic Church and its role in providing substantial governing functions. The church has continuously substituted the state in the provision of education, health and welfare services and through this gained immense legitimacy and political leverage. Although some of these functions diminished over the years, the church used its political influence to remain a dominant actor in the domain of sexual and reproductive health, both as a moral authority and a veto player in legislative politics. Avramovska concludes that while the Philippines showed strong commitment to international covenants on sexual and reproductive rights, in terms of the spiral model we observe only a 'partial prescriptive status' when it comes to adjusting the national legislation to these norms. Ultimately, this led to incomplete norm compliance with regards to sexual and reproductive health, with progress stuck with an incomplete realisation of stage four of the spiral model.

In Chapter Five, Chiba argues that her study of the diffusion of comprehensive sexuality education (CSE) in Thailand can be regarded as an example of 'locally-mediated diffusion' (Bacon & Nakamura, 2021). The external norm senders of CSE, such as UN agencies, the Global Fund and international NGOs played the roles of direct and indirect diffusers of the CSE norm in Thailand through advocacy of adolescents' sexual and reproductive health and rights (SRHR), the development of the CSE curriculum and human resources, and support and implementation of the project to promote school-based CSE. Through interaction with these organisations, the local agents of norm diffusion, predominantly the Ministry of Public Health (MoPH), was convinced of the benefits of CSE and engaged in persuasion and socialisation of other local agents, such as the Ministry of Education (MoE) and schools. The MoPH was indispensable in local norm diffusion, particularly contributing to the MoE's instrumental adaptation of promoting school-based CSE through the creation of domestic pressure. At the community level, school principals and CSE teachers, including those who used to be sceptical about the value of CSE, were persuaded and in turn acted as norm entrepreneurs, who socialised other teachers and parents into the CSE norms. During this process, student peer educators were also mentored to become norm diffusers. Parents in the schools with such active local norm diffusers were eventually persuaded of the merit of CSE through subjective recognition of its positive outcomes and understanding the needs of CSE for adolescents' pregnancy prevention.

In Chapter Six, Hayashi investigates Cambodia's diffusion of inclusive education norms. She argues that this norm is not being delivered and is not being accepted, adopted and internalised in the way intended at both international and national policy levels. Norm reception and diffusion in this context refers to the intermediary role played by the teachers who are currently accepting, adopting and internalising inclusive education norms, firstly through special education. In contrast to what Hayashi calls the one-track approach to inclusive education, the present status of Cambodia's internalisation of inclusive education norms lies in its strong recognition of the need to follow a 'two-track approach'. Although teachers have been positively socialised into accepting the idea of inclusive education at a general level, in terms of delivery on the ground teachers have localised the content of this norm, and adapted their practice to reflect the reality of limited resources, by adopting a two-track approach. This implies that the contestations as expressed by teachers and other norm receivers and diffusers of inclusive education demand resolution in the form of further investment in the development and use of special education resources, including teacher education and training on the special education curriculum and textbooks. However, Hayashi claims that although inclusive education as intended is not the norm or the practice in Cambodia at present, partially inclusive practices are positively implemented. Yet at the same time, positive practices also encounter contestation at the classroom level. It is necessary to combine medium-term aspirations for the fuller achievement of the norm of inclusivity with a short-term perspective which is realistic about Cambodia's adaptation and internalisation of inclusive education.

In Chapter Seven, Kawaguchi and Kuroda offer strikingly similar findings in their case study of Malawi, to those of Hayashi with regard to Cambodia. Although the Malawi government has adopted an inclusive education policy at the national level, implementation has been inadequate. Schools and teachers are left to enact the policy while facing the realities of the current educational situation, leading to various issues. While Malawi's unique approach to disability and education suggest that a shared philosophy of inclusive education exists, the reality in the classroom is that inclusive education is not often practiced. Instead, educators faced with practical and structural barriers strive to provide the best education possible through a combination of special and integrative education. What Kawaguchi and Kuroda refer to as 'Malawian-style inclusive education' has been enabled in part by inadequate preparation of schools due to lack of funding and support for teacher training at the national level. There have been no resolutions to issues of teacher training or the scale of inclusive education practice, such as who will be responsible for teaching inclusive education or whether a whole-school or classroom-based approach is appropriate. Further, they argue, a lack of continuous government funding for inclusive education initiatives means that public schools are unable to meet the needs of the community. Therefore, the norm of 'inclusive education' as recognised at the global level is diluted at every layer of society until transformed into integrated education at the local level, where only the students who can keep up with general education classes are included. For the rest, they are left to search for a school that can meet their needs.

In Chapter Eight, Radjai focuses on factors that affect the diffusion of Global Citizenship Education (GCED) in higher education policies in Japan. Although as she notes, GCED has been integrated into the global SDG framework, its implementation reflects different local realities. This is notably the case in Japan, where concerns about GCED have been interwoven with ongoing higher education policy conversations and reform efforts. Policies aimed at the internationalisation of higher education have seen the SDG-sponsored norm come into contact with local norms reflecting distinctive agendas. Internationalisation of higher education in Japan is a national strategy, and as a result, the term 'global' has been used for naming newly established programmes at the universities selected for these projects. There are many 'global' courses and programmes intended to develop students' global competencies. However, there appears to be hesitation to use and diffuse the term 'global citizenship' in Japan. In this chapter, Radjai attempts to identify factors that are preventing the 'global citizenship' norm from being diffused in Japan's higher education policy. She explains that in higher education policy the term 'global human resources' (GHR) is used and discussed frequently in Japan. Although GHR and the concept of a global citizen sound similar they are very different concepts that emerged from a different set of problems and perspectives. While global citizens are intended to have a sense of belonging to a common humanity, Radjai demonstrates that the Japanese concept of GHR emphasises 'a deep understanding of Japanese culture' and 'identity as a Japanese', aiming to nurture people who can work internationally in the global market for Japan as Japanese. GHR therefore offers a quite nationalistic portrait of the type of people Japanese higher education policy is aiming to cultivate. Contrary to Cambodia and Malawi, where educational authorities would like to implement international norms but lack the resources, Japan is proposing a more distinctive concept which differs from prevailing international norms.

Moving to the third section of the book, on decent work, in her discussion of the diffusion of gender-related SDG norms in Chapter Nine, Souza argues that Japan has not managed to eliminate, or even satisfactorily improve issues such as indirect discrimination in the workplace, the considerable and stagnant gender-pay gap, the persistent M-shaped curve in the ratio of women's labour participation, the fact that employment rates in all age groups remain lower for women than for men, that most working women are in lower positions, that they are more prone to taking low paying part-time jobs, that a dual track career system persists, and that sexual harassment and detrimental treatment due to marriage, pregnancy and childbirth, etc. persist. She also notes that the lack of intention to create an independent national human rights institution, and to ratify the Convention on the Elimination of All Forms of Discrimination Against Women (CEDAW) Optional Protocol or ILO Convention No. 111, and the refusal of male-dominated Japanese courts to even apply these or other international women's rights norms in their judicial decisions also deserves criticism. In terms of the spiral model, Souza argues that it is clear that Japan has been lacking in commitment to and compliance with international women's rights norms and thus remains stuck far below the level of rule-consistent behaviour, stage five of the model. Even though Japan has tried to bring the topic of gender equality in labour and society to the forefront with policies and laws, these have not achieved the expected success. Japan can therefore be positioned at phase four of the spiral model, that of prescriptive status, when it comes to the right to work.

In Chapter Ten, Bacon and Usayapant demonstrate that in Thailand, the EU has successfully diffused SDG norms relating to decent work and forced labour. This resulted in behavioural change by the Thai government, the ratification of several important international treaties and conventions, the transposition of the content of these treaties into Thai domestic law and substantial compliance with SDG standards on forced labour inside Thailand. In terms of the spiral model, the diffusion of the anti forced labour norm reached stage five. Concretely, the working conditions and living standards of those working in the

Thai fisheries industry have improved considerably, and it is possible to trace this improvement through an analysis of the Baseline and Endline reports of the ILO. Furthermore, the ILO Ship-to-Shore project was at the core of these positive developments, and this project was heavily and exclusively funded by the EU. A combination of EU conditionality and Capacity-building has therefore proved highly successful. Bacon and Usayapant argue that various actors within Thailand have been socialised into respecting labour rights. Finally, the work of the ILO and the various Thai human rights NGOs on the ground is an example of 'mediated local diffusion', where actors funded by the EU engage in direct SDG norm diffusion in the territory of the target state. Although Börzel and Risse claimed that Capacity-building is not particularly important the further away we move from Europe, Bacon and Usayapant found several examples of Capacity-building being useful, the most obvious of which is the Ship-to-Shore project. And although Börzel and Risse suspect that direct methods of norm diffusion are unlikely to be successful the further one travels away from Europe, conditionality, Capacity-building and socialisation are all direct forms of norm diffusion. Ultimately, Bacon and Usayapant show that the EU *was* able to exercise a significant degree of normative power and to successfully diffuse SDG norms related to decent work in Thailand.

In Chapter Eleven, Koyama demonstrates the usefulness of the spiral model in understanding the dynamics, processes and actors in the early phases of labour rights norm diffusion in Georgia. She focuses on the repression, denial and tactical concessions phases (stages one, two and three of the spiral model). Additionally, Koyama shows the importance of examining the roles and dynamics of local actors other than the state and other formal actors, in order to better understand factors in the norm diffusion phases beyond tactical concessions (stages four and five of the model). The Georgia example in this chapter suggests that a more nuanced understanding of local actors is required in order to better analyse factors which could drive the norm diffusion process from the tactical concessions phase, to prescriptive status and rule-consistent behaviour. Koyama's analysis of the bottom-up rights-based movement suggests that the traditional strategy of labour strikes still has a certain leverage in forging improvements in labour rights practices. What the case of Georgia also shows is that traditional labour activism has now been joined by a new generation of social activists who carry European identity. For the young generation, labour rights and other human rights are not something external to be adopted, but rather an integral part of their 'own' identities. This way, instead of 'localising' the international labour rights norms, these local actors take the rights as an integral part of their own European identity. For local actors in Georgia, the rights-based norms are not foreign norms but something that they are equipped with naturally due to their European identity. The case of Georgia also demonstrates the close interaction and collaboration between local civil society actors and international actors, especially through transnational networks.

In Chapter Twelve, Ghislain explains that while animal welfare is not explicitly mentioned in the SDGs, in fact animal welfare is widely recognised as an important dimension of sustainability. This normative connection has also been underlined in EU trade policy, but the first explicit reference to it can only be found in the recently signed EU–UK TCA. While it is too early to reach an overall assessment of the EU's norm diffusion efforts on animal welfare and the SDGs, the EU's normative outreach around animal welfare in the context of trade policy provides several important case studies. The experience of the EU in using Free Trade Agreements (FTAs) to diffuse its animal welfare norms has so far met with mixed results. This is mostly due to the weakness of the tools the EU has relied upon—in most cases, cooperation mechanisms. In terms of the spiral model of norm diffusion, the EU has only reached the final stage of rule-consistent behaviour on animal welfare with one partner, mainly because of the partner's willingness to adopt the projected norm, which had been fostered by a localisation process around this norm. When the EU has met resistance, it has been unable or unwilling to use the required levers to lift entrenched opposition. The EU has thus a capacity and does engage in norm diffusion using soft policy tools, but there is no willingness to level up this effort and engage more political capital. So far, EU trade policy has been able to put animal welfare on the agenda of its partners—achieving socialisation around this norm—but not always to shape how its partners consider animal welfare and how they behave. Nevertheless, the successes that the EU has achieved in diffusing norms related to animal welfare has clearly contributed to the achievement of the SDGs, as animal welfare is strongly connected to most of the SDGs and their objectives.

Each of the chapters in the book offers a distinctive and original contribution to our understanding of the challenges and opportunities that we face in diffusing the SDGs. We can see that the spiral model remains an extremely helpful theoretical framework within which to understand norm diffusion; this framework was used productively by most of the contributors to the volume. More broadly, we can see in many of the case studies the problems that remain in moving from 'commitment to compliance'—moving from a state of affairs where target states sign up to commitments, to a point where these commitments are implemented in a meaningful way. The identification of this commitment/compliance gap is a core attribute of the spiral model framework (Risse & Ropp, 2013). We can also see that a lack of resources can have a profound impact on norm diffusion. It can often be the case that the target state is committed to implementing an SDG norm, but has to compromise through a lack of funding or knowledge, as in the cases of inclusive education in Cambodia and Malawi.

We can also see that there are often several SDG norms in play. Sometimes this can offer a productive multiplier effect, but it can sometimes be a significant barrier to progress. In an example of the former phenomenon, Chiba demonstrates that comprehensive education with regard to the prevention of HIV/AIDS in Thailand was facilitated by the fact that parents embraced the idea of CSE in order to mitigate the risk of unwanted teenage pregnancy. In an example of the latter phenomenon, Bacon and Usayapant showed that it is commonly assumed that victims of forced labour are also victims of human trafficking, when in fact this is frequently not the case. In Thailand, these assumptions were built into

Thai law, making it very difficult to prosecute those guilty of imposing forced labour in the fisheries industry.

Finally, most of the chapters in this volume are based on extensive fieldwork. We have suggested that it is necessary to engage in such granular fieldwork, in order to fully understand the locally-mediated nature of SDG diffusion. To conclude, we believe that we have demonstrated that conceptualising the SDGs as norms and analysing the implementation of the SDGs through a norm diffusion lens has been a productive exercise. There is tremendous scope to use this approach as the basis for a comprehensive research programme on the implementation of the SDGs.

References

Acharya, A. (2018). *Constructing global order: Agency and change in world politics*. Cambridge University Press.

Asian Development Bank. (2018). Localizing the SDGs. *Governance Brief*, *33*. www.adb.org/sites/default/files/publication/472021/governance-brief-033-sdgs-implementation-2030-agenda.pdf

Bacon, P., & Nakamura, H. (2021). Diffusing the abolitionist norm in Japan: EU 'Death Penalty Diplomacy' and the gap between rhetoric and reality in EU–Japan relations. *Journal of Common Market Studies*, *59*(5), 1230–1246. https://doi.org/10.1111/jcms.13177

Börzel, T. A., & Risse, T. (2012). From Europeanisation to diffusion: Introduction. *West European Politics*, *35*(1), 1–19.

Fukuda-Parr, S., & Muchhala, B. (2020). The Southern origins of sustainable development goals: Ideas, actors, aspirations. *World Development*, *126*, 104706. https://doi.org/10.1016/j.worlddev.2019.104706

Jetschke, A., & Liese, A. (2013) The power of human rights a decade after: From euphoria to contestation? In T. Risse, S. C. Ropp, & K. Sikkink (Eds.), *The persistent power of human rights: From commitment to compliance* (pp. 26–42). Cambridge University Press.

Keck, M. E., & Sikkink, K. (1998). *Activists beyond borders*. Cornell University Press.

MOFA. (2016). *Japan: Sustainable Development Goals implementation guiding principles*. www.mofa.go.jp/files/000252819.pdf

Risse, T. & Ropp, S. C. (2013). Chapter 1 – Introduction and overview. In T. Risse, S. C. Ropp, & K. Sikkink (Eds.), *The persistent power of human rights: From commitment to compliance* (pp. 3–25). Cambridge University Press.

Index

Note: Page locators in **bold** and *italics* represents tables and figures, respectively.